CW00687691

THE POLITICAL SELF

THE POLITICAL SELF
Understanding the Social Context for Mental Illness

Edited by
Rod Tweedy

KARNAC

Quotes from pp. 2–8, 11–17, 38–41, 75–6, 82–3, 154–6, 158–9 [6666 words] from *We've Had a Hundred Years of Psychotherapy—And the World's Getting Worse* by James Hillman and Michael Ventura. Copyright © 1992 by James Hillman and Michael Ventura. Reprinted by permission of HarperCollins Publishers.

First published in 2017 by
Karnac Books Ltd
118 Finchley Road
London NW3 5HT

Copyright © 2017 to Rod Tweedy for the edited collection, and to the individual authors for their contributions.

The rights of the contributors to be identified as the authors of this work have been asserted in accordance with §§ 77 and 78 of the Copyright Design and Patents Act 1988.

All rights reserved. No part of this publication may be reproduced, stored in a retrieval system, or transmitted, in any form or by any means, electronic, mechanical, photocopying, recording, or otherwise, without the prior written permission of the publisher.

British Library Cataloguing in Publication Data

A C.I.P. for this book is available from the British Library

ISBN-13: 978-1-78220-409-1

Typeset by Medlar Publishing Solutions Pvt Ltd, India

Printed in Great Britain

www.karnacbooks.com

To David Smail (1938–2014)
A great man and an inspiration

There is an old Buddhist story (or if there isn't, there should be): two monks are walking beside a fast-flowing river. Suddenly, they hear a shout and see a man being carried helplessly downstream. Wading into the water, they manage to pull him out and are tending to him on the bank when they hear a woman's voice and realize that she too is struggling in the torrent. Again, they manage to pull her out; but then they see a whole group of people being swept along. One of the monks is about to wade in for the third time when he realizes that his companion is not with him; instead she is running upstream as fast as she can. "Where are you off to?" he demands. "These people need help!" Without slowing, the other monk shouts over her shoulder, "I'm going to find the bastard who's throwing them in!"

This pretty much sums up one central justification for bringing politics together with psychotherapy: that it is not possible properly to understand, or address, individual suffering (people being carried downstream) without looking at the context of power relationships in which it occurs (someone throwing them in).

—Nick Totton, *The Politics of Psychotherapy*

From a psychological point of view, the world is making people unwell; it follows that, for people to feel better, the world's situation needs to change. But perhaps this is too passive: perhaps for people to feel better, they have to recognize that the human psyche is a political psyche and hence consider doing something about the state the world is in.

—Andrew Samuels, *Politics on the Couch*

CONTENTS

PART II: OUTSIGHT

ACKNOWLEDGEMENTS

My thanks to Uta and Alastair Smail for all of their help and encourage-
ment for this project, and to Heather Allan at PCCS Books for her kind
permission to cite from David Smail's *Power, Interest and Psychology:
Elements of a Social Materialist Understanding of Distress* (© 2015, PCCS
Books). I would also like to thank Oliver Rathbone, Alex Massey, Kate
Pearce, Cecily Blench, Constance Govindin, and everyone at Karnac
Books for their support and assistance, and all of the contributing
authors for their tremendous generosity and advice, which has been
invaluable in putting this book together.

Finally, I would like to take this opportunity to thank Sarah Wheeler,
the remarkable founder and director of the user-led mental health
organisation Mental Fight Club. Sarah was one of my inspirations,
an energetic angel and a practical visionary, and her death earlier this
year has diminished my world. But her work and her legacy live on
through the remarkable organisation she founded, Dragon Café, in
south London. For me, Mental Fight Club and the Dragon Café are the
model for effective, sustainable, and compassionate therapy and care

in the twenty-first century: user-led, community-based, and genuinely transformative. I hope that the present volume, in its own small way, might live up to the galvanising and inspiring ethos of the Dragon Café: "Create, Relate, Integrate".

Rod Tweedy
London

ABOUT THE EDITOR AND CONTRIBUTORS

Joel Bakan is a professor of law at the University of British Columbia, and an internationally renowned legal scholar and commentator. A former Rhodes Scholar and law clerk to Chief Justice Brian Dickson of the Supreme Court of Canada, Bakan has law degrees from Oxford, Dalhousie, and Harvard. His critically acclaimed book, *The Corporation: The Pathological Pursuit of Profit and Power*, was published in more than twenty languages and became a bestseller in several countries. The book inspired a feature documentary film, *The Corporation*, written by Bakan and co-created with Mark Achbar, which won numerous awards, including best foreign documentary at the Sundance Film Festival, and was a critical and box office success. Bakan's highly regarded scholarly work includes *Just Words: Constitutional Rights and Social Wrongs* (1997), and *Childhood Under Siege: How Big Business Targets Children* (2012), as well as textbooks, edited collections, and numerous articles in leading legal and social science journals. Recognised with awards for both his writing and teaching, Bakan has worked on landmark legal cases and government policy, and serves regularly as a media commentator, and is a frequent public speaker for a wide range of audiences.

John Beveridge is a UKCP registered, attachment-based psychoanalytic psychotherapist, supervisor, and trainer working in private practice in Central London. His thirty-four years in recovery from addiction, and further training in the treatment of sex addiction and trauma reduction with Pia Melody at The Meadows, Arizona and at The Sensorimotor Institute, informs his work with people in recovery from trauma, chemical dependency, sex and relationship addiction, emotional anorexia, and co-dependency. He enjoys public speaking and sharing his clinical expertise on the connections between attachment, trauma, and addiction. John is a trustee with ATSAC—a nonprofit-making professional association dedicated to providing education and information about sex addiction and compulsivity.

Nick Duffell is the pioneer theorist on the psychotherapeutic understanding of residential education. Two television documentaries have featured his work with "Boarding School Survivors", and his book *The Making of Them: the British Attitude to Children and the Boarding School System* appeared in 2000 to wide acclaim. He is also the author of *Wounded Leaders: British Elitism and the Entitlement Illusion—A Psychohistory* (Lone Arrow Press, 2014), and co-author (with Thurstine Basset) of *Trauma, Abandonment and Privilege: A Guide to Therapeutic Work with Boarding School Survivors* (Routledge, 2016). Born in 1949, he has a degree in Sanskrit and has been a schoolteacher, carpenter, psychotherapist, management consultant, and trainer. He writes frequently for psychological journals, contributed to the University of Surrey Human Potential Group's *Dictionary of Personal Development*, and is committed to the development of psychohistory as a tool for understanding current world problems. He is the father of two grown-up sons. In 1996, he and his wife Helena Løvendal-Duffell founded the Centre for Gender Psychology in London, offering specialist training for professionals in the field of relationships, sex, and gender. Their 2002 book, *Sex, Love and the Danger of Intimacy* (HarperCollins Thorsons), has been translated into several languages and supports their training of CreativeCoupleWork therapists. They live between London and a remote corner of SW France.

Sue Gerhardt has been a psychoanalytic psychotherapist in private practice since 1997. She was educated at Newnham College, University of Cambridge, where she studied English literature; she was an active feminist and campaigned successfully for women to be given places in the previously single sex men's colleges. She later trained as a psychotherapist and achieved an MA in child observation at the Tavistock Clinic in London. In 1998 she co-founded the Oxford Parent Infant Project (OXPIP), a pioneering charity that today provides psychotherapeutic help to hundreds of parents and babies in Oxfordshire and is now the prototype of many new "PIPs" around the country. Her books include the bestselling and critically acclaimed *Why Love Matters: How Affection Shapes a Baby's Brain*, and *The Selfish Society: How We All Forgot to Love One Another and Made Money Instead*.

Lt. Col. Dave Grossman is an internationally recognized scholar, author, soldier, and speaker who is one of the world's foremost experts in the field of human aggression and the roots of violence and violent crime. He is a former sergeant, platoon leader, general staff officer, and company commander, as well as a former West Point psychology professor and chair of the Department of Military Science and Leadership at Arkansas State University. His classic book *On Killing: The Psychological Cost of Learning to Kill in War and Society* was nominated for a Pulitzer Prize and is required reading in classes at West Point and the U.S. Air Force Academy. He is also the author of the acclaimed work *On Combat: The Psychology and Physiology of Deadly Conflict in War and in Peace*, and co-author of *Stop Teaching Our Kids to Kill: A Call to Action Against TV, Movie and Video Game Violence*.

James Hillman (1926–2011) was a psychologist, scholar, international lecturer, and the author of numerous books. He studied with the great Swiss psychiatrist Carl Jung in the 1950s and later became the first director of studies at the Jung Institute in Zurich. After returning to the United States in 1980, he taught at Yale, Syracuse, and the universities of Chicago and Dallas. He also became editor of *Spring Publications*, a small Texas publisher devoted to the work of contemporary psychologists, as well as writing some twenty books of his own. As one of the key proponents of archetypal psychology—a school of thought aimed at "re-visioning" or "re-imagining" psychology—Hillman argued that the therapy business needs to evolve beyond reductionist "nature" and "nurture" theories of human development. Over a period of almost five decades—until his death in October 2011—he wrote, taught, and lectured about the need to get therapy out of the consulting room and into the real world. Conventional psychology, he argued, has lost touch with what he called "the soul's code" and become reduced to "a trivialized, banal, egocentric pursuit, rather than an exploration of the mysteries of human nature."

Joel Kovel is an American scholar and author who studied at Yale University, Columbia University College of Physicians and Surgeons, and the Psychoanalytic Institute, Downstate Medical Center Institute, New York. He was director of residency training at the Department of Psychiatry, Albert Einstein College of Medicine (where he was also professor of psychiatry); adjunct professor of anthropology at the New School for Social Research; and visiting professor of political science and communications at the University of California, San Diego. Kovel became involved in political activism in the 1960s as a result of the Vietnam War, and later became involved with the environmental movement, having a brief career with the Green Party of the United States, under which he ran for the U.S. Senate in 1998, and was also former editor-in-chief of *Capitalism, Nature, Socialism*. His works include *White Racism* (nominated for a National Book Award); *A Complete Guide to Therapy* (1976); *The Age of Desire* (1981); *Against the State of Nuclear Terror* (1984); *In Nicaragua* (1988); *The Radical Spirit: Essays on Psychoanalysis and Society* (1988); *History and Spirit* (1991); *Red Hunting in the Promised Land* (1994); *Overcoming Zionism* (2007); and *The Enemy of Nature: The End of Capitalism or the End of the World?* (2003). His memoir, *The Lost Traveller's Dream* (Peter Lang, New York) will be published in 2017.

Iain McGilchrist is a former fellow of All Souls College, Oxford, a fellow of the Royal College of Psychiatrists, a fellow of the Royal Society of Arts, and former consultant psychiatrist and clinical director at the Bethlem Royal & Maudsley Hospital, London. He has been a research fellow in neuroimaging at Johns Hopkins Hospital, Baltimore, and has published original articles and research papers in a wide range of publications on topics in literature, philosophy, medicine, and psychiatry. McGilchrist is the author of *Against Criticism* (Faber, 1982), *The Master and his Emissary: The Divided Brain and the Making of the Western World* (Yale, 2009), *The Divided Brain and the Search for Meaning: Why Are We So Unhappy?* (Yale, 2012), and is currently working on a project entitled *When the Porcupine Is a Monkey*, to be published by Penguin. He lives on the Isle of Skye.

Jonathan Rowson is co-founder and director of Perspectiva. He was until recently director of the Social Brain Centre at the RSA where, over the course of six years, he authored a range of influential research reports on behaviour change, climate change, and spirituality, and curated and chaired a range of related events. Jonathan is an applied philosopher with degrees spanning a range of humanities and social sciences from Oxford, Harvard, and Bristol universities. In a former life he was a chess grandmaster and British champion (2004–6) and views the game as a continuing source of insight and inspiration. His book, *The Seven Dimensions of Climate Change: rethinking the world's toughest problem* will be published by Palgrave Macmillan in early 2017. He lives in Putney, London, with his wife Siva, an academic lawyer from South India and their two sons, Kailash and Vishnu. His recent work includes *Money Talks: Divest, Invest and the Battle for Climate Realism* and *Spiritualise: Revitalising Spirituality to Address 21st Century Challenges.*

David Smail (1938–2014) was born in Putney, London, and studied philosophy and psychology at University College London, where he was awarded a PhD in psychology in 1965. He entered the National Health Service as a clinical psychologist in 1961, and in 1964 joined Tom Caine's psychology department at Claybury Hospital in Essex, which was at that time pioneering the "therapeutic community" approach to the treatment of mental disorder. David moved to Nottingham in 1968, where he remained as head of clinical psychology services until 1993. He retired fully from the NHS in 1998, and held the honorary post of special professor in clinical psychology at the University of Nottingham from 1979 until 2000. His books include *Power, Interest and Psychology: Elements of a Social Materialist Understanding of Distress* (2005), *Illusion and Reality: The Meaning of Anxiety* (1984), *Taking Care: An Alternative to Therapy* (1987), and *The Origins of Unhappiness: A New Understanding of Personal Distress* (1993).

Nick Totton has been working as a therapist, supervisor, and trainer since 1981, having originally trained as a Reichian body therapist. He has an MA in psychoanalytic studies and has worked with process oriented psychology and trained as a craniosacral therapist. He has authored or edited seventeen books, mostly on psychotherapy-related topics, including *Embodied Relating: The Ground of Psychotherapy*; *Vital*

Signs: Psychological Responses to Ecological Crisis; *Psychotherapy and Politics*; and *Wild Therapy: Undomesticating Inner and Outer Worlds*.

Rod Tweedy is the editor for Karnac Books and the author of *The God of the Left Hemisphere: Blake, Bolte Taylor and the Myth of Creation*, a study of William Blake's works in the light of contemporary neuroscience. He has written a number of articles on the relationship between analysis and creativity, bihemispheric lateralization, Romanticism and popular culture, and the social and environmental contexts for individual distress. He is an active supporter of Veterans for Peace UK and the user-led mental health organisation, Mental Fight Club.

Michael Ventura is an American novelist, screenwriter, essayist, and cultural critic. He commenced his career as a journalist at the *Austin Sun*, a counterculture biweekly newspaper that published in the 1970s. Ventura is best known for his long-running column, "Letters at 3 A.M.", which first appeared in *L.A. Weekly* in the early 1980s and continued in the *Austin Chronicle* until 2015. He has published three novels: *Night Time Losing Time* (1989), *The Zoo Where You're Fed to God* (1994), and *The Death of Frank Sinatra* (1996). He is currently completing another novel, about Miriam of Magdala, an excerpt from which was published in the third issue of the CalArts literary journal *Black Clock*. He is the author of two essay collections, *Shadow-Dancing in the U.S.A.* (1985) and *Letters at 3 A.M.: Reports on Endarkenment* (1994). With psychologist James Hillman, Ventura coauthored the bestseller *We've Had a Hundred Years of Psychotherapy—And the World's Getting Worse* (1992).

FOREWORD

Andrew Samuels

The political turn taken (or should that be re-taken?) by the psychotherapies since the end of the 1980s is illuminated in this vital, informed, and inspiring collection of classic (yet still cutting-edge) papers, creatively and expertly selected by the editor who has provided a succinct summary of the main lines to be discovered in each chapter. This makes the job of the person charged with writing a Foreword both easier and more difficult. Easier, because I am released from the task of summarising the book (and inevitably, if inadvertently, annoying the contributors). Difficult, because I have to find something to say that does not aspire to being another chapter.

So—what I want to offer is a dissection of what might be meant by this tag "psychotherapy and politics", which is, boiled down, what the book is presenting to us. I am going to suggest that there are *seven types* of "psychotherapy and politics" to consider—each of them interesting and valuable, but sufficiently different from each other to warrant a list-making, classificatory—almost nosological—exercise.

I hope my seven types will be a reliable guide to people whose knowledge of the field is mostly of an enthusiastically curious kind—and sufficiently wrong to draw people such as the contributors into some kind of debate. For, as Robert Musil once put it, "I am convinced not only that what I say is wrong, but that what will be said against it will be wrong as well". (I used this quote as the epigraph to *The Political Psyche* back in 1993.)

The number seven is a homage to the title of the great work of literary criticism by William Empson—*Seven Types of Ambiguity* (1930). Empson says that significance and beauty in a literary work relate to the ambiguity of its language. For a work to have beauty and even for it to be artistic, there needs to be a multiplicity of possible meanings for it. Empson lists seven types of ambiguity, from simple double meanings right across to direct contradictions.

I think that what Empson says applies also to psychotherapy and politics. Specifically, given that *everyone* in the "psy" field is talking about "politics" these days, I suggest that something significant and beautiful is lost if we do not reflect—and act on—the ambiguities in the phrase "psychotherapy and politics".

We need to recall that the list's compilation would not be possible without the elasticity in the notion of "politics" that feminism has made possible. And there has also been a general epistemological shift in Western thinking wherein experience is seen as being as valid a source of knowledge as empirical data or pedagogical authority. Psychotherapy is a prime generator of this shift as well as a beneficiary of it.

I. The politics of the professions of psychotherapy (and psychoanalysis)

Linking—or re-linking—psychotherapy and politics still brings us up against the politics of the profession itself. In particular, assertions from the upper sections of our various hierarchies about what constitutes "good practice" have a huge impact on clinical work. To engage with one's client on a political matter has long been castigated as "bad practice" and political activity itself sometimes referred to as acting out. Would you want actively to try to become a bad therapist? Or, as Nick Totton and James Hillman suggest, is it "bad practice" to ignore and internalise potential "political" concerns as they arise, or to pretend that the therapeutic encounter is not itself in some senses already a politicised one?

*II. The application of psychotherapeutic ideas ("therapy thinking")
in a quest for deeper understandings of political processes and
problems*

Turning now to the question of the application of psychotherapeutic
ideas to politics, there is a general problem, which I must say I found
occasionally in the chapters of this book. It's there in my own work, too.
If one uses cutting-edge psychotherapeutic ideas too readily and in too
sophisticated a way, there will be an understandable response from the
political world that this is just psychobabble—and from the intellectual
world that it is just reductive. But if one finds a more popular, emotive,
and common-sense related way to express the insights of therapy thinking on politics, then the response is often that you don't have to be a
highly trained psychotherapist to come up with such obvious formulations. Any journalist can do it.

My slogan has for many years been: let's have a psychotherapist on
every Government committee or commission—but, please God, not a
committee of therapists! On these committees, there would be a spectrum of skills with the therapist at one end and someone like a statistician at the other end. Neither of these would be the most popular
nor most influential member of the committee—but, I would argue, the
presence of the psychotherapist could become as essential as the presence of the statistician.

*III. The usage by politicians and political groupings of therapy
thinking for furtherance of their own aims and objectives*

As far as the usage of psychotherapeutic ideas by politicians and political groupings is concerned, we have to remember that the history of
psychoanalysis includes a number of regrettable collusions with the
powerful. C.G. Jung fell foul of this temptation and recent historical
researches show that much the same was true of Anna Freud and Ernest
Jones in the 1930s.

There is a distinction to be made between the taking up of psychological ideas without the participation or presence of the theorist and
a situation wherein a therapist offers her or himself in the service of a
particular cause or as part of a job. For example, I have done numerous consultations for politicians and activist groupings in many countries, as have other psychotherapists. All would agree that it can be a

wonderful (and frustrating and humbling) experience. But interesting questions of definition, integrity, and identity arise.

For if one gets involved as a therapist with a politician or a political movement, is one doing it as a psychotherapist or as a citizen who happens to be a psychotherapist? Or both? And what are the relevant ethics?

IV. Political projects of whatever kind undertaken by organisations of psychotherapists

I turn now to organisations of psychotherapists (and counsellors) that seek to make an impact on the political scene, speaking with a coherent political voice that rests on a degree of professional expertise. For reasons of space, I will focus on two issues only.

The first concerns whether or not such organisations are (or should be) inevitably left-leaning, or "progressive" in whatever ways that might be defined in an age that claims to have gone beyond left and right. If being part of the left is an inevitability, then the organisation has to accept that it cannot claim to "represent" a consensual professional view (though it may some of the time) and certainly cannot speak for the profession as a whole. An eminently discussable example would be that of an organisation of psychotherapists that spoke out against a candidate in an important election.

In terms of political impact, there's a second issue. Isn't it necessary to get a balance between engaging with the traditional "psychological" areas ("soft" areas) such as family policy, education, and so forth—and less traditional areas ("hard" areas) such as economics, violence in society, leadership, and foreign policy? The environment and issues such as climate change and species depletion have often turned out to be a linking area of interest because ecological concern is (rightly, in my opinion) both a soft and a hard policy area.

Another example of a move by a therapists' organisation into a "hard" policy area has been the discussions in the UK within Psychotherapists and Counsellors for Social Responsibility over the "models of human nature" that underpin economic policy. (For an account of the early history of PCSR in the UK, see Samuels 2003, pp. 150–153.)

V. Psychotherapeutic understandings of the growth and development of the political dimensions of the subject-as-citizen

We are gradually moving from the non-clinical to the clinical aspects of the principal themes of the book. In this section, I want to question why it is that psychotherapy (as opposed to social psychology) has so little to say in recent years about topics such as "the political self", "political development", even, to use a tag of mine that I am still somewhat embarrassed by, "the inner politician". Don't we need to know more about where we (the therapist and the client) got our politics from, of the relative importance of the politics of father and mother, of the ways in which social class operates at an unconscious level, of how ethnic, national, and religious factors transmogrify into political attitudes and behaviours, and—in an imaginative return to the bedrock of psycho-therapeutic exploration—how issues of sex, sexuality, and gender play into the formation of the political subject? We need to be careful not to get hooked up on facts here for much political autobiography is personal myth.

VI. The struggle to apperceive the micro-politics of the therapy session itself—the power, vulnerability, and differing experiences in the therapy and in the social world of both participants

This section and the next are overtly clinical. Regarding the micro-politics of the session, I would like to suggest that the usual sophisticated, politically conscious contemporary focus on the therapist's power over the client is insufficient (though certainly not wrong). For if we turn to the traditional idea of the Wounded Healer, we see that it underscores the opposing idea that therapists (like shamans and other healers) are basically very vulnerable people. Such vulnerability may be carried by somatic/physiological factors, such as their proneness to illness. Maybe their choice of the profession stems from such vulnerabilities. Maybe that is also why they often seem so into power. But what we need is a psycho-political analysis of the power *and* the vulnerability of both the therapist *and* the client and how these evolve over the course of a therapy. In general, I think that many therapists have a problem in realising that they are both powerful and vulnerable—it is not always a case of either powerful or vulnerable. In other words, much thinking about who has the power and who has the vulnerability in the politics of the therapy relationship may have been rather binary.

VII. Devising responsible ways to engage directly with political, social, and cultural material that appears in the clinical session

Finally, we come to the question of how to work with political, social, and cultural material in clinical sessions. Going back to what I said in my first point about "bad practice", it is clear to me that yesterday's bad practice is set to become today's good or good-enough practice. The question will soon cease to be, "Why did you get involved in that political discussion?" but, "Why did you collude in evading the political discussion that the client was seeking?" I would like to see this matter of politics being part of clinical material become a rather ordinary, everyday matter, nothing special—in the sense that for a therapist to hear about and engage in dialogue over sexuality, relationships, etc. is nothing special; not "nothing special" in the sense of "no big deal" but in the sense of something familiar. We surely don't want to limit political discussion only to those moments of war or attack that make avoidance of the world "out there" impossible (and never was there a binary more in need of deconstruction than "in here" and "out there").

What we need to do is to highlight the therapeutic value of political discussion undertaken in a responsible and relational way that acknowledges the dangers. It is not going to be the same as discussion held in a bar or over dinner or at work. The clinical frame—what the Jungians call the *vas* (alchemical vessel) or *temenos* (temple precinct)— guarantees that even mundane occurrences within it acquire transformative potential.

Politics as the ground of psychotherapy

That concludes my seven types of psychotherapy and politics. Up to now, I have kept to the pathways trodden by the authors in the book. But I'd like to end by throwing out a tentative idea (also floated in Samuels, 2015) for further discussion. Therapist and client are nearly always citizens in the same polity. But they will occupy different citizen-positions due to economic, cultural, and other differences. Nevertheless, despite such differences, they are linked by social bonds. Would any of us, thinking as psychotherapists, want to regard the common state of citizenship as it applies to therapists and clients within an exclusively social understanding? Could it be the case that what makes unconscious to unconscious communication, transference–countertransference dynamics, and therapeutic dialogue *possible* is this *shared experience of citizenship*? Could it be the political relationship of therapist and client that leads to their psychological relationship? If this is the case, then politics is the very ground of the depth relational and embodied aspects of the psychotherapy project.

References

Empson, W. (1930). *Seven Types of Ambiguity: A Study of Its Effects on English Verse*. London: Chatto and Windus.

Samuels, A. (1993). *The Political Psyche*. London & New York: Routledge.

Samuels, A. (2003). Psychotherapists and counselors for social responsibility (UK). *Journal for the Psychoanalysis of Culture and Society, 8*(1): 150–153.

Samuels, A. (2006). Working directly with political, social and cultural material in the therapy session. In: L. Layton, N. C. Hollander & S. Gutwill (Eds), *Psychoanalysis, Class and Politics: Encounters in the Clinical Setting* (pp. 11–28). London & New York: Routledge.

Samuels, A. (2015). *A New Therapy for Politics?* London: Karnac.

Where three roads meet

Rod Tweedy

> *Oedipus*: If I understand you, Laïos was killed
>   At a place where three roads meet.
>   *Iocaste*: So it was said; We have no later story.
> *Oedipus*: Where did it happen?
>   *Iocaste*: Phokis, it is called: at a place where the Theban Way
>   Divides into the roads toward Delphi and Daulia.
>   —Sophocles, *Oedipus Rex*

> Individuals live not only their own lives but also the life of the
> times … Once we see that there is a political self who has devel-
> oped over time, we can start to track the political history of that
> self—the way the political events of a lifetime have contributed
> to forming the individual's political myth.
>   —Samuels, *Politics on the Couch*

This book explores how our social and economic contexts profoundly
affect our mental health and well-being, and how modern neuroscientific and psychodynamic research can both contribute to and enrich our
understanding of these wider discussions. It therefore looks both inside
and outside—indeed one of the main themes of *The Political Self* is that

the conceptually discrete categories of "inner" and "outer" in reality constantly interact, shape, and inform each other. Severing these two worlds, it suggests, has led both to a devitalised and dissociated form of politics, and to a disengaged and disempowering form of therapy and analysis.

Like Oedipus, we are standing at a crossroads, facing on the one hand remarkable new discoveries about how our brains work and are shaped and sculpted by the world around us, and on the other hand an increasing awareness of the deeply dysfunctional and divisive nature of many of our traditional political and economic institutions. This convergence—a bringing together and alignment of the inner and outer—is one of the defining characteristics of this age; and what makes this period of history particularly exciting in terms of psychoanalysis and psychotherapy is the new receptivity and willingness among many mental health practitioners and professionals to address and engage with social reality as part of the necessary therapeutic process.

As Andrew Samuels, one of the pioneers of this new integrated approach to psychotherapy, has observed: "From a psychological point of view, the world is making people unwell; it follows that, for people to feel better, the world's situation needs to change. But perhaps this is too passive: perhaps for people to feel better, they have to recognize that the human psyche is a political psyche and hence consider doing something about the state the world is in" (2001, p. 21). This recognition requires seeing that the human psyche is not some abstracted entity operating in splendid isolation from the world, but is on every level profoundly involved in the world: we are embedded, embodied, and embrained, and the world—for better or worse—is hardwired and mirrored within us.[1] "For us to feel better" we therefore need to adjust not only ourselves but our worlds, our surrounding contexts—the powerful matrix of forces, pressures, ideas, and interests constantly acting upon us. And for this to happen, Samuels notes, we also need to adjust and update our model of the human psyche from the crude seventeenth-century version—conceived as a separate, atomised, rationalised unit (which unfortunately still drives mainstream political, and indeed psycho-analytic, discourse)—to a more twenty-first-century dynamic model, based on a deeper and more sophisticated understanding of the inter-dependent, interactive nature of our psyches: we need to recognise, as Samuels puts it, that "the human psyche is a political psyche."

As the symbolic "father" of the psychoanalytic and therapeutic industries—as well as one of the most influential and important of the early explorers of the modern psyche—the figure of Sigmund Freud is particularly significant at this juncture. Freud's pioneering work profoundly challenged the mechanistic, rationalising, literalist world of nineteenth-century science—opening up the vast symbolic realms of the human unconscious onto the unsuspecting materialism and respectability of Viennese and Victorian bourgeois living rooms, and transforming our appreciation of the human mind in the process. Freud drew powerful attention to the role of repression in concealing uncomfortable—unspoken—truths about society. And the method he instigated to reveal and resolve these repressions and hidden realities, which became the basis of "the talking cure", heralded a new emancipatory role for analysis in addressing and transforming them. As Adam Phillips—one of the ablest proponents of Freud's thought today—has remarked, while the *aims* of therapy (in helping people) are fairly conventional, "the method is revolutionary": "It dawned on Freud very early, that what he was opening up by letting people say what they thought and felt, was really very very explosive—and would really have unpredictable consequences" (Phillips interview, 2014). It is this aspect of Freud's discovery that the present book draws on in suggesting a new multidisciplinary, integrated, and contextualized model of therapeutic practice for the twenty-first century. Letting people say what they think and feel still has unpredictable consequences.

100 years of therapy: an analysis of psychoanalysis

Freud's concept of repression is particularly useful in understanding the reasons for psychoanalysis's own history of disengagement from social reality. As we'll see, this disconnection or "dissociation" from reality has been observed by a number of commentators. "The great illusion of psychoanalysis", notes Joel Kovel (see Chapter Three), "has been to imagine itself free from society." By abstracting itself from society and turning "inwards"—literally—psychoanalysis forged for itself a more respectable role in the turbulent decades of the mid-twentieth century, especially in America, but in doing so it also lost its earlier radical, genuinely liberating, therapeutic role, as it quickly became co-opted by the social and economic structures it inevitably came to serve. "The main theme of the history of psychoanalysis," Kovel therefore notes, is "that of the absorption of critique by the dominant culture" (p. 64).

Many others have drawn the same conclusion: the eminent psychoanalyst and social philosopher Horst-Eberhard Richter, for example, observed that orthodox psychoanalysis lacks "social analysis": for Richter, "the traditional psychoanalytic near-exclusive focus on the inner world of the individual … is negligent when it ignores the socio-economic dynamics that contextualize the person's experience" (Warnecke, 2015, p. 11). Indeed, this lack of context—or rather deliberate severing and *de*-contextualising of the person's experience—led to a form of therapeutic dissociation that was itself rather pathological. "It was in fact as if the world had split in two," notes David Smail, whose remarkable and compelling analysis of the root causes of this fracturing of analytic consciousness, post-Freud, forms the opening chapter of the present collection.

> The most striking thing of all is how "psychotherapy", in becoming one of the greatest cultural and commercial success stories of the Western world, remained over the past hundred years almost hermetically sealed off from the rest of reality. (p. 3)

And where psychoanalysis did engage with social reality, it was often in order to bolster the very systems of political control and commercial exploitation that were generating much of the distress and ill health in the first place: as Kovel notes, "It was Edward Bernays, Freud's nephew and the founder of public relations, who spearheaded the appropriation of psychodynamics by advertising and the mass media in general" (p. 65). If psychoanalysis itself was reluctant to incorporate social reality, social reality was only too happy to co-opt psychoanalytic thinking in order to help sell us washing machines, cars, and holidays—as Joel Bakan's compelling analysis of the rise of the corporation, in this book (Chapter Nine), brilliantly demonstrates.

Thus, despite its promising beginnings and radical potential, Sue Gerhardt notes (see Chapter Four), "Psychological discoveries have more often been used … to manipulate customers, and to increase our consumption through advertising, with its empty promises of sexual fulfilment. In other words, like so much else in this phase of human history, psychology has been subordinated to material pleasure and comforts" (p. 77). One of the aims of the present book is to show how deeply this manipulation occurs: how these everyday processes of advertising and consumption rely for their success on reshaping our desires, our psyches—how, as Sue Gerhardt's research shows, corporate capitalism shapes our brains and reworks our nervous systems in its own image. Indeed, as a number of contributors in this volume suggest, economic practices are necessarily and simultaneously *psychological* practices—encouraging and embodying specific ways of relating to or attending to the world—which is another reason why the current dislocation of inner and outer, "economic" issues (percentage rates, algorithms, taxes, productivity) and "mental health issues" (addiction, compulsion, autism, depression, trauma) is so misleading and unhelpful. Within every economy, to paraphrase Neil Postman (1992), there is always embedded a psychology, an ideology, a way of doing things.[2]

It's important to note that many individual therapists and analysts were, and still are, often wholly unaware of this process of co-option, and of the deeper social currents acting on their profession—in part due to the very dissociation and conscious uncoupling of psychoanalysis from these broader contexts—and were therefore largely unable to prevent this powerful drift. As David Smail notes, "The capitalist counter-revolution of the late twentieth century in the West co-opted therapy as part of a technology of profit, and it did so so swiftly—in part by engaging the interests of therapists and counsellors themselves—that many, perhaps most, practitioners still find it hard to accept their complicity in a political and economic system they in all likelihood deplore" (p. 24). The most persuasive reason for this historical lack of awareness, or unconsciousness, as Smail suggests, is actually a familiar one to the profession: repression—in this case, the repression of powerful but largely unconscious interests, as his chapter compellingly demonstrates. It is, perhaps ironically, Freud's own concept of repression that therefore provides the crucial key to understanding the process by which therapy became "a central tool of ideological power" in the latter half of the twentieth century. To blame individual therapists and analysts for this, Smail adds, is to completely miss the point—is precisely to "psychologise" an issue which is collective and political at heart: "This would of course be to *psychologise* the account in exactly the way I am arguing against throughout: it is not that the individuals *decide* to act in accordance with interest (theirs or others'), but rather that, not least because interest is repressed, they find themselves caught up in a system in ways they cannot fully understand and would—if they could under-stand it—undoubtedly deplore" (p. 14).

On those comparatively rare occasions where psychotherapy has directly engaged with social issues and political reality the results to date have been rather disappointing, to say the least. Freud himself, as Adam Phillips notes, was a "politically naïve liberal" for whom "political participation was unthinkable", as indeed it was for so many Jews of his generation. But this marginalisation and internalised sense of isolation unfortunately became written into his theorising about psychoanalysis itself, and fed into his disengagement with the political realities of his own day. As Phillips notes, he was "a man who, most strikingly, couldn't take the Nazis seriously until it was almost too late", and who even dedicated a copy of his book to Mussolini (Phillips, 2014, p. 33; see also Belilos, 2016).[3] "Politics", concludes Phillips, "was one of Freud's blind spots" (op. cit., p. 34). Unfortunately, it was also a "blind spot" of Jung's. "I couldn't help liking Mussolini," the founder of ana-lytical psychology once remarked, and he had similarly positive words for Hitler: "There is no question but that Hitler belongs in the category of the truly mystic medicine man" (cited in Masson, 1989, p. 147; see also Samuels's penetrating discussion of Jung's politics in his chapter "Jung, anti-Semitism and the Nazis", 1993, pp. 287–316). How could these founding fathers of psychology have got things so wrong—could have so poorly analysed what was going on? The clue perhaps lies pre-cisely in the decontextualising of experience that they presided over. By so completely severing the inner and outer, the psychological and the political, they were largely unprepared and unable to understand or engage with the major historical movements of their time, or the forces acting on their profession. As Smail trenchantly observes: "The twentieth century, after all, exploded into revolution and war on an unprecedented scale, but you would hardly know it from examining the theoretical speculations of Freud and Jung at the time—and so far as outer events did concern them, it was nearly always as an expressions of inner 'psychic' conflicts of some kind (a stance still widely evident among some psychoanalytic writers)" (p. 4).

It is this legacy of disconnect that has been so limiting and harm-ful both to the theoretical formulations and the practical applications of therapy. From its disastrous pathologising of homosexuality in the twentieth century (only formally declassified as a "mental illness" by the American Psychiatric Association in 1987), to its complicity in the torture programmes of the Pentagon and the CIA in the "war on terror", and its contemporary involvement in such toxic practices as "psychocompulsion", psychotherapy has sadly shown itself to be only too amenable as a "tool of ideological power".[4]

Therapy as a political act: let's talk about power

The difficulty in recognising and addressing the ideological role of therapy within these wider political and ideological systems is also what makes the work of many contemporary therapists and analysts who *are* engaged with challenging the movement of ideological power so impressive and exciting. Psychotherapist Nick Totton has perhaps done more than anyone to reveal how issues of power profoundly shape our contemporary therapeutic institutions as well as the actual practice of psychotherapy. As he notes, "The structure of psychotherapy builds in stubborn problems of power and control, irrespective of the good intentions or otherwise of the practitioner." These problems manifest at every level of the psychoanalytic industry: from inequalities in the therapeutic encounter itself, to structural and institutional issues of control and hierarchy, to the cultural status of therapy as a value system or ideological set of beliefs—with many of these beliefs, he notes, often being unconsciously held. "In one way or another, I suggest, all therapists are carrying out a political programme in their work with clients." The reason for this, he points out, is that "… therapists have their own, often highly developed, beliefs about how people should be and live":

> These beliefs are essentially political in nature; they are also often unconscious and implicit. For us to hold such beliefs is an inevitable part both of our lives as citizens and of our whole approach to interacting with our clients. This is very obvious with therapy styles that think explicitly in terms of cure and adjustment: people *should* be healthy, *should* be well adjusted—and, of course, each school and each practitioner has their own set of small print about what "healthy" or "well adjusted" actually means. "Well adjusted" to what? Each practitioner believes their clients should adjust to whatever aspects of life they themselves see as natural or acceptable. (p. 35)

Given the ineluctable presence and potency of these beliefs—which of course constitute and underwrite the very idea and practice of "therapy"—the profession is therefore faced, he observes, "with a fundamental political problem at its heart".

Totton's analysis is an eye-opening account of how issues of power and control inevitably operate at the heart of all our practices, therapeutic ones included. "For psychotherapy to respond helpfully, on a clinical and on a social level," he observes, "it needs to think seriously about the power politics of its own practice." As he notes, it is not the presence of "power politics" in itself but rather the failure to address the issues they generate that constitutes "bad practice": "What I *do* think is bad practice is to pretend that we are *not* operating from a set of beliefs or that those beliefs are different from what they really are. Then we confuse both our clients and ourselves." His chapter is both a remarkably honest account of "the struggle over power" within the therapeutic relationship and the wider institutions of psychotherapy, and also an ultimately optimistic analysis of the social role of therapy—providing that we have the courage to talk about these issues and not avoid or repress them. *"By making the struggle over power a central focus of the therapeutic encounter,"* he adds, "we can do as Freud did with transference: turn a structural problem into a creative aspect of therapy." Indeed, he observes, this "may actually be a necessary condition for a positive therapeutic outcome" (p. 30).

Issues of power arise whenever there is inequality or imbalance, and in the present economic system these inequalities are unfortunately structural and therefore unavoidable. As David Smail observes, *"Power,* which may be defined broadly as the means of obtaining security or advantage, is the fundamental dynamic of social structure" (p. 9). Politics and power are inextricably interwoven, as Totton's discussion of "power politics" suggests. This means that the "self" which is engaged with these dynamics and structures is necessarily a "political" self: "a point in social space-time *through which* powers flow" (Smail, p. 19). The principal kinds of power are coercive (direct use of force), economic or financial, and ideological (i.e., control of meaning, language, information, and horizon): "In other words, it is what shapes and maintains a society that forms, from our current Western perspective, a pyramidal hierarchy, at the peak of which is a small corporate plutocracy and at the bottom of which is a vast, largely politically atomised collectivity of consumers" (p. 9). Institutions, those of psychotherapy necessarily included, work within this broader gravitational hierarchy, either con-sciously or—perhaps more often—unconsciously and unknowingly. As Totton notes in his compelling discussion of how the flow of power manifests itself, "This goes beyond the issue of the individual power relationship between client and therapist and raises questions about how therapy works to support and endorse the power relations of society as a whole" (p. 34). Indeed, a number of cultural commentators have pointed out how the therapy industry has historically operated to "endorse the power relations of society as a whole", acting as an instru-ment of social control. The influential philosopher and social theorist Michel Foucault, for example, observed that the state manages the indi-vidual through a process of controlled "subjectivisation", noting that in such a system the practice of psychoanalysis is ultimately a "political technology of the self" (cited in Warnecke, 2015)—a point reiterated by Nikolas Rose in his study of "the management of subjectivity" through psychotherapy in *Governing the Soul: The Shaping of the Private Self* (1999, p. 2). More recently, the cultural and social historian Frank Furedi has developed this critique, showing how the therapy industry is par-ticularly serviceable to current economic and political interests both by "distracting people from engaging with the wider social issues in favour of an inward turn to the self", and also by "cultivating a sense of vulnerability, powerlessness and dependence", through its promo-tion of the patient as a traumatised "victim", or even as a "child" (2004, p. 203). As Hillman notes, traditional psychotherapy tends to infantilise us through its emphasis on "the child archetype", which is "by nature apolitical and disempowered" (p. 192). In both these respects, as Kovel observes, "… therapy has in some respects been even more success-ful than religion in deflecting energy from the need for radical social change" (p. 43).

From social brain to "political brain": how society shapes who we are

The new understanding of the "self" as a "political self", intimately and unavoidably involved in issues of power, control, agency, and social formation, is also a development of recent psychological and neuroscientific research into what has been termed the "social brain", and an increasing awareness of the importance of secure attachments and supportive social relationships in the formation of who we are.

"Right from the start," notes Sue Gerhardt, "we are all responsive to other human beings":

> Even newborn babies have a basic capacity to imitate others and to resonate with other people's feelings through their brain's mirror neurons. If you copy a smile, you often feel happier, and if you copy a yawn, you are likely to feel more tired. We need this ability to be social creatures. To the brain, self and other are part of the same process. In fact, it's the same area of the brain—the right frontal insula, in particular—which lights up whether we are being aware of our own body states or other people's. (p. 69)

The discovery of these deep empathic networks in the right hemisphere of the brain, including the existence of "mirror neurons" which effectively collapse the conceptual distinction between "me" and "you" on a neurological level, is transforming our understanding not only of our brains but also of our identities as fundamentally social beings. As Louis Cozolino, one of the leading researchers in this field, has observed:

> Like every living system—from single neurons to complex ecosystems—the brain depends on interactions with others for survival. Each human brain is dependent on the scaffolding of caretakers and loved ones for its growth and well-being. So we begin with what we know: *The brain is a social organ of adaptation built through interactions with others.* To write the story of this journey, we must begin with the understanding that *there are no single brains—brains only exist within networks of other brains.* (2006, p. xiv, italics in original)

"There are no single brains": this understanding of the brain as a fundamentally "social organ" is in many ways a development of Winnicott's earlier pioneering observation that "there is no such thing as an infant" (i.e., that babies cannot survive, develop, or even be understood outside a relationship with another; Winnicott, 1960), and will have similarly far-reaching consequences for our therapeutic models of who we are in the twenty-first century. As Allan Schore, another architect of this new model of the self, has remarked, neuroscientists are concluding that even brain structure itself "is experience-dependent and influenced by

social forces". Indeed, because of the deep pervasiveness of these "social forces" in the development and structure of the brain, neuropsychiatrists are now, he notes, referring to the "social construction" of the human brain (2012, p. 225). Brains are where the inner and outer worlds collide and interconnect, mutually shaping and sculpting each other, and these interactions and dependencies occur both within and between brains. Recent advances in interpersonal neurobiology, affective neuroscience, developmental neuropsychiatry, and social neuroscience are revealing the depth of this interdependency and mutual entanglement. Indeed, as neuroscientist David Eagleman (2015) observes, the human brain relies on other brains for its very existence—the concept of "me", he notes, is dependent on the reality of "we":

> We are a single vast superorganism, a neural network embedded in a far larger web of neural networks. Our brains are so fundamentally wired to interact that it's not even clear where each of us begins and ends. Who you are has everything to do with who we are. There's no avoiding the truth that's etched into our neural circuitry: we need each other.

Dependency is built into the fabric of who we are as social and biological beings, hardwired into our mainframe: it is "how love becomes flesh", in Cozolino's striking phrase: "Through the biochemical alchemy of template and transcription genetics, experience becomes flesh, attachment takes maternal form, and culture is passed through a group and carried forward in time … *It is the power of being with others that shapes our brains*" (2006, pp. xv–xix, italics in original). This deep dependency, far from being a weakness, is therefore a necessary and primary source of our strength and resilience, whereas "independence" and "isolation" actually serve to undermine and atomise us—the ideology of independence may be a highly serviceable mythology to control and segregate populations (the familiar psychology of "divide and conquer"), but it is unscientific and also unhealthy for our selves and our chances of social happiness, both of which rely on and require strong social bonds and support systems. As McGilchrist observes, "The main determinants of happiness are not economic in nature. The single most common finding on the correlates of life satisfaction is that happiness is best predicted not by wealth, or even health, but by the breadth and depth of one's social connections" (2009, pp. 434–435).

Eagleman notes that the mutual reciprocity and interweaving of our brains has significant social and political—as well as psychoanalytic—implications, and is based on a new dynamic networking model of identity that profoundly challenges, indeed reverses, the old Enlightenment idea of the self as some sort of self-standing and discrete unit. Twenty-first century neuroscience is significantly upgrading this old, rather quaint, view of the isolated, "rational" individual (*homo economicus*), and also revealing a far richer and more sophisticated understanding of human development, through increased knowledge of "right hemisphere" intersubjectivity, unconscious processes, group behaviour, the role of empathy and mentalization in brain development, and the significance of context and socialisation in emotional and cognitive development.[5] One of the most exciting developments of these new ideas is the RSA's Social Brain project, which places notions of social context and neuroscience at the centre of its formulation of an updated version of Enlightenment ideas—what it terms "21st century enlightenment". As Jonathan Rowson (the former director of the Social Brain Centre) observes (2011), the old idea of an independent, "rational" individual "who makes decisions consciously, consistently and independently is, at best, a very partial account of who we are":

> Science is now telling us what most of us intuitively sense: humans are a fundamentally social species. We are embedded in complex social networks. However, recent social, political and environmental challenges fail to grasp that social context is not an afterthought, a variable to be controlled, but the defining feature of how we think, learn and behave.

That social context is not an afterthought but the defining feature of who we are: this new understanding of the social nature of the brain is central to the paradigm shift that is now occurring in many areas of contemporary thought and practice, and one which needs to be incorporated into the new therapeutic thinking and clinical understanding if psychoanalysis is to remain relevant and able to engage creatively with the challenges of the twenty-first century.

Social disorders, mental disorders

As Nick Totton notes, at a fundamental level both politics and psychotherapy share a similar concern: a desire to engage with and improve the well-being of others, a concern "about how people should be and live". Indeed, as James Hillman remarks (Chapter Ten), given the relational basis and "social construction" of who we are, the *psyche* and the city (the *polis*) are necessarily intertwined and mutually interdependent spheres:

> It took the last several decades for therapy to learn that body is psyche, that what the body does, how it moves, what it senses is psyche. More recently, therapy is learning that the psyche exists wholly in relational systems. It's not a free radical, a monad, self-determined. The next step is to realize that the city, where the body lives and moves, and where the relational network is woven, is also psyche. City strongly affects psyche. Better said: city *is* psyche. (p. 197)

As he explains, "What goes on in the city is not merely politics or economics or architecture. It's not even 'environment'; it's psychology. Everything 'out there' is you." And that's why, as he also points out, the sickness is also "out *there*"—in the environmental destruction, the homelessness, the relentless consumption, even, he notes, in the fluorocarbon cans and fluorescent lighting—manifesting as symptoms of a sick world.

> By removing the soul from the world and not recognizing that the soul is also *in* the world, psychotherapy can't do its job anymore. The buildings are sick, the institutions are sick, the banking system's sick, the schools, the streets—the sickness is out *there*. (pp. 190–191)

As he acutely shows, we need a therapy that can do justice to this sickness, that can start to heal it—to integrate these fissured and broken worlds.

Mental illness is now one of the biggest causes of individual distress and misery in our societies and cities, comparable in levels to poverty and unemployment. "There are now more mentally ill people drawing incapacity benefits", notes Layard, "than there are unemployed people on Jobseeker's Allowance" (2005, p. 2), and this huge weight of misery imposes heavy costs both on individual lives and on the economy (2 per cent of GDP) and the Exchequer (also about 2 per cent of GDP according to Layard's LSE research). Mental illness is currently estimated to cost the UK economy as much as £100billion a year in terms of healthcare, lost jobs, unemployment benefits, homelessness support, police time, and prisoner places (Johnson, 2016). Kovel (Chapter Three) refers to the "colossal burden of neurotic misery in the population, a weight that continually and palpably betrays the capitalist ideology, which maintains that commodity civilization promotes human happiness":

> If, given all this rationalization, comfort, fun and choice, people are still wretched, unable to love, believe or feel some integrity to their lives, they might also begin to draw the conclusion that something was seriously wrong with their social order. (p. 58)

A poignant and powerful illustration of Kovel's point is that one in ten children aged between five and sixteen now suffers from a diagnosable mental health disorder, almost half of adults will suffer from a mental health condition, and more than a third of GP surgery consultations are now due to mental problems (Campbell, 2016; *YoungMinds*, 2016). That something is profoundly wrong with the "social order" is also suggested by the fact that the UK has the seventh highest prescribing rate for antidepressants in the Western world, with around four million Britons taking them each year—twice as many as a decade ago.

The close correlation between depleted and dysfunctional social contexts and the prevalence of mental illness has been observed by many researchers. "Unequal societies", as Professor Richard Bentall starkly observes, "have more psychiatric disorders." His compelling talk for the Institute of Art and Ideas, "Why Society Drives You Mad" (2013), suggests that the presence of factors such as social inequality, racism, and the physical environment have a far more significant role to play in mental illness than the biomedical establishment would like to acknowledge. Living in a modern city, he notes, "makes you 15% more likely to be psychotic"—a striking confirmation of Hillman's link between city and psyche, and a correlation also confirmed by the work of psychoanalyst Christopher Bollas, who observes that "The rate of schizophrenia is two and a half times higher in urban metropolitan areas than it is in rural areas. So it ain't genetic" (Bollas interview, 2015). Treating such illnesses through a narrow biomedical approach (one that, it has to be said, allows huge profits for "Big Pharma") not only fails to address the primary drivers of such distress, but has also been shown to increase the stigma associated with mental illness—a double whammy.

> The more that ordinary people think of mental illness as a geneti-
> cally determined brain disease, and the less they recognise it to
> be a reaction to unfortunate circumstances, the more they shun
> psychiatric patients. (Bentall, 2016)

Medicating populations may drive up profits for large pharmaceutical corporations, support the decontextualised "personal responsibility" rhetoric of governments, and help turn citizens into what Hillman calls "docile plebs", but it does little to help those actually suffering distress, because it does little to actually address the conditions and determinants of mental illness.[6]

As Bentall acutely notes, "Given the evidence, we should be able to dramatically reduce the prevalence of mental health problems by, for example, addressing childhood poverty and inequality, figuring out which aspects of the urban environment are toxic … and by aiming to ensure that all our children experience benign childhoods." Linking "childhood poverty and inequality" with "mental health problems" is a striking illustration of the new embodied and contextualised vision of both mental health and childhood, and one that is slowly beginning to permeate psychoanalytic thinking. Attending to the actual social conditions and drivers of mental distress has only just begun to be recognised and explored: as Bentall (2016) again notes, "Some potential influences on mental health (e.g., the way we organise our schools) have hardly been studied. We cannot create a mentally healthier world if we spend all our time peering into test tubes." Living in a society founded on profound structural inequality is increasingly being recognised as a significant driver of mental illness. "Lip service is paid to the social inequalities that create and maintain mental distress," remark Anne Cooke and Jay Watts, "and society increasingly sees suffering as an individual, psychological issue with a technical fix" (Cooke & Watts, 2016). The intense forms of cognitive dissonance, distress, and even psychosis that social inequality generates has been observed by a number of leading psychoanalysts. Salomon Resnik, for example, observes that "Psychosis can be seen as the sign or symptom of disturbances within our present cultural situation in the world. For a significant number of people, it is a way of escaping from unbearably destructive and maddening social situations" (2016). We live in a maddening world, and it is perhaps unsurprising that so many of us internalise the neuroses, dysfunctions, and alienations of a system that, as Resnik notes, is in many ways psychotic itself. The impact of these wider "social situations" on the prevalence of psychosis is especially concerning since, as Kallert and Leisse's research suggests, those suffering from psychosis are particularly susceptible to contextual and environmental clues and rely on outer structures to contain their inner chaos (Kallert & Leisse, 2000).

Given the powerful impact of environmental conditions on mental health and the correlation between social disorders and mental disorders (from depression and neurosis to addictive behaviours and psychosis), an increasing number of researchers are challenging the way that current funding into mental health operates. Bentall persuasively argues that too much money is currently being spent on technological, pharmaceutical, and genetic research and not enough on addressing the actual triggers for illness, which lie in social contexts and life experiences. Over the past decade, he points out, funding bodies such as the Medical Research Council have spent hundreds of millions of pounds investing in technologies such as brain scanners and gene sequencing machines but only 3 per cent of its budget on funding studies into mental illness:

> It's a tragedy actually. The UK Medical Research Council is one of the biggest funders of medical research in the UK but if you look at the things that they fund ... almost none of it is going towards understanding psychological mechanisms or social circumstances by which these problems develop. It is impossible to get funding to look at these kind of things. (cited in Knapton, 2016)

This preference for funding technological options and solutions strongly reinforces McGilchrist's argument that we live in a rather psychotic and dangerously "left hemisphere" world that would prefer to throw money at machines and temporary quick fixes, however irrelevant they are, than on engaging with the more nuanced and contextualised realities actually driving mental illness. "Both schizophrenia and the modern condition", he suggests, "deal with the same problem: a free-wheeling left hemisphere" (2009, p. 403). But it is also indicative of the presence of repressed interests again, since for the established political and indeed medical elites to formally recognise the "social circumstances by which these problems develop" would mean that they would have to take responsibility for them, as engineers and architects of social and political policy.

A new self, a new politics

Rather than separating our understanding of economic and social practices from our understanding of affective development and human development, we need to bring them together, to align them: we need to realise that politics, the external world, is not a world without an "inner". And for this to happen, we need a new integrated model for mental health, and a new politics: we need a new dialogue between the political and personal worlds, and a recognition of how psychotherapeutic practice and the psyche both shape and are powerfully shaped by existing structures and interests.

As Gerhardt observes (Chapter Four), "As a psychotherapist, I argue that we must bring a deeper understanding of the role of emotional development into our political awareness, and recognise that political behaviour in general is not something separate from other forms of human relationship and is influenced by the same emotional dynamics" (p. 82). *That political behaviour is not something separate from other forms of human relationship*: this is what this integrative vision is all about. These wider social and political contexts are after all made up of human beings, subjective presences, and are constituted by familiar forms of relationships, desires, and behaviours.[7] As Bakan's chapter suggests, the psychological and the economic, the political and the personal, in reality constantly interact and interweave: psychology may indeed "provide a better account of business executives' dual moral lives than either law or economics" (p. 184). If the psyche is necessarily political, embedded in systems of power and control—part of a wider body of social interaction and choice—then the political is simultaneously psychological, is psyche. The particular nature of the current economic and political "psyche" has been suggested by a number of commentators. Anita Roddick, for example, notes that the language of contemporary business is "a language of indifference; it's a language of separation, of secrecy, of hierarchy"—one that, she adds, "is fashioning a schizophrenia in many of us" (p. 184). It's a correlation we should not take lightly: Robert Hare, one of the world's leading authorities into psychopathy, has remarked that psychopathy is not simply a list of internal psychological behaviours but also a set of economic practices. The difference, he notes, is that "serial killers ruin families", whereas "… corporate and political and religious psychopaths ruin economies. They ruin societies" (cited in Ronson, 2011, p. 117).

Applying a psychodynamically informed and neuroscientifically grounded approach to our understanding of social and political behaviours and practices—to issues as various as education, consumerism, sexual addiction, and militarisation (as the commentators in the present book show)—can both significantly enrich our understanding and evaluation of these practices, and also reveal a deeper dimension to their influence and impact. As Gerhardt observes, "The challenge now is to integrate the scientific knowledge that psychology and neuroscience offer us, information about how people develop and how their emotions are played out in the public sphere, with action: only then will we have a chance of moving towards the right solutions" (p. 77). The key word here is *integrate*: whereas our current, left-brain world would prefer to compartmentalise, to divide and rule, to segregate and silo, we must apply a reconciliatory, compassionate, holistic model in order to be of genuine therapeutic benefit and value.[8]

"I sense that people are sick of the current worldview in the West," observes McGilchrist in his compelling discussion with Jonathan Rowson. "We have been sold a sadly limiting version of who we as human beings are, and how we relate to the world." Like Duffell, Gerhardt, Smail, Kovel, and Hillman, McGilchrist argues for a "complete re-think of what our lives are about", one that includes transcending the current alienated and dysfunctional economic and ontological model—what he calls the "morally bankrupt system of competitive capitalism". "We will never solve the major global problems we face", he notes, "by tinkering with the current model" (p. 102). As Duffell (Chapter Six) similarly remarks, this need for a complete shift in perspective also applies to our educational and political structures. "British elitism supports an out-dated leadership style that is unable to rise above its own interests, perceive the bigger picture and go beyond a familiar, entrenched and unhealthy system of adversarial politics":

> Such a leadership style is not to be recommended—it may well be dangerous. It is manifestly unfit for purpose, given the demands of the current world in which, increasingly, problems are communal—indeed global—and in which solutions urgently demand non-polarised cooperation and clear focus on the common good, in order to take effect on a worldwide scale. (p. 119)

As he notes, the problems of the twenty-first century are "communal—indeed global" in nature, and therefore require "non-polarised cooperation and clear focus on the common good"—an outlook completely at odds with the current, crude, seventeenth-century model of atomised individuals competing against each other in glorious isolation. This concept of the self, he suggests, is one ultimately rooted in egoic and dysfunctional left-brain modes of thinking—what he terms the *"Entitled Brain"*, denoting one that is "over-trained in rationality, has turned away from empathy and has mastered and normalised dissociation in its most severe dimensions; it is consequently incapable of recognising the fault in its own system" (p. 119). This form of "normalised dissociation", he notes, characterises contemporary political debate and discussion, a peculiarly manipulative and unempathic form of the "reality principle", and one that—like all such left-brain thought-systems—is ultimately unconscious and narcissistic. McGilchrist makes the salient point that it is both the virtue and the limitation of the left brain that it "doesn't know what it doesn't know", which is why, as Duffell notes, it is "incapable of recognising the fault in its own system".

It is surely time for us to take back our view of ourselves as compassionate and connected human beings, and to develop a new, integrated, and dynamic world in which the values of empathy, compassion, cooperation, and community are not seen as luxuries or incidental to human progress or happiness, but as actually driving our psyches, our evolution. "Developing a new politics based on practical caring and mentalizing", notes Gerhardt, "is an urgent task" (p. 77). And also a necessary task, if we are to seriously engage with the sorts of brains, and lives, we want for our children—one which will depend on reintegrating the economic and the psychological, the inner and the outer, in order to create more robust, resilient, and caring communities and contexts for them to grow up in. This requires thinking differently—as McGilchrist notes, it requires "a complete shift in perspective"—and it also requires practical changes, so that our economic policies and decisions are based on empathy and humanity, not on financial profit. Gerhardt writes:

> At a time when we need to adjust our values and expectations away from a world economy based on growth and the exploitation of fossil fuels towards a world based on greater empathy for others and care for our natural resources, we will need to understand why we behave as we do and what drives us. I would suggest that we need the more collective values of empathy, care and thoughtful collaboration, if we are going to solve the problems that face us. (p. 84)

The need for this adjustment—this shift from exploitation to empathy, from content to context, from narrowly left-brain practices and approaches to right-brain (whole brain) ones—is the challenge for us in the twenty-first century.

Insight and outsight: an overview of the book

This book is divided in two parts, just like the human brain, each one focusing on a different aspect or mode of engagement with the world, also like the human brain. Integrating these two approaches is very much part of the overall purpose of the book. The first part, "Insight", provides an analysis of psychoanalysis and its history, including the reasons for its historical separation from social reality, the political aspects and nature of therapeutic practice, its function within the wider ideological framework, and its transformative potential. The chapters also demonstrate how compelling and illuminating contemporary therapeutic approaches can be when applied to wider social contexts. All the contributing authors are, I think, remarkable and important pioneers of a new model for therapy.

The book opens with David Smail's penetrating examination of the social contexts for individual distress. His work is the inspiration for this whole book—an enormously cogent analysis of how psychology has "served ideologically to detach people from the world we live in", the reasons for this, and how a less "idealistic" and abstracted view of the psyche is necessary both for the health and reputation of psychoanalysis as a profession and for the well-being of each of us as citizens. The depth of his critique makes for uncomfortable reading at times, but it is always galvanising and thought-provoking, and the brilliance of his analysis is only matched by the humanity contained within it. David's pioneering concept of "Outsight"—the subject of the second half of this book—is a formidable tool for anyone engaged not only in mental health but in understanding better how the wider exercise of power and concealed interests operates in our society.

Nick Totton extends this analysis by revealing how these "stubborn problems of power and control" manifest within the consulting room itself, and within the very institutions and ideology of psychotherapy. He suggests how this exercise of power affects not only the clients but also the therapist, and psychotherapy as a project. If anyone believes that these problems do not exist, or that practitioners are not already involved in a "political" programme, they need to read his chapter. As he acutely shows, it is not the presence of these wider issues in therapy that is the problem, but their denial or concealment. However, his approach, like that of Smail's, is ultimately positive, providing that—as with all good therapy—these issues are addressed, not repressed. "By making the struggle over power a central focus of the therapeutic encounter," he notes, "we can do as Freud did with transference: turn a structural problem into a creative aspect of therapy." Indeed, as he points out, making these stubborn, structural problems a central focus "may actually be a necessary condition for a positive therapeutic outcome" (p. 30). By bringing issues of power and interest into awareness—by making the unconscious conscious—he is not only reaffirming and extending the basic impulse of all psychodynamic approaches, but also outlining a new model for psychotherapeutic and political practice for the twenty-first century. For the "political self" of this book's title is also the "therapeutic self".

Joel Kovel's chapter, "Therapy in Late Capitalism", provides a compelling framework with which to understand the social and economic forces acting on all our practices, therapeutic ones included. Because of the homogenisation and commercialisation of intellectual culture, this framework is generally little known today—Kovel provides an empowering lexicon for anyone wanting to engage with the wider social structures and approaches that are currently dismantling and commodifying welfare. He also provides a glimpse of what a socially aware psychology of the self might look like: how issues of the "social unconscious", the "rationalised reality principle", and the ubiquity of neurosis under the present economic system, might be incorporated into a more contextualised and relevant model of the psyche. His chapter also contains a wonderfully grounded illustration of how this "flux of capitalist relations" is no mere theoretical abstraction but is manifest and embodied in the very institutions and relationships of society: his analysis of "the burden of becoming Mum" will strike a chord with every family.

Indeed, the social and political significance of these familial environments and close attachments is the theme of Sue Gerhardt's remarkable exploration of how a modern understanding of developmental psychology can help us comprehend the "connections between our infancies and the kind of world we create". For the issue of parenting—the form of attention we give to our children—not only "affects our psychological development and our brain structure, but also the society and culture in which we live". Her chapter persuasively demonstrates how the "emotional dynamics" of childhood profoundly shape the brain, which then in turn shapes society. This analysis therefore works both ways, allowing her to simultaneously analyse the dysregulated, narcissistic, and sometimes pathological culture of contemporary politics. She has previously written:

> As a psychotherapist I am often struck, when observing the behaviour of those in power, by their remarkable similarity to those less powerful people who are designated as "patients". Whether people are depressed, unhappy or could even be diagnosed as having borderline, narcissistic or anti-social personality psychopathology, the bottom line is that they have difficulties with the quality of their attachments to other people and often find it a struggle to think of others' needs. The same lack of emotional connection to other people is often seen on the public stage. (2010, pp. 45–46)

There is, she notes, "no neat divide between 'private life' and 'public life', since the people who lead the banks, governments or corporations bring their psychological attitudes and values to their public tasks. They shape the culture in their own image" (p. 84). Gerhardt's analysis again points to the high levels of dysfunction operating within these apparently successful and powerful organisations, whose symptoms are nevertheless everywhere apparent. Her concern as a psychotherapist is therefore to understand these connections so that we can make more empathic, integrated, and enriched worlds.

Making connections, and integrating different worlds and approaches, is the theme of the following chapter. The discussion between Iain McGilchrist and Jonathan Rowson about the nature of the human brain and what neuroscience can tell us about its relationship with the world, forms the central chapter of the book. As McGilchrist notes, the brain is an organ that exists to make connections—"The power of the brain consists precisely in the number and complexity of its connections"—so it is perhaps fitting that this chapter should go at the centre of the book, connecting inner and outer, insight and outsight. It is, as he explains, primarily the "right hemisphere" of the brain that is adept at integrating and making relational connections: the right hemisphere "has richer connection with the body via the limbic system" than the left, it "takes into account more and better integrated information, over a broader range", it regulates our capacity for empathy and creativity, and "is the basis of our nature as the 'social animal'". If the paradigm shift that we considered earlier were to be incarnated as anything bodily, it would be a shift from the "left hemisphere" (compartmentalised, manipulative, power-based, and devitalised) to the "right hemisphere" (holistic, empathic, relational, and interconnected). This new awareness of the role of the right brain in delivering a socially integrated and collaborative society will be key both to twenty-first century politics and to the new model for psychotherapy that is now emerging, as demonstrated in the pioneering work of Schore, Cozolino, Siegel, and others. The dynamic and contextualised understanding of the brain not only grounds the present discussion about the "political self" but also suggests that many of our current dysfunctions are the result of being rooted not in neurology, but in ideology. In this sense, as Rowson notes, the chapter illustrates "the social and political relevance of neuroscience" (p. 87).

And as Nick Duffell's illuminating "psycho-historical overview" of boarding schools suggests, the current elite educational system exists in many ways precisely in order to reproduce and replicate these dysfunctions—the specific left-brain psychodynamics relating to dissociation, entitlement, and hyper-rationality. His book, *Wounded Leaders: British Elitism and the Entitlement Illusion—A Psychohistory*, provides a compelling profile of the type of political, judicial, and corporate "leader" that British boarding schools and public schools have traditionally been so good at manufacturing. More than half of the members of the British cabinet in 2010–2012, he points out, came from this hot-housing process, and the influence of these dissociative backgrounds on their subsequent attitudes towards policy and media is subtle, complex, and extensive. Many commentators have remarked on the homogeneity of thinking that these schools exhibit: as one Etonian acutely put it, Eton is like "a factory churning out the same sort of people, over and over again" (*Cutting Edge*, 1991). Duffell reveals the logic behind this "industrialised" educational model in his fascinating analysis of the "Rational Man Project"—the Enlightenment promotion of peculiarly left-brain, compartmentalised, unempathic modes of thinking, rooted in concepts of superiority, disengagement, manipulation, and instrumental reasoning. The formation or mass production of this type of divided, hyper-rational "self"—"the standardised production of rational gentlemen" as

Duffell aptly refers to it—was in many ways a necessary requirement and product of industrialisation and empire. Indeed, in a particularly thought-provoking observation he notes that "Dissociation is the original 'divide and rule' strategy in its individual and pre-political form"—a strategy that became "the unconscious driveshaft of the engine of colonialism" and underwrote the psychic mechanisms that "made slavery possible", again pointing to the implicit impact of the personal on the political. "From the mid-18th century onwards," as he remarks, "we can observe dissociation operating on a massive, global scale." "Rational Man", Duffell concludes, "is permanently at war. He was at war with himself and with the world he had created" (p. 136).

As if to give graphic form to this profound self-alienation, Lt. Col. Dave Grossman's analysis of war, and the culture of violence and militarism that lies behind it, reveals its latent psychological dimension—its origins and consequences. His chapter does to the subject of killing what Freud a hundred years ago did to the subject of sex. Grossman makes the salient point that society often has a "blind spot", a subject it represses: "A century ago it was sex … Today that blind spot is killing." His discussion lifts the lid on this "new repression": a society that neither understands nor talks about the complex and lasting psychological consequences of military engagement (killing), and a society that both plugs itself into *Call of Duty*, *Black Ops*, and *Grand Theft Auto* while simultaneously unplugging itself from any discussion or understanding of the discernible effects of violence on the human brain and wider culture.[9] Despite the ubiquity of violence in late capitalism we are as a society, he observes, largely ignorant of the precise processes and psychology of killing. We have a misconception, for example, that it's easy to kill, or that it's natural to kill—the widespread myth of humans as "natural born killers"—and he shows how this popular delusion is rooted not in neuroscience, sociology, or anthropology, but in fiction:

> The media in our modern information society have done much to perpetuate the myth of easy killing and have thereby become part of society's unspoken conspiracy of deception that glorifies killing and war. There are exceptions … but for the most part we are given James Bond, Luke Skywalker, Rambo, and Indiana Jones blithely and remorselessly killing men by the hundreds. (p. 145)

His chapter effortlessly tears these illusions apart, exposing the vulner-ability, trauma, and resistance to killing that our species experiences. Throughout history, he notes, the military has spent enormous resources, effort, and training to overcome this innate resistance, in order to desen-sitise and dehumanise combatants. Even with this massive arsenal of psychological training and conditioning, the military's own research into firing rates during World War II found to its surprise that only 10 to 15 per cent of soldiers during military engagements actually fired their weapons at the enemy (the "Marshall statistic", which has fundamen-tally redefined how we understand the "death instinct"). When soldiers do participate in killing, unlike in the rather pitiful James Bond and Luke Skywalker franchises, it often leaves deep and devastating mental scars, sometimes lifelong. Unfortunately, this extensive research on the actual nature and costs of warfare rarely penetrates psychoanalytic thinking. There is, in the words of philosopher-psychologist Peter Marin, "a mas-sive unconscious cover-up" in which society hides from itself the true nature of combat. This collective cover-up—our refusal to speak about what is happening in wars—is one of the reasons, he powerfully notes, why we constantly misdiagnose PTSD as if it was a "disorder". His chapter ends by noting the disturbing way in which methods devised by the US military to overcome the Marshall statistic—including the development of operant conditioning firing ranges, pop-up targets, and immediate interactive feedback, "shoot/no shoot training programs", and "symbolic modeling"—have now been made commercially avail-able to young children by huge multinational corporations, in the form of interactive video games which reproduce these same distancing and dehumanising techniques. "The same tools that more than quadrupled the firing rate in Vietnam", he acutely notes, "are now in widespread use among our civilian population" (p. 150).

John Beveridge picks up these themes in his compelling discussion not of death but of sex, showing how internet pornography similarly rewires the brains of users. His chapter persuasively suggests how contemporary technologies, in symbiosis with corporate and com-mercial interests, profoundly and intimately shape our brains—our neural pathways, neurotransmitters, dopamine levels, relational net-works, and the deep processes of the limbic system. For, as Gerhardt noted earlier, "We would miss much of what capitalism is about if we overlook its role in restructuring and marketing desire and impulse themselves" (p. 47). A striking example of this neural "restructuring" is the prevalence of addictive behaviours and attention deficits as a result of extended access to pornography: Beveridge, Gerhardt, and Smail all persuasively demonstrate how consumer capitalism breeds "addictive psychologies" through a deliberate manipulation of the "human brain's dopamine reward systems", and the deregulation of pleasure.

> It is, for example, a particular strategy of modern consumer capitalism to reduce as far as possible inhibitions standing in the way of the self-indulgence and greed upon which an ever-expanding market depends—what might be called the deregulation of pleasure. (Smail, p. 10)

This "deregulation of pleasure", the driving engine of the materialistic basis of the current economic system, is in many ways reified and epitomised in pornography: a manipulative, fetishistic, devitalised mode of attention to others characterised by endless craving and instrumental reasoning. And as Beveridge observes, the impact of this mode of attention is not confined to the internet: "A pornographic sensibility has permeated films, billboards, fashion, television, magazine adverts, and music videos, affecting how people have sex with themselves, how men and women see each other, and how we relate—and it is affecting young people growing up." His chapter shows how the promotion of this form of adrenalised arousal constantly shapes and reshapes our neurological maps and connections—he compares it to a sort of reverse psychoanalytic "training session"—deregulating neurotransmitters such as dopamine and impairing "the white matter fibres in the brain connecting regions involved in emotional processing, attention, decision-making and cognitive control". "With many pre-teen children regularly accessing sexual material on the Internet," he adds, "it has been said that there is a tidal wave of addiction heading towards the therapeutic world" (p. 168). Beveridge's chapter provides an invaluable guide to anyone working with addiction, as well as providing practical advice to mental health professionals in the treatment of addiction. Like the internet itself, the effects of addictive pornography are wrapped around our collective nervous systems: as the title of his chapter suggests it is a "tangled web" we weave.

Both Grossman's and Beveridge's chapters point to the role that contemporary corporations play in driving certain forms of behaviours and relationships, and in Joel Bakan's chapter the fundamentally exploitative and invasive nature of the corporation is analysed, in his remarkable psychological profile of the world's dominant economic institution. "The corporation's legally defined mandate", he notes, "is to pursue, relentlessly and without exception, its own self-interest, regardless of the often harmful consequences it might cause to others." It is programmed to exploit, in other words—rather like the freewheeling and schizophrenic left hemisphere which it in many ways resembles. By its own legal definition, therefore, the corporation is "a pathological institution", and Bakan helpfully lists the diagnostic features of its default pathology (lack of empathy, pursuit of self-interest, grandiosity, shallow affect, aggression, social indifference) to show what a reliably disturbed patient the corporation is. "Most people", he adds, "would find its 'personality' abhorrent, even psychopathic, in a human being, yet curiously we accept it in society's most powerful institution." As we've seen, Anita Roddick (in her interview here with Bakan) describes the language of contemporary business as "a language of separation, of secrecy, of hierarchy"—a language that is "fashioning a schizophrenia in many of us":

> So using child labor or sweatshop labor or despoiling the environment … is legitimate in the maximizing of profit. It's legitimate to fire fifteen thousand people to maximize profits, keep the communities in just such pain. (p. 184)

Therapists looking for drivers of schizophrenia might well look to these vast behemoths and soulless leviathans for the drivers of psychosis in our society: what formerly passed for Enlightenment "rationality" and aggressive management now looks increasingly like profoundly disturbed and dysfunctional psychotic behaviour. "I shouldn't have done my research just in prisons," concluded psychologist Robert Hare, the originator of the widely accepted "Hare Checklist" used to test for psychopathy. "I should have spent some time inside the Stock Exchange as well" (cited in Ronson, 2011, p. 117).

The final chapter of this volume, a conversation between Jungian analyst James Hillman and writer and activist Michael Ventura, beautifully and movingly suggests how the fissured and fractured worlds of the inner and outer might become healed, if psychotherapy can be reintegrated back into the real world. This is the world, he says, that psychotherapy has "left out": "*Hillman makes a wide gesture that includes the oil tanker on the horizon, the gang graffiti on a park sign, and the fat homeless woman with swollen ankles and cracked skin asleep on the grass about fifteen yards away*" (p. 190). It is the world in which psychoanalysis is situated, and needs to re-engage with. Because, notes Hillman, that's where the sickness lies: in the homelessness, in the banking systems, in the corporations, in the oil tankers, in the repressions, in the dissociation and devitalisation. "The world has become full of symptoms"—but then, who better to recognise, diagnose, and treat these symptoms, than therapists? "All our pathologies are imaginings, and so therapy's job is primarily to deal with the symptoms, just as Freud tried at the beginning, but now because the symptoms are the imaginings of the psyche seeking a better form." These "symptoms"—the displayed symbols of our broken world—are, as every therapist knows, both indicators of sickness and also latent signs of life: "the irrepressible imagination breaking through our adapted mediocrity" (p. 196). By engaging with this irrepressible social imagination, this vast interconnected and unconscious sea of being that lives within and through us, Hillman suggests that we can start to transform it, work through it, both in the "external" structures and within ourselves, within our "psyches". For, he observes, it has been the splitting away of the one from the other that has been so disastrous and damaging: the compartmentalisation, dissociation, and severance of the world from us, and us from the world—disastrous and damaging for our politics, for our environment, for our societies, and for our dislocated and severed psyches, struggling to integrate and make sense of the world.

Integrating these divided worlds will have profound implications, which makes this period of history so exciting, so unique. By incorporating social reality into therapy, and therapy into social reality—putting the psyche back in the world—we can enrich and extend both. Moreover, by taking seriously the role of "social influence in the generation of distress" we will finally be able to engage in the prevention, as well as the treatment, of mental illness. For the psyche is necessarily embedded and embodied in this world: it is a social self, and a political self, shaped by powerful economic and social forces but also shaping them in return. The political self is the place where the three roads meet: capitalism, mental illness, and therapy. What route we decide to take is completely up to us, but as Oedipus discovered, our choices will be better the more conscious they are. "You see, Michael, at last therapy is going to have to go out the door with the client, maybe even make home visits, or at least walk down the street" (Hillman & Ventura, 1992, p. 81).

Notes

1. The phrase "splendid isolation" derives, perhaps significantly, from Freud himself, whose own acute sense of personal and political disengagement in Vienna was to significantly affect, and indeed become mirrored, in his psychoanalytic theories. As Adam Phillips notes in his penetrating discussion of this dynamic, "Freud's suspicions about sociability—his paradoxical sense that the very thing that sustained us could ruin us—would permeate psychoanalytic theorizing" (Phillips, 2014, p. 63).

2. "Embedded in every tool is an ideological bias, a predisposition to construct the world as one thing rather than another, to value one thing over another, to amplify one sense or skill or attitude more loudly than another" (Postman, 1992, p. 13). See also McGilchrist's compelling exposition (Chapter Five) of how the attitude, values, and skills of the instrumental "left hemisphere" are being increasingly incarnated and manifested in society, through technology and contemporary economic practice. As a number of contributors in this volume note, the very presence of a therapeutic industry is in itself testimony to the high levels of neurosis and dysfunction embedded within the current system: "A most striking feature of neurosis within capitalism", observes Kovel, "is its ubiquity" (p. 46).

3. See also Phillips's acute observation of the impact of anti-Semitism on the political dimension of early psychoanalytic thinking: "It is not incidental that, at the very time when Freud is, in a sense, not taking the Nazis seriously—because of course he wasn't the only person who did this—he was writing almost entirely about how people refuse to perceive the things that matter most to them, and the ways in which people are skilled at refusing, denying, foreclosing, very evident knowledge" (Phillips interview, 2014).

4. For an illuminating discussion of "psychocomplusion" see Auestad (2016); Friedli & Stearn (2015); Hughes (2015); Ipswich Unemployed Action (2015); Rhodes (2015). For articles on the American Psychological Association's involvement in torture, see Ackerman (2015); *Democracy Now* (2015); *The Economist* (2015); and for the DSM's belated

declassification of homosexuality see Burton (2015); Surís, Holliday, & North (2015).

5. "Our tacit acceptance of homo-economicus may be partly the result of an over-reliance on rationality at the cost of reason ... There is abundant evidence that we do not behave like 'homo economicus', and it is peculiar that we continue to vaunt a model of rationality that directly and consistently contradicts human judgement. Instead we need to move towards a more reasonable form of reflexive rationality, in which we no longer express surprise at humans persistently behaving irrationally in classical economic terms, and begin instead to encourage people at every level of society to make plans and take decisions on the basis of what we know about the social influences, biases and heuristics that shape our framing of choices" (Rowson, 2011, pp. 30, 26).

6. In their contributions to this volume, Gerhardt, Beveridge, and Smail all powerfully challenge the crude and decontextualised traditional rhetoric of "responsibility": "The notion of 'responsibility' lies at the heart of what one might well call our suppression of the social ... For the purposes of understanding how and why people experience and act in the world as they do, and what freedom they may have to act otherwise, the concept of 'responsibility' has become virtually useless. What we need is a psychology that switches its attention from a metaphorical 'inner world' to try instead to elaborate the ways in which powerful influences in the external environment of social space-time serve to liberate or enslave us, as well as to shape our consciousness of ourselves" (Smail, p. 20). As Gerhardt and Beveridge similarly note, what we need is a less moralistic and a more socially nuanced and effective understanding of how the self is engaged with and dependent on deeper environmental conditions and contexts—to realise that we are all embodied and embedded beings, that no man is an island.

7. As Gerhardt notes, in this sense "Each society is a sort of mega-family," transmitting "underlying beliefs and attitudes, simply through the way things are done and the way things are" (p. 72).

8. "In siloed intellectual frames, we chop up human beings into fragmented pieces while deluding ourselves that we're making them whole," notes Batmanghelidjh (2015): "There is a reticence to cross boundaries in the belief that thought and talking should be separated from the body and that the body should be separated from its social environment" (Batmanghelidjh, cited in Warnecke, 2015, p. 58). The systematic and multidisciplinary care model pioneered and developed

by Batmanghelidjh at Kids Company was a remarkable attempt at developing a genuinely integrative model for child welfare and mental health in this country. As she acutely notes, "The history of siloed packages of care is a perverse by-product of Cartesian thinking, where the mind and body are separated for attention. The biggest challenge in understanding the repercussions of childhood maltreatment is in the separation of social, biological and cognitive concerns, reflecting administrative divisions in public management" (ibid., pp. 50–51). It is precisely this Cartesian "separation of social, biological and cognitive concerns" that needs to be addressed if we are ever to establish a system of care that is beneficial to children rather than to the administrators of management systems. Her project for an alternative, more holistic system, "See the Child: Change the System", sought to replace the current dissociative model of welfare (which even the government admits is in crisis and "unfit for purpose") with a more joined-up, integrative, and socially contextualised model of mental health. Indeed, one wonders whether the forced closure of the company, driven by the political and ideological interests in Whitehall and Westminster and a spineless British media, was because of its remarkably cogent and coherent challenge to the existing "siloed" and compartmentalised approach to child abuse and child welfare in this country.

9. See also von Radowitz, 2015: "A report from the APA task force on violent media concludes: 'The research demonstrates a consistent relation between violent video game use and increases in aggressive behaviour, aggressive cognitions and aggressive affect, and decreases in pro-social behaviour, empathy and sensitivity to aggression.'"

References

Batmanghelidjh, C. (2015). Clinical snobbery—get me out of here! New clinical paradigms for children with complex disturbances. In: T. Warnecke (Ed.), *The Psyche in the Modern World: Psychotherapy and Society*. London: Karnac.

Belilos, M. (Ed.) (2016). *Freud and War*. London: Karnac.

Cozolino, L. (2006). *The Neuroscience of Human Relationships: Attachment and the Developing Social Brain (2nd edn.)*. New York: W. W. Norton, 2014.

Duffell, N. (2014). *Wounded Leaders: British Elitism and the Entitlement Illusion—A Psychohistory*. London: Lone Arrow Press.

Furedi, F. (2004). *Therapy Culture: Cultivating Vulnerability in an Uncertain Age*. London: Routledge.

Gerhardt, S. (2010). *The Selfish Society: How We All Forgot to Love One Another and Made Money Instead.* London: Simon & Schuster.

Hillman, J., & Ventura, M. (1992). *We've Had a Hundred Years of Psychotherapy—And the World's Getting Worse.* San Francisco, CA: HarperCollins.

Kallert, T., & Leisse, M. (2000). Schizophrenic patients' subjective needs for care during community-based treatment. *Psychiatria Danubina, 12*(3–4): 253–265.

Marin, P. (1981). Living in moral pain. *Psychology Today, 6*(11): 68–80.

Masson, J. (1989). *Against Therapy.* London: HarperCollins.

McGilchrist, I. (2009). *The Master and His Emissary: The Divided Brain and the Making of the Western World.* New Haven, CT: Yale University Press.

Phillips, A. (2014). *Becoming Freud: The Making of a Psychoanalyst.* New Haven, CT: Yale University Press.

Postman, N. (1992). *Technopoly: The Surrender of Culture to Technology.* New York: Alfred A. Knopf.

Ronson, J. (2011). *The Psychopath Test: A Journey through the Madness Industry.* London: Picador.

Rose, N. (1999). *Governing the Soul: The Shaping of the Private Self.* London: Free Association.

Samuels, A. (1993). *The Political Psyche.* London: Routledge.

Samuels, A. (2001). *Politics on the Couch: Citizenship and the Internal Life.* London: Karnac.

Schore, A. N. (2012). *The Science of the Art of Psychotherapy.* New York: W. W. Norton.

Smail, D. (2005). *Power, Interest and Psychology: Elements of a Social Materialist Understanding of Distress.* Ross-on-Wye, UK: PCCS.

Totton, N. (Ed.) (2006). *The Politics of Psychotherapy: New Perspectives.* Open University Press.

Warnecke, T. (Ed.) (2105). *The Psyche in the Modern World: Psychotherapy and Society.* London: Karnac.

Winnicott, D. W. (1960). The theory of the parent–infant relationship. *International Journal of Psychoanalysis, 41*: 585–595.

Web resources

Abramovitz, M. & Albrecht, J. (2014). The Community Loss Index: A New Social Indicator. https://www.researchgate.net/publication/259727693_The_Community_Loss_Index_A_New_Social_Indicator [last accessed 26.6.16].

Ackerman, S. (2015). Three senior officials lose their jobs at APA after US torture scandal. *The Guardian*, 14 July 2015. https://www.

theguardian.com/us-news/2015/jul/14/apa-senior-officials-torture-report-cia [last accessed 25.6.16].

Auestad, L. (2016). And This Time It's Personal: Psychocompulsion and Workfare. WellRedFilms. http://lawritings.net/film/ [last accessed 11.6.16].

Bentall, R. (2013). Why Society Drives You Mad. Institute of Art and Ideas. https://www.youtube.com/watch?v=ufHO3zlY3qk [last accessed 26.6.16].

Bentall, R. (2016). Mental illness is a result of misery, yet we still stigmatise it. *The Guardian*, 26 February 2016. https://www.theguardian.com/commentisfree/2016/feb/26/mental-illness-misery-childhood-traumas [last accessed 26.6.16].

Bollas, C. (2015). Interview with Matt Olien. Prairie Plus. https://www.youtube.com/watch?v=Qy9LAyhwNZo [last accessed 26.6.16].

Burton, N. (2015). When homosexuality stopped being a mental disorder. *Psychology Today*. https://www.psychologytoday.com/blog/hide-and-seek/201509/when-homosexuality-stopped-being-mental-disorder [last accessed 2.7.16].

Campbell, D. (2016). Two-thirds of parents fear child's mental illness "a life sentence". *The Guardian*, 28 June 2016. https://www.theguardian.com/society/2016/jun/28/parents-children-mental-illness-life-sentence-yougov-survey [last accessed 5.7.16].

Cooke, A., & Watts, J. (2016). We're not surprised half our psychologist colleagues are depressed. *The Guardian*, 17 February 2016. http://www.theguardian.com/healthcare-network/2016/feb/17/were-not-surprised-half-our-psychologist-colleagues-are-depressed [last accessed 11.6.16].

Corbyn, J. (2016). More funding needed for mental health in stressful modern Britain. *The Mirror*, 18 February 2016. http://www.mirror.co.uk/news/uk-news/jeremy-corbyn-more-funding-needed-7397591 [last accessed 11.6.16].

Cutting Edge (1991). Class of '91: Eton College documentary. Channel 4: *Cutting Edge*. https://www.youtube.com/watch?v=r75ajf6UEhU [last accessed 3.7.16].

Democracy Now (2015). No More Torture: World's Largest Group of Psychologists Bans Role in National Security Interrogations. http://www.democracynow.org/2015/8/10/no_more_torture_world_s_largest [last accessed 25.6.16].

Eagleman, D. (2015). The Brain with David Eagleman: Part 5, Why Do I Need You. https://www.youtube.com/watch?v=6VwIQq9aOkQ [last accessed 11.6.16].

Economist, The (2015). How America's psychologists ended up endorsing torture. http://www.economist.com/blogs/democracyinamerica/2015/07/terror-torture-and-psychology [last accessed 25.6.16].

Friedli, L., & Stearn, R. (2015). Positive affect as coercive strategy: conditionality, activation and the role of psychology in UK government workfare programmes. *BMJ Medical Humanities.* http://mh.bmj.com/content/41/1/40.full [last accessed 11.6.16.

Hughes, J. H. (2015). Psychology and the unemployed. The British Psychological Society. http://www.bps.org.uk/blog/presidential/psychology-and-unemployed [last accessed 25.6.16].

Ipswich Unemployed Action (2015). Unemployment a Mental Health Problem to Solve by "Psycho-Complusion"? https://intensiveactivity.wordpress.com/2015/06/10/unemployment-a-mental-health-problem-to-solve-by-psycho-compulsion/ [last accessed 25.6.16].

Johnson, S. (2016). The cost of mental illness. *The Guardian*, 17 May 2016. http://www.theguardian.com/healthcare-network/2016/may/17/economic-cost-of-mental-illness?CMP=share_btn_fb [last accessed 26.6.16].

Knapton, S. (2016). Mental illness mostly caused by life events not genetics, argue psychologists. *The Daily Telegraph*, 28 March 2016. http://www.telegraph.co.uk/news/2016/03/28/mental-illness-mostly-caused-by-life-events-not-genetics-argue-p/ [last accessed 11.6.16].

Layard, R. (2005). Mental health: Britain's biggest social problem? The London School of Economics and Political Science. http://eprints.lse.ac.uk/47428/ [last accessed 26.6.16].

Phillips, A. (2014). On the Couch: Adam Phillips and Daphne Merkin, 92Y Plus. https://www.youtube.com/watch?v=i2RRA1sQ274 [last accessed 11.6.16].

Resnik, S. (2016). Madness dispersed or disseminated: A re-actualization. *Karnacology*, February 2016. https://karnacology.com/2016/02/08/madness-dispersed-or-disseminated-a-re-actualization-by-salomon-resnik/ [last accessed 26.6.16].

Rhodes, E. (2015). Is unemployment being rebranded a psychological disorder? *The Psychologist*, August 2015. https://thepsychologist.bps.org.uk/volume-28/august-2015/unemployment-being-rebranded-psychological-disorder [last accessed 11.6.16].

Rowson, J. (2011). Transforming Behaviour Change: Beyond Nudge and Neuromania. RSA Projects. https://www.thersa.org/globalassets/pdfs/blogs/rsa-transforming-behaviour-change.pdf [last accessed 26.6.16].

RSA Social Brain Centre. https://www.thersa.org/action-and-research/rsa-projects/social-brain-centre/social-brain/about [last accessed 11.6.16].

Surís, A., Holliday, R., & North, C. S. (2015). The Evolution of the Classification of Psychiatric Disorders. MDPI (Multidisciplinary Digital Publishing Institute). www.mdpi.com/2076-328X/6/1/5/pdf [last accessed 2.7.16].

von Radowitz, J. (2015). Study finds that violent video games may be linked to aggressive behaviour. *The Independent*, 17 August 2015. http://www.independent.co.uk/news/science/study-finds-that-violent-video-games-may-be-linked-to-aggressive-behaviour-10458614.html [last accessed 6.7.16].

YoungMinds (2016). Mental Health Statistics. http://www.youngminds.org.uk/training_services/policy/mental_health_statistics [last accessed 6.7.16].

PART I

INSIGHT

CHAPTER ONE

Understanding the social context of individual distress*

David Smail

Introduction

Therapeutic psychology has been going long enough now for it to have a discernible history. The story of its development since the last quarter of the nineteenth century is in fact a familiar one and I am not going to repeat it here (an excellent all-round account of the development of therapeutic psychology can be found in Dilys Davies, *Counselling in Psychological Services*). There are, however, just a few features of this story that I would like to pick out for particular comment.

The most striking thing of all is how "psychotherapy", in becoming one of the greatest cultural and commercial success stories of the Western world, remained over the past hundred years almost hermetically sealed off from the rest of reality. It was in fact as if the world had split in two: the West introvertedly preoccupied with the workings of the individual psyche, the East extrovertedly concerning itself with the machinery of material relations within society.

---

*This chapter is an edited version of *Power, Interest and Psychology: Elements of a Social Materialist Understanding of Distress* by David Smail (2005) and is reprinted by kind permission of PCCS Books, Ross-on-Wye.

But it was not as though the real world wasn't happening as we Westerners searched for the meaning of our actions in our secret wishes and unconscious motives. The twentieth century, after all, exploded into revolution and war on an unprecedented scale, but you would hardly know it from examining the theoretical speculations of Freud and Jung at the time—and so far as outer events did concern them, it was nearly always as expressions of inner "psychic" conflicts of some kind (a stance still widely evident among some psychoanalytic writers).

This indifference to the mundane operations of external materiality by no means meant that the great psychologists were above such things—it was just that they appeared not to attach much psychological significance to them. It is a particularly poignant irony that Freud's concept of repression is probably the best explanation one can find for his apparently failing to notice the importance to him (and indeed to us all) of the means of material survival.

This is nowhere clearer than in the correspondence Freud maintained with his friend Wilhelm Fliess during the years in which the foundations of psychoanalysis were laid (Masson, 1985a). The extraordinary thing is (if hardly unexpected from common sense) that while refining a theory which carried its subjects further and further from the real concerns of the outer world, when it came to his personal life Freud over and over again in his letters betrayed a consuming anxiety about that most mundane of preoccupations: money.

In his letter to Fliess of 2 November 1896, for example, Freud expresses worry about "the state of my practice this year on which my mood always remains dependent". While as an explanation of psychological unease this would have had the full understanding of almost any nineteenth-century European novelist, it seems not to have occurred to Freud to countenance such a material basis for the troubles of his patients.

However, his personal circumstances have improved somewhat by 6 December, "after having for once enjoyed the full measure of work and earnings *that I need for my well-being* (ten hours and a hundred florins) …"[1] And a couple of months later (8 February 1897) things are even more promising:

> I now have ten patients in treatment, including one from Budapest; another one from Breslau is due to arrive. It is probably one hour too much, though otherwise I feel best precisely when I am working a lot.

Last week, for example, I earned 700 florins—you don't get that for nothing. Getting rich must be difficult.

In one of the most interesting letters in the collection (21 September 1897)—that which announces to Fliess the beginnings of a shift in Freud's theory of neurosis, from the view that his patients were sexually molested as children to the idea that they imagined it all—there is a continuous theme of financial insecurity running alongside his reasons for abandoning some of his previously key contentions (e.g., that fathers could so often be involved in "widespread perversions"). The letter opens with Freud's observation that he is "… impoverished, at present without work", and acknowledges later on that: "The expectation of eternal fame was so beautiful, as was that of certain wealth, complete independence, travels, and lifting the children above the *severe worries that robbed me of my youth.*" Towards the end he regrets—prematurely as it turned out—that "It is a pity that one cannot make a living … on dream interpretation!"

Jeffrey Masson, in his excellent account of this period of Freud's life, suggests that Freud's retraction of the seduction theory and substitution of it with the idea that sexual events in the patient's past were fantasy, represented a failure of moral courage (Masson, 1985b). But maybe one can see other, more tangible, more material factors at work here. Could it be that Freud's gradual shifting of the burden of blame for his patients' "neuroses" from the fathers and uncles of his "hysterical" female patients to, eventually, themselves (via, incidentally, the lower orders in their household—the servant girls), might have been something to do with who was paying his bills?

A letter of 21 September 1899—as fine a piece of self-analysis as one could wish for—would appear to give weight to the view that money was for Freud as strong a motivator as it is for most of the rest of us:

A patient with whom I have been negotiating, a "goldfish", has just announced herself—I do not know whether to decline or accept. *My mood also depends very strongly on my earnings. Money is laughing gas for me.* I know from my youth that once the wild horses of the pampas have been lassoed, they retain a certain anxiousness for life. Thus *I have come to know the helplessness of poverty and continually fear it.* You will see that my style will improve and my ideas will be more correct if this city provides me with an ample livelihood.

It would surely be very hard in these circumstances for Freud to pursue a theory that threatened to cut off the very source of his income.

It is perhaps a particularly twentieth-century form of prudery that money as a *personal* motivation is not something alluded to in polite society, and to "accuse" Freud of being influenced by material concerns can still easily be taken as at least tasteless and at most outrageous. But is it not precisely outrage, indignation, and accusations of unworthiness— the idea, in short, that some things are just too tasteless to suggest— which generates and masks the operations of repression?

Repression

What seems to me particularly significant is that a psychologist focally concerned with our most basic fears and motivations—one, moreover, famously given to self-analysis—should not find a fundamental place in his theoretical structure for factors *"on which my mood always remains dependent"*, which he feels *"I need for my well-being"*, and which created *"the severe worries that robbed me of my youth"*.

This may be revealing, but it need not be surprising. For what it reveals is not a shameful flaw in Freud's character, but the extent to which we all manage to avoid reference to the way our actions are governed by our interest—the way, that is, we need always and everywhere to struggle with and adjust to the material demands of our existence. And "avoiding reference to" is precisely what is meant by repression, as Freud himself made very clear.[2]

In my view, the nineteenth-century theoretician who best understood the relation of people to their world, and what this meant (among other things) for their conscious as well as unconscious understanding of themselves, was Karl Marx. While "dialectical materialism" helped fuel the struggles against oppression of the peoples of Eastern (and some of Western) Europe, the intellectual preoccupations and philosophical tastes of the intelligentsia to which the theories of Freud and Jung appealed were far more equivocal. One could not say that the founders of therapeutic psychology had no interest in material science, but that their interest was always fused with a penchant for magical authority that attempted—and in a way largely succeeded in—lifting theory beyond the reach of empirical criticism. In this Freudians and Jungians typified a cultural strain already evident in the West for some time, and which flowered most colourfully at about the turn of the twentieth century in a strange mixture of scientific curiosity, fascination with the occult, aestheticism, religiosity, and obsessive sexual interests and experimentation. This, of course, is what we tend to mean when we speak of *"fin de siècle"*.[3]

It is not hard to identify the currents in nineteenth-century literary and artistic, philosophical and scientific culture that resonated with the thought of Freud and his followers, and it is also of interest to note those that didn't. Both Freud and Jung, I would suggest, swim in the same stream as, for example, Nietzsche, Blavatsky, and Yeats, the Pre-Raphaelites, Wagner, Bergson. In other words, theirs is a kind of amalgam of Romantic, occult, mystical, and "scientific" ideas, where, however, science is attractive more for the mysterious authority it may bestow than for its empirical transparency (witness, for example, Freud's enthusiasm for Charcot's hypnotism).

On the other hand, what one might call the materialist line of nineteenth-century culture—including (as more or less random examples) Dickens, Tolstoy, and indeed most of the great English, Russian, and French novelists, Proudhon, Marx, and slightly later writers like Sinclair and Tressell—pursues a line that finds almost no echo at all in psychoanalysis and its offshoots. While a materialist understanding of society was at the centre of uprising, war, murder (e.g., of Rosa Luxembourg) and the Russian Revolution, the conceptually much more slippery mixture of interior "psychic" mysteries and the magical power of the expert took root among a Western intelligentsia whom these huge events of the world stage appeared almost to pass by. With only a few minor setbacks in the mid-twentieth century, this essentially idealist current flows unabated into the twenty-first.

It is not as if the swirling fashions of thought that made and make up this current are characterised by any noticeable unanimity: the principal psychological approaches, for example, spent and continue to spend many years in bitter dispute. Psychoanalysis, behaviourism, positivist "science", "humanistic" approaches of the mid-twentieth-century such as those of Carl Rogers, Abraham Maslow, Fritz Perls, and others, existentialism and phenomenology, plus the cognitivist, social constructionist, and postmodernist approaches of more recent times, may often seem to have very little in common, and have certainly fought hard to carve out their distinctive territory. And yet at the centre of this quarrelsome mishmash of ideas and practices is a gaping nothingness that, paradoxically, serves in one respect to unify them all. This is that *none* of them has anything to say about how the apparatus of power and interest that so clearly operates at the level of society comes to be reflected in the subjectivity of individuals—or even *whether* it does.

It is true, of course, that until the capitulation of Eastern communism in the late 1980s, Marxism enjoyed a strong vogue in sociology and some other academic disciplines, and it is true too that some of Foucault's ideas took root (somewhat belatedly) in a rather far-flung corner of post-modernist psychology; but all the same power and interest *as inescapable material factors* in the lives and minds of human beings (as opposed simply to features of "discourse") have just not figured in psychological thinking. Such an oversight, I would argue, can only reflect the operation of repression on a massive scale.

In my view the effects of this repression can be observed at the most general, public level as well as in quite specific, private social exchanges. In popular culture, for example, the "reasons" for events are nearly always sought in the conduct and intentions of individuals (usually in the form of "blame"). This is largely an *interior* matter, i.e. a question of psychological causes originating in individuals' heads that have, so to speak, escaped out into the real world by way of their actions. Attempts to reverse the direction of this causation, so that individuals' conduct is seen as *reactive to* events originating outside them, are likely to be seen as "excuses".

Explanations that take an exterior (from outside in) as opposed to an interior (from inside out) point of view are thus likely to evoke both incomprehension and disapproval. And it is precisely these reactions that one can often see on the faces of those to whom power and interest are offered as *explanatory* concepts in the course of private conversation. For example, when I have suggested to colleagues or students that Freud's retraction of the seduction hypothesis in favour of *fantasised* sexual abuse as the generator of "hysteria" was a factor of his need to earn a living (see above), I have often felt that they have simply not been able to comprehend what I am saying, but see it as a kind of below-the-belt slur on Freud's character—rather as if I had uttered an obscenity so out of context that people couldn't be quite sure they'd heard it right. I've often had the same feeling when I've suggested to groups of professionals that therapists and counsellors (among whom, after all, I count myself) shy away from an explanation of our activities in terms of interest because it would seem to undermine our very *raison d'être*—i.e. it would undermine the "scientific" rationale for our practice. This idea seems to be seen often not just as uncomfortable but as, literally, unthinkable. "Yes, but what do you *mean* by interest?" people say, puzzlement written all over their faces; "Could you *define* it?"

Power, interest, and psychology

In my view, *power*, which may be defined broadly as the means of obtaining security or advantage, is the fundamental dynamic of social structure. Apart from the latent violence that constitutes the ultimate sanction of every society (and is making an ominous reappearance at the present time), the dominating power in the modern Western world is that of money. In other words, it is what shapes and maintains a society that forms, from our current Western perspective, a pyramidal hierarchy, at the peak of which is a small corporate plutocracy and at the bottom of which is a vast, largely politically atomised collectivity of consumers (the traditional working class of industrialised Western countries having been fractured and to a considerable extent exported to other parts of the globe). Distributed through the middle ranges are diminishing numbers of public-service workers and professionals, and an expanding bureaucracy of managers of various grades.

Power, though historically omnipresent, is mercurial; if its structures were stable it would become too predictable and hence too easily undermined. What can be said about the role of therapeutic ideology in the maintenance of dominating power here and now cannot remotely be thought of as standing for all time, either past or future. Indeed, successfully to maintain its advantage, power needs to catch us off balance, to stay one step ahead. And it almost certainly will. The principal kinds of power that operate within social space-time are: biological, coercive, legal, economic, and ideological (i.e., control of meaning, language, perspective, and horizon). The control of meaning (ideological power) is of course an immensely important aspect of social control. The degree to which people can analyse and understand their situation and the influences that shape it depends upon their access to knowledge and information that exist largely in organisations and institutions which tend to have an interest in keeping them to themselves. The mass media of news and entertainment, again semi-independent of national control, constitute an enormous influence on our lives, and they are clearly about much more than simply the provision of objective information and innocent cultural stimulation and fun. The actual interests they serve are, however, largely opaque to the mass of their consumers.

Interests, I suggest, are, like drives and needs, determined by our nature as embodied beings, and stem from such biological necessities as food, sex, security, pain avoidance, and pleasure, and shade into the rather more obviously social requirements for attachment, association, money, and status. But interests, seen in this sense, are not *additional to* needs and drives so much as *replacements of* them. The crucial theoretical point I'm trying to make is that by conceiving of "drives" as "interests" we turn traditional psychology *inside out*, so that rather than seeing individuals as *pushed from within* by various urges and desires for which, ultimately, they are personally responsible, they are *pulled from without* by the social manipulation of, in the last analysis, inescapable biological features of being human. I am arguing, therefore, not for an entirely new psychological concept called "interest", but for a change in *perspective* that conceives of "motivation" not as individual and internal, but as social and environmental.

Powers may be *received* (by interests) or *resisted* (by counter-powers). Reception affords by far the most efficient transmission of power. It is, for example, a particular strategy of modern consumer capitalism to reduce as far as possible inhibitions standing in the way of the self-indulgence and greed upon which an ever-expanding market depends—what might be called the deregulation of pleasure.

Magical voluntarism

In the world of twentieth-century therapeutic psychology, people do things because of impulses, intentions, cognitions, or conditioned reflexes of which they may or may not be aware. This inevitably means that, at least implicitly, they are *responsible* for their actions and that change can be brought about only through some kind of *decision* on their part. Such decisions may not be easy, they may need to be based on "insight" brought about by therapeutic interpretation or intervention; but when all is said and done, "It's up to *you*." Only a very small proportion of therapies take cognisance of influences upon the subject that are both social and material, while pretty well all the conventional mainstream approaches cluster in the individual/idealist approaches. The best name I can think of for the philosophy that underlies this phenomenon is "magical voluntarism". The central contention here is that, with perhaps the expert help of your therapist or counsellor, *you* can change the world *you* are in the last analysis responsible for, so that it no longer causes you distress. The way may certainly be hard, possibly (at the expensive end of the therapeutic spectrum) necessitating Odyssean ventures into the Unconscious, but ultimately salvation depends upon personal acts of will.

This was the principal achievement of the founders of modern psychotherapy: to turn the relation of person to world inside out, such that the former becomes the creator of the latter. With many postmodernist approaches (e.g., "narrative therapy") magical voluntarism reaches its apotheosis: the world is made of words, and if the story you find yourself in causes you distress, tell yourself another one.

From any rational, scientific standpoint, this kind of view is completely incoherent—indeed it is psychotic. And yet the universe of discourse in which it is put forward *is*, essentially, a rational, scientific one: the propositions of "psychology" purport to be statements about our own nature and the nature of our world, and in this specific case it is asserted that our world is made of words and can be remade through rearranging words. That such a preposterous notion could be seriously put forward and maintained by people considered to be social scientists is inexplicable unless one introduces into the explanatory framework the notion of *interest*. In other words, it cannot be that the proposition in question is *true*; it can only be that it is *useful*, i.e., that it *suits the interests* both of those who assert it and those who assent to it. As long as consideration of interest is repressed we are likely to remain utterly mystified about the causes and cures of our psychological ills, trying instead to find our way in a make-believe world while looking for guidance principally to the adepts of magical voluntarism.

But once we make *interest* our focus, things become much clearer.

The stake counsellors and therapists have in maintaining an individualist and idealist account of emotional distress is obvious, for only such an account can legitimate the role of professional practitioner. Early in his career, Freud himself nearly stumbled into the dilemma posed for therapeutic practice by the realisation that psychological distress is in essence nothing more than unhappiness brought about by adverse circumstances. (His oft-quoted observation that "neurotic misery" is merely the mask of "common unhappiness" was made in 1895,[4] well before he had perfected the complex psychic apparatus that justified the professional practice of psychoanalysis.)

Clearly, any such insight as this points in a very different direction from that implied in the professional practice of therapy. A therapist can hope to act only upon the sufferer, and is in no position to act upon the sufferer's *world*. Therapeutic interest will therefore dictate that reasons for distress are found within, and not outside the person; if they are not, therapy will have to be abandoned (Freud, let it be noted, duly "found" such reasons). Furthermore, not only must the causes of distress be both personal and interior, they must also be subject in one way or another to the influence of the therapist. At this point, I suggest, therapists find themselves uncomfortably close to magicians, and it is not surprising if the concepts and rituals of therapeutic cure (e.g., "interpretation of the transference") bear a strong resemblance to the spells and incantations of sorcerers.

However, it is not just the interests of therapists that are in play here, but also the interests of their clients, as well as those of the wider society.

One has only to consider the typical ingredients of religious belief, or indeed the bulk of the output of Hollywood, to appreciate the fundamental appeal of magic to pretty well all of us. Reconciling ourselves to the harshness of life, the inevitability of death, and the resistance of the world to our efforts to change it are things none of us finds easy, and anything that promises to increase our personal power over fate can anticipate an enthusiastic reception from most of us. Our interest in there being accessible solutions to the troubles that beset us could scarcely be stronger, and any guru, therapist, or celebrity who tells us we can do anything we want, overcome any obstacle, change ourselves from the inside out, is likely to get an attentive audience.

The alternative to magical voluntarism—for example, that the world is unyielding to mere wishes, and must be worked upon in patient collaboration with others—is likely to get the thumbs down, and proponents of "material realism" tend not to find themselves elevated to cult status at all quickly. For this is, in comparison, a somewhat bleak philosophy, recognising that even with blood, sweat, and tears a good outcome is not assured, and that damage once done may well be irreparable. How much more attractive is the idea that a relatively brief association with a sorcerer, priest, astrologer, or therapist can heal the wounds of the past or unleash a golden future, than that the conditions of our existence are to a great extent the outcome of material forces far beyond our personal control, historically unchangeable, and with an uncertain future only amendable at best to the efforts of concerted, communal (*political*) effort.

Therapy, then—as has been abundantly demonstrated in recent years—is likely to be a popular option,[5] but it is not only to the interests of therapists and their clients that it appeals. Arguably, those who stand to benefit most from its underlying philosophy are those likely to feel themselves least in need of it. For if therapy offers a magical solution to the majority who suffer the world's cruelties, it also provides handy advice for them to be given by the minority who inflict them: suffering is to be lessened not by attacking social injustice, but rather by *personal* readjustment of the disadvantaged themselves. Whether such readjustment is to be achieved through "counselling" or through half-baked political philosophies such as "communitarianism",[6] in which moral exhortation replaces practical help, the message is the same: wealth and privilege have nothing to do with a brutally unbalanced social system, but are available to all who achieve the right psychological balance and act "responsibly". It is surely no coincidence that the increasing disparities in wealth and power, both within and between countries over the past twenty-five years or so, have been accompanied by an explosion in the advocacy and provision of therapies and political prescriptions that have magical voluntarism at their core.

It is, then, only by taking into account the networks of *interest* that glue society together that we can really understand the undoubted success of counselling and psychotherapy, which are otherwise empirically unsupported, philosophically incoherent, and mutually contradictory.[7]

Scientism, CBT, and the myth of mental illness

But there is another factor that we need to consider if a fair account is to be given of the rise of therapy, especially around the middle of the twentieth century, and how it was that many well-informed and well-intentioned people—particularly of course professionals in the field—embraced and defended the "therapeutic ethos" with passion, and sometimes courage. For it would certainly be wrong of me to give the impression that therapists and counsellors themselves are nothing but a bunch of consciously self-interested charlatans out to exploit human weakness and legitimate social inequality. This would of course be to *psychologise* the account in exactly the way I am arguing against throughout: it is not that the individuals *decide* to act in accordance with interest (theirs or others'), but rather that, not least because interest is repressed, they find themselves caught up in a system in ways they cannot fully understand and would—if they could understand it—undoubtedly deplore.[8]

Those of us who applauded the mid-century challenges that the likes of Carl Rogers, George Kelly, Fritz Perls, and "existential" writers issued to orthodox psychiatry, psychoanalysis, and behaviourism, no doubt did so because they introduced much less mechanistic, objectivist, and inhumane accounts of personal distress. But what we didn't notice was that, even though there was a new emphasis on the importance of decent personal relationships—both within and outside therapy—as well as on exploring the individual's subjectivity, we were still stuck with the same model of therapist–patient "treatment" in which "change" would come *from within*, almost certainly greatly facilitated by some kind of "intervention" on the therapist's part. In other words, though some principles of "the treatment of mental illness" were hotly disputed, and some quite important gains made in terms of humanising "the therapeutic relationship", the fundamental paradigm shifted not one iota: we were still dealing with an individual (now "client" rather than "patient") expected, with of course therapeutic help, to seek salvation through personal change. Furthermore, absolutely no progress had been made in reducing the confusion which inevitably flows from representing an interest-soaked enterprise as a scientific procedure—if anything, "humanistic" approaches made things worse, as they introduced into therapeutic psychology ethical and aesthetic elements which are impossible to square with a model of dispassionate, professional advice.

The attack on the "medical model" that coincided with the burgeoning of the new therapies was no doubt a reaction against the heartless scientism of psychiatry, orthodox psychoanalysis, and "behaviour therapy". All of these, in their own way, claimed an objectivity and scientific validity that was in fact quite bogus. Patients were "diagnosed" with "illnesses" for which extraordinarily haphazard "treatments" such as electro-convulsive therapy, insulin comas, brain surgery, and drugs were prescribed; a minority might be subjected to the supposedly neutral, technical procedures of Freudian analysis; others would undergo the relatively newer, "scientifically established" behavioural techniques based on the conditional learning experiments of Pavlov and Skinner. In every case there was the same emphasis on the aloof indifference of the clinician to anything but the technical modifications of "symptoms", and almost no attention would be paid to the circumstances of patients' lives beyond the immediate family (and by no means always that); neither was any serious consideration given to the subjective experience of "mental illness".

Any critical and sensitive observer walking into almost any psychiatric institution in the 1950s would thus find him- or herself confronted with a population of bemused and desperate "psychotic" and "neurotic" patients, whose always disturbed and often devastating life circumstances simply didn't figure as causal elements in the theory and practice of those responsible for their care.

Hardly surprising, then, that so many of us embraced the new therapies with such enthusiasm: at least we could talk to patients as human beings about the issues that mattered to them and respond with compassion. But instead of developing a critique of the society that gave rise to our clients' difficulties, we replaced the dead scientism of conventional approaches with moralising critiques of individual development and theories about ideal human being. Instead of considering the material circumstances of people's lives, we got into "relationships" and "spirituality". Whether followers of Carl Rogers, Fritz Perls, Eric Berne, Albert Ellis, George Kelly—or any other of the many therapeutic gurus who came to prominence in the second half of the twentieth century—the emphasis was always on what the *individual* should do to overcome or compensate for personal inadequacies of one kind or another. Even though such inadequacies might be considered with (Rogerian) "warmth, empathy, and genuineness" in a setting where the therapist made no attempt to hide behind a mask of cold impersonality, the onus nevertheless was always on the client to "take responsibility" and make the necessary personal changes indicated by therapy.

In fact, this placed a new burden on people to whom life had already been less than kind. For failure to be "cured" (not a term anyone used, but which nevertheless lurks at the heart of the whole idea of "therapy") meant *personal* failure: either a moral failure of will (refusal to take responsibility) or falling short as a human being (failure to reach the aesthetic standards set up by, for instance, such arbiters of "self-actualisation" as Abraham Maslow and Fritz Perls). If the scientific pretensions of the "old treatments" resulted in a frightening impersonality and neglect of subjectivity, at least they didn't (intentionally) tamper with your soul; in contrast, the new therapies assigned themselves a scope more characteristic of religion than science and, at least tacitly, invested themselves with an authority that went well beyond the objective and technical.

Margaret Thatcher's much-cited view that "There's no such thing as society, only individuals and their families," finds an unacknowledged echo in almost all approaches to therapy, including those that continued throughout the second half of the twentieth century to wrap themselves in the mantle of "science". For example, in asserting its claim to "evidence-based" credibility, cognitive behavioural therapy (CBT) takes no more note of social influence in the generation of distress than do the "humanistic" therapies.

CBT—in fact more a kind of rhetorical construction than a serious, theory-based practice—is perhaps the least convincing of all therapies from the standpoint of a critical onlooker. In combining the "scientific rigour" of behavourism with the mentalism of, essentially, popular psychology, CBT is par excellence the product of professional interest; it appeals to common-sense ideas of how people do things (action follows deliberation) while attempting to preserve the technical mystique that behaviourism managed to establish within academic psychology precisely on the grounds of *anti*-mentalism. This opportunistic marriage of incompatible approaches is then supported by its doctors through the judicious highlighting of a handful of research studies from the huge, chaotic, and contradictory literature[9] that has developed in the psychotherapy field over the past fifty years or so.

In some ways the concessions made by behaviour therapists to "cognitive" factors, in order to give birth to the more "credible" hybrid CBT, is paralleled by the development of postmodernist approaches in therapy (and indeed psychology more generally), in which the implausible constraints imposed by a too-rigid scientism yield to a framework more generously accommodating of the needs of the therapy market.

There is no doubt that many dissenters from the ruling positivist/ behaviourist line suffered under its domination, undergoing years of frustration as they struggled in vain to get a hearing for therapeutic approaches that paid proper respect to subjectivity. For some, the advent of postmodernism seemed to provide exactly the breakthrough they had longed for, ushering in a "new paradigm" (House, 2003) that would at last allow an unfettered exploration of crucial therapeutic issues. But, I think, one only needed to step for a moment outside the consulting room to see that this was not so much a new dawn of reflective insight and intellectual tolerance as a deregulation of the academic and therapeutic orthodoxies. The coming of postmodernism had more to do with market expansion than with the progress of psychological understanding.

Although it is quite common for academic psychologists as well as therapists to feel that they are still fighting old battles, in fact there is no longer much sign either in academia or the wider culture of the dominance of rigid scientism. The final two decades of the twentieth century saw a relaxation of control in which, for example, psychoanalysis emerged from long years of scornful neglect and dismissal, "alternative" forms of medicine and therapy suddenly found themselves flourishing, and "blue sky" thinking could all but pass for research. Academic psychologists could discuss "grounded theory", "action" and "qualitative" research, "discourse analysis", and other forms of uncontrolled and even speculative investigation in ways that would have been unthinkable only a short while before. Philosophers expressed their contempt for any notions such as "truth" or "right" that was not translated into a kind of linguistic illusion (Derrida, in Norris, 1987) or the pragmatic construction of a particular self-interested group (MacIntyre, 1981; Rorty, 1980). At the same time, university provision expanded dramatically (interestingly, in Britain, mainly through a simple rebranding of already existing educational facilities) and with it the provision of counselling courses of every hue. The direction of pretty well all public institutions, including of course education and health, became subject to a uniform business culture.

Business is instinctively antipathetic to the "old" academic values of scholarship, intellectual rigour, and the disinterested search for truth, which in fact not only do not facilitate, but actually stand in the way of market expansion and moneymaking. Many of those working in health and education thus found themselves completely disorientated and bemused as the crass "philosophies" and techniques of business management suddenly came to be imposed on them from the highest levels of their organisations. The conceptual flaccidity and generously inclusive nature of postmodernism was ideally suited as an underlying rationale for creating and running new markets where what mattered was "wealth creation" and not critically rigorous thought.[10]

What we witnessed, I would argue, was not the tortured, hard-won emergence of a new paradigm, but the (counter-revolutionary) imposition of a "new" orthodoxy. Orthodoxies are about power, not truth, which perhaps is why for many of us the changes that overcame our places of work had an uncomfortably familiar feel about them: the message might seem different but the medium was the same, and in fact our freedom to think independently about our discipline and to develop our practice creatively was greatly curtailed—not, as before, by a kind of doctrinal bullying, but by the deliberate application of (non-professional) managerial control.

Thus, although markets were deregulated, control of production was not, and the new managerial classes, blindly responsive to the interests of neoliberal capitalism, were assiduous in making sure that, at least as they saw it, all business-unfriendly practices were eradicated from professional and academic institutions, and procedures of discipline and surveillance were introduced into middle-class occupations that formerly had been applied only to workers. Although in the clinical field "quality" was supposedly "assured" through the establishment of "tough targets", "evidence-based practice", and "clinical governance", etc., the managers' visceral hostility to knowledge, combined with their unawareness of their own ignorance, meant that in fact the field quickly became an incoherent collage of ideas and practices whose only common feature was a superficial market credibility. But that, of course, was all that mattered.

In this way, the turning of the millennium marked no great progress in psychological understanding, but rather, compared with what had existed only a few years before, an enormous expansion in the market for counselling and therapy. No longer constrained by a "medical model" to limit their attentions to the manifestation of a handful of "neuroses", therapists and counsellors are now able to claim as their legitimate province huge swathes of human conduct[11] ranging from grief to criminality, family discord to international conflict.

The fact that this individualist/idealist bandwagon rolls on so successfully is testament to how little truth matters in this sphere (as in so many others). Magical voluntarism may be difficult to support rationally, but it pays, and at a time in history when the bottom line is—not for the first time—paramount, we are unlikely to see any diminution in its sway.

The illusion of the autonomous self

In all this "psychology"—a central tool of ideological power—plays its crucial part. If people are to be diverted from criticising the material circumstances that condition their lives, they must believe those circumstances to be irrelevant, and psychology has over the past century invented and sustained a magical theology in which it seems that people may choose themselves and shape their future by eradicating their past.

Our self-as-centre culture makes it very difficult for us to conceive of responsibility as anything other than the application of personal influence which has its origin entirely within the individual agent. It takes quite an effort of imagination to see the person as a point in social space-time *through which* powers flow. Though, as an individual, I am indeed that point through which whatever powers and resources available to me may be, so to speak, refracted back into the social world, I certainly did not personally create them out of nothing.[12] It is with the sphere of ideality that traditional therapeutic psychology has mainly concerned itself, and as a consequence has become lost in a magical realm which in fact has no chance of impacting upon the real world of material space-time. Thus what we take to be "psychology" in this respect *hypostatises* an immaterial world based on linguistic constructions, inevitably giving rise to a mythology of magical voluntarism that is, though highly plausible, doomed to impotence.

It is not that "selves" cannot or do not change; it is simply that significant change comes about as the result of shifts in the pattern of environmental influence, not because of the individual's personal wishes or efforts. The extent to which you can alter your "self" will depend upon the powers available to you to alter your world. "Therapy" may help someone to redeploy more effectively than before what powers and resources are available to him or her (which explains the oft-cited research finding that young, attractive, verbal, intelligent, and successful people gain most from psychotherapy). Therapy may also provide the person with much-needed support and solidarity at times of great trouble. Beyond these entirely "ordinary" (in the sense used by Peter Lomas, 1999) services, however, there is no magic about therapy, and no reason to justify its becoming a professional form of "treatment".

The notion of "responsibility" lies at the heart of what one might well call our suppression of the social. Whatever it is we seek to understand—ranging from the reasons for personal distress to the "evil" of spectacular crime or the failure of public servants to avert some social disaster—it is always to an unanalysed and unanalysable individual, internal world (where "blame" is harboured) that we turn our gaze. As essential cogs in the vast economic machine designed to extract profit for the minority at the top of the social pyramid, politicians have an important role in representing disadvantage as personal moral failure. For the purposes of understanding how and why people experience and act in the world as they do, and what freedom they may have to act otherwise, the concept of "responsibility" has become virtually useless. What we need is a psychology that switches its attention from a metaphorical "inner world" to try instead to elaborate the ways in which powerful influences in the external environment of social space-time serve to liberate or enslave us, as well as to shape our consciousness of ourselves. As things are, it is not at all clear how far individuals are able to marshal and control the influences that flow through them. Furthermore, in our attempt to understand the processes involved we are constantly misled by the assumption that our commentary refers directly to them.

Insight and outsight: societal perspectives within therapy

This is not to say, however, that the individualism and idealism of orthodox approaches to psychotherapy have not had their critics, right throughout the period we have been considering. The world view implicit in Freudian psychoanalysis is so bizarre that it is not surprising that from the very beginnings of modern psychotherapy rational sympathisers found it impossible to swallow whole.[13]

For example, even though still focused very much on the individual, Alfred Adler soon left the camp Freud was endeavouring to set up because he was unable to overlook the fact that our place in *society* is just about our most fundamental concern from a psychological point of view. Subsequent apostates from orthodox psychoanalysis in the first half of the twentieth century included the once-familiar trio of Erich Fromm, Karen Horney, and Harry S. Sullivan,[14] all of whom placed great emphasis on the ways in which we are social products whose distress can neither be understood nor fully dealt with if divorced from its social context. Although prominent and even influential around mid-century, their perspective did not take permanent hold in the field (students of clinical psychology these days are quite likely not to have heard of them). A more recent proponent of a social perspective within psychiatric disorder (notably "schizophrenia"), coupled with a subtle and profound consideration of subjectivity, was of course R. D. Laing.[15] Briefly influential, as with the others, Laing's work seems now to be regarded more as a kind of "typical" Sixties extravagance than an important contribution to our understanding of serious distress.

The "therapeutic community" movement, at its peak (in Britain) in the 1960s constituted an attempt to take social factors into account in the treatment of "mental illness", such that several previously conventional psychiatric institutions were transformed into mini-societies in which the chief therapeutic focus was on how the inmates—patients and staff—related to each other. While this represented a laudable attempt to get beyond "individuals and their families", the project foundered (among other reasons) because of the inevitable insularity of the communities themselves: as it does with individual therapy, the world that had originally generated patients' difficulties lay in wait beyond the hospital doors to re-inflict its injuries once they were discharged. (Asylum would indeed be the "treatment of choice" for most forms of psychological distress were it not for its impermanence.)

More recently, the development of "community psychology"[16] as an offshoot of clinical psychology reflects (and contributes to) an awareness of the issues raised above and tries to counter the insulating effects of "treatment" by extending its influence into the actual communities in which people live. In this way "community psychologists" and other community workers may try to help people tackle some of the noxious features of their social environment that are amenable to communal action, involving if they can those powers within the community (local authorities, etc.) that bear responsibility for them. At this point the role of psychologist or community worker begins to shade into that of politician, and what the implications of this might be is not clear, but in any case it does in my view reflect a more accurate appreciation of the causes of distress than just about any other "clinical" discipline.

All these forms of practical dissent within psychoanalysis, psychiatry, and clinical psychology constitute an at least implicit critique of magical voluntarism, and attempt to take social factors seriously. In parallel with, but not necessarily allied to them, there has since mid-twentieth century been a constant stream of criticism both of the conceptual foundations of conventional therapies as well as of the inadequacy of evidence of their effectiveness. The motives of such critics—ranging from H. J. Eysenck in clinical psychology and Thomas Szasz in psychiatry to more recent writers such as Robert Fancher (1995), William Epstein (1995), and Donald Eisner (2000)—have varied considerably, but they represent a very large body of opinion that questions the soundness of the very basis of therapeutic psychology.

At an even broader conceptual level have been the critiques such as those of Michel Foucault (1979) and Christopher Lasch (1985) of the whole apparatus of "treatment", seeing them as the result of an essentially *disciplinary* political exercise. This kind of critique has laid the foundations for a widespread awareness of the social consequences—indeed the whole socio-economic and socio-political aims—of an ideology of "therapy" which is closely allied to the interests of corporate capitalism.[17]

Though not focally "therapeutic", the "critical theory" developed throughout much of the twentieth century by thinkers and researchers of the Frankfurt school of social criticism, essentially Marxist in its approach, probably constitutes the most thoroughgoing and intellectually challenging attempt to focus on the societal origins of individual malaise. Herbert Marcuse's *One-Dimensional Man* (1964), for example, offers a brilliantly powerful demonstration of late capitalism's crippling effect on our subjectivity, while Jürgen Habermas (e.g., 1987) has worked assiduously over the years (and in my view with great success) to rescue truth from the postmodernists. Russell Jacoby's *Social Amnesia* (1975) is an appreciative account of the Frankfurt thinkers' assault on the social blindness and individualism of much mainstream and psychological writing.

However, I find it puzzling—even paradoxical—that so many of the Frankfurt writers, in order to theorise the influence of material, societal conditions on personal subjectivity, felt it necessary to turn for help to psychoanalysis. The attempt to marry Marxism and psychoanalysis was of course encountered more or less from the outset in the writings of left-wing Freudians such as Reich and Fenichel and is found more recently in the work of a range of more directly therapeutic writers (e.g., Joel Kovel, 1983; and the British therapists grouped around the journal *Free Associations*), much of whose work deserves respectful attention. The basic argument (as put, for example, by Jacoby) seems to be that in psychoanalysis Freud posits an (essentially pessimistic) view of the human psyche as shaped culturally and historically by forces beyond the reach of the individual's autonomous control. While that may superficially point to some common ground between Freud and Marx, the fundamental differences seem to be overwhelming. What can be gleaned from his writings of Freud's political views is more typical of the saloon bar than of dialectical materialism, and though certainly

Freud refers to himself on occasion as a "revolutionary", this is certainly meant in an intellectual rather than a political sense. Jacoby states the case well (and, somewhat strangely, cuts the ground from under his own feet):

> Psychologism is the constitutional failing of psychology, *psychoanalysis included*. Social process and conflicts are read as psychological and individual ones. Society is conceived as simply an individual or psychological pact between men, not as a piece of reality with its own social gravity. (op. cit., p. 65, my italics)

No matter how intelligent and accurate critiques of the therapeutic orthodoxy have been, they have been dealt with easily enough by the rhetorical devices of the ruling magical-voluntarist orthodoxy. This would of course be puzzling if the debate were truly the scientific one it pretends to be, but in fact even at its most sharply divided, any argument between idealists/individualists on the one hand and social materialists on the other is almost bound to be vacuous because, once again, the criterion of validity is not truth, but power.[18] Virtually all the critics of the orthodoxy, however impeccable their credentials, have sooner or later been marginalised not because their arguments are untrue, but because they are inconvenient.

If the world we live in were really constructed of "discourse" none of this would matter very much, and "reality" would change shape and colour according to the flow of power and interest. The success of "spin" and the apparent absence of any serious consequences of our cavalier treatment of old notions such as right and truth might suggest that we can indeed get along very well without pursuing these "grand narratives" of the Enlightenment. Alternatively (which is my view), it may be that our indifference to material reality leads to an increasingly depleted environment, unbalanced society, and tortured subjectivity. The last of these three—and the one with which this chapter is of course principally concerned—is a function very largely of the first two, and to understand how we come to suffer avoidable psychological distress we are going to have to extend our gaze beyond the "inner worlds" of individuals to take account not only of social structure, but also of the limitations placed on our imaginings by the real world.

Notes

1. My emphasis in this and following quotations.
2. "We now seem to know all at once what the difference is between a conscious and an unconscious presentation. The two are not, as we supposed, different registrations of the same content in different psychical localities, nor yet different states of cathexis in the same locality; but the conscious presentation comprises the presentation of the thing plus the presentation of the word belonging to it, while the unconscious presentation is the presentation of the thing alone … Now, too, we are in a position to state precisely what it is the repression denies to the rejected presentation in the transference neuroses: what it denies to the presentation is translation into words, or a physical act which is not hypercathected, remains thereafter in the Ucs in a state of repression" (1915e, p. 201).
3. For a brilliant study of aspects of Freud's political and cultural background, see Schorske, 1961.
4. See Freud and Breuer, 1895d, p. 393.
5. For a powerful critique of the psychology industry see Tana Dineen, 1999.
6. For a particularly crass exposition of this "movement" see Amitai Etzioni, 1995.
7. This proposition will, I know, strike many as contentious. The best single source I can think of to cite in its support—even if only indirectly—is Colin Feltham, 1999.
8. The capitalist counter-revolution of the late twentieth century in the West co-opted therapy as part of a technology of profit, and it did so so swiftly—in part by engaging the interests of therapists and counsellors themselves—that many, perhaps most, practitioners still find it hard to accept their complicity in a political and economic system they in all likelihood deplore (neo-conservative therapists certainly exist, but they are thin on the ground).
9. Some of the nature of this is conveyed in the excellent volume edited by Dryden and Feltham (1992).
10. For an excellent critique see Philo and Miller, 2001.
11. A number of critics have lined up against this tendency. See for example Dineen, 1999; Furedi, 2003; Hansen, McHoul, and Rapley, 2003; and Pupavac, 2004.
12. "The psychology of leaders", Chomsky writers, "is a topic of little interest. The institutional factors that constrain their actions and beliefs

are what merit attention" (1989, p. 19). And that is precisely the point: circumstances choose the person, not vice versa. Since circumstances decree that there can be only one leader, we make the mistake of concluding that the leader who emerges—Hitler, say—is unique, either (at the time we adulate him) in his virtue or (after his fall from grace) in his evil. It is, however, the office (and what sustains it) that is unique, not the person. Just look at the politician who is voted from power or the pop star who falls out of the charts—victims of instant ordinariness! Here, before our very eyes, we observe what happens when social power ceases to flow through the embodied locus which constitutes our individuality. In fact, as the cynical manipulators of the popular culture industries well recognise, the "unique star" can be elevated from a very wide range of ordinary people, but, having been selected, it takes a rare and exceptionally balanced head for the manufactured celebrity not to believe in his or her own image.

13. Two of the best critics of Freud that I know are Gellner (1985) and Webster (1995).

14. Works by these writers are too numerous to cite. I have listed the most important on my website at http://www.davidsmail.info.

15. See, for example, Laing, 1967.

16. A good account is to be found in Orford, 1992.

17. See, again, the works of Dineen; Furedi; and Hansen, McHoul, and Raply—all cited above.

18. Just how vacuous the argument can be may be judged from an examination, once again, of the contributions to Colin Feltham's (ed.) *Controversies in Psychotherapy and Counselling*, cited above, in which quite often the *same* research evidence is cited to support fundamentally opposed views.

References

Chomsky, N. (1989). *Necessary Illusions: Thought Control in Democratic Societies*. London: Pluto Press.

Davies, D. (1997). *Counselling in Psychological Services*. London: Open University Press.

Dineen, T. (1999). *Manufacturing Victims: What the Psychology Industry is Doing to People*. London: Constable.

Dryden, W., & Feltham, C. (1992). *Psychotherapy and its Discontents*. London: Open University Press.

Eisner, D. A. (2000). *The Death of Psychotherapy: From Freud to Alien Abductions.* Westport, CT: Praeger.

Epstein, W. M. (1995). *The Illusion of Psychotherapy.* New Brunswick, NJ: Transaction Publishers.

Etzioni, A. (1995). *The Spirit of Community: The Reinvention of American Society.* London: Fontana.

Fancher, R. T. (1995). *Cultures of Healing.* New York: W. H. Freeman.

Feltham, C. (Ed.) (1999). *Controversies in Psychotherapy and Counselling.* London: Sage.

Foucault, M. (1979). *Discipline and Punish: The Birth of the Prison.* London: Penguin.

Freud, S. (1915e). The unconscious. *S. E., 14.* London: Hogarth.

Freud, S., & Breuer, J. (1895d). *Studies on Hysteria.* London: Penguin, 1974.

Furedi, F. (2003). *Therapy Culture: Cultivating Vulnerability in an Uncertain Age.* London: Routledge.

Gellner, E. (1985). *The Psychoanalytic Movement: The Cunning of Unreason.* London: Paladin.

Habermas, J. (1987). *The Philosophical Discourse of Modernity.* Cambridge: Polity Press.

Hansen, S., McHoul, A., & Rapley, M. (2003). *Beyond Help: A Consumer's Guide to Psychology.* Ross-on-Wye, UK: PCCS.

House, R. (2003). *Therapy Beyond Modernity: Deconstructing and Transcending Profession-Centred Therapy.* London: Karnac.

Jacoby, R. (1975). *Social Amnesia: A Critique of Conformist Psychology from Adler to Laing.* Hassocks, UK: Harvester.

Kovel, J. (1983). *Against the State of Nuclear Terror.* London: Pan.

Laing, R. D. (1967). *The Politics of Experience and The Bird of Paradise.* London: Penguin.

Lasch, C. (1985). *The Minimal Self: Psychic Survival in Troubled Times.* London: Pan.

Lomas, P. (1999). *Doing Good? Psychotherapy Out of Its Depth.* Oxford: Oxford University Press.

MacIntyre, A. (1981). *After Virtue: A Study in Moral Theory.* London: Duckworth.

Marcuse, H. (1964). *One-Dimensional Man: Studies in the Ideology of Advanced Industrial Society.* Boston, MA: Beacon Press.

Masson, J. M. (Ed.) (1985a). *The Complete Letters of Sigmund Freud to Wilhelm Fliess 1887–1904.* Cambridge, MA: Harvard University Press.

Masson, J. M. (1985b). *The Assault on Truth: Freud's Suppression of the Seduction Theory.* London: Penguin.

Norris, C. (1987). *Derrida.* London: Fontana Modern Masters.

Orford, J. (1992). *Community Psychology: Theory and Practice.* Chichester, UK: Wiley.

Philo, G., & Miller, D. (2001). *Market Killing: What the Free Market Does and What Social Scientists Can Do about It.* London: Longman.

Pupavac, V. (2004). Psychosocial interventions and the demoralisation of humanitarianism. *Journal of Biosocial Science, 36*: 491–504.

Rorty, R. (1980). *Philosophy and the Mirror of Nature.* Oxford: Blackwell.

Schorske, C. E. (1961). *Fin-de-Siècle Vienna: Politics and Culture.* Cambridge: Cambridge University Press, 1981.

Smail, D. (1995). Power and the origins of unhappiness working with individuals. *Journal of Community and Applied Social Psychology, 5*: 347–356.

Smail, D. (2005). *Power, Interest and Psychology: Elements of a social materialist understanding of distress.* Ross-on-Wye, UK: PCCS.

Webster, R. (1995). *Why Freud Was Wrong: Sin, Science and Psychoanalysis.* London: HarperCollins.

CHAPTER TWO

Power in the therapeutic relationship*

Nick Totton

> *Can anyone do effective therapy without becoming an instrument of social control, without participating and contributing, often unknowingly, to the construction or the maintenance of a dominant discourse of oppression?*
>
> —Cecchin, 1993, p. ix

> *Psychotherapy is the only profession where the practitioner can be insensitive, evasive, patronising, arrogant, discourteous, self-righteous or just plain wrong and where clients' observations of this can be taken to be an expression of* their *problems, evidence that what they really need is more of the same therapy.*
>
> —Sands, 2003, p. 15

---

*This chapter was originally published in *The Politics of Psychotherapy: New Perspectives*, edited by Nick Totton (© Open University Press, 2005), and is reproduced with the kind permission of Open University Press. All rights reserved.

Introduction

The psychotherapy relationship is vulnerable to the abuse of power, from hard-to-define but nonetheless damaging emotional manipulation to very concrete behaviours such as financial and sexual exploitation. These abuses are fairly common; but how far are they part of the *structure* of the psychotherapy relationship and the feelings it fosters— exaggerated versions, perhaps of something underlying every therapeutic encounter? I will focus on how the structure of psychotherapy builds in stubborn problems of power and control, irrespective of the good intentions or otherwise of the practitioner.

Like the fact of abuse itself, these structural issues have often been pointed out—often, understandably, as part of an argument against therapy per se. My own position is much more optimistic than this. I believe that *by making the struggle over power a central focus of the therapeutic encounter*, we can do as Freud did with transference: turn a structural problem into a creative aspect of therapy. In fact, this is what many therapists and their clients are already doing. It may actually be a necessary condition for a positive therapeutic outcome.

Abuse of power

Outright therapeutic abuse is serious and widespread. According to the UK charity POPAN (2004), 50 per cent of calls to its phone helpline are alleging abuse within the talking treatments; this amounts to around 300 people each year and—since many clients have never heard of POPAN—must represent only a small proportion of what actually occurs. Several different forms of abuse have been documented, including such things as clients being unable to tell their counsellor that the counselling is not being helpful or being afraid to quit therapy because of the anticipated response of the counsellor (Dale, Allen, & Measor, 1998); gay users of counselling reporting that their therapists advised them to change their sexual orientation (Garnets, Hancock, Cochran, Goodchilds, & Peplau, 1991; several psychoanalysts freely admit to this, e.g., Socarides, 1996); and—far more researched than any other abuse— sexual activity between therapists and their clients.

Many different figures are quoted for sexual abuse, probably the highest being a finding that 9 per cent of male psychotherapists anonymously admitted to having had sexual involvement with clients

(Pope, Keith-Spiegel, & Tabachnik, 1986). According to Prozan's (1993, pp. 354–356) collation of American research on sexual abuse in therapy, around 5 per cent to 7 per cent of therapists admit anonymously to sexual contact with clients, while 65 per cent to 70 per cent of therapists report hearing from a client that a previous therapist has had sexual contact with them. Pope's recent survey (2001) indicates 4.4 per cent of therapists admitting to sexual abuse and argues that the incidence may be declining; it is also possible that the tightening of accepted standards means that, even anonymously, fewer practitioners will admit to sexual abuse (i.e., more self-deception is being practised). Sexual abuse happens at the top of the therapeutic hierarchy at least as often as lower down (for instance, Noel & Watterson, 1992).

Sex in therapy is a difficult subject to address soberly, being subject to the "moral panic" effect (Pearson, 1983). Denman offers a valuable reconceptualisation of therapist–client sex that, without condoning it, positions it as one of a *range* of harmful activities in therapy and suggests that its prohibition is "a politically necessary evil rather than as a personally difficult good" (in Totton, 2006, p. 68). One might also suggest that like child or adult rape, sex between therapist and client is symptomatic of an inability to perceive or imagine the other person's experience and needs and that this inability is unacceptable in a psychotherapist at work.

Structural problems of the therapy relationship

Critics often argue that the sorts of abuse just outlined are related to how therapy is structured and how this makes clients feel. Many focus specifically on the power imbalance that accrues around transference (see, for example, Sands, 2000). Generally speaking, clients arrive at therapy hoping and expecting that the therapist will be able to help, through their wisdom, understanding, and expertise: in a very natural way, they tend to give power to the therapist. In Krause's words: "There is always the possibility of conflict in communication. There is therefore also always the possibility that the most powerful will persuade, command, or event terrorize the less powerful" (1998, p. 153).

Many familiar therapy techniques intensify the transferential power imbalance: not only do clients give power to the therapist, the therapist acts so as to grab power with both hands. As Sands points out, the rules of conversation are strikingly different within therapy from outside it: "... for example, they do not follow the conventions which cover 'turn-taking' ... in normal speech" (2000, p. 39). The client has to learn what sort of communication is expected and accepted. In this and many other ways (for example, therapists' obsession with precise punctuality and their apparent belief that clients can control the traffic), the unfamiliar situation throws the client off balance—in David Smail's phrase, it creates "social dislocation" (2003, p. 22). I recently watched a video of an assessment interview conducted by a psychoanalytic therapist, which started approximately as follows: after a long pause, the clearly uncomfortable client asked the very reasonable question, "So should I just tell you about why I'm here?" The therapist's response was, "Is there something else that you feel should happen?"—a familiar and comprehensible move from an "insider's" viewpoint, but from the prospective client's perspective, a humiliating and mystifying one.

It is this sort of interaction that leads Mearns and Thorne to say that, at the start, "[T]he counsellor holds nearly all the cards in a game of which the client does not even know the rules" (1988, p. 98). As Hinshelwood argues (1997, pp. 101–102), no genuinely informed consent to undertake psychotherapy is possible: no one can appreciate in advance what it will be like, however much it is explained. And even when the client learns the rules, they are not her rules, but those of the therapist, or of the therapy "game" itself.

> It is always the analyst ... who establishes the rules that govern behaviour in this primal space. However much these rules may be constructed to enable the patient's cure, the analyst is their maker and enforcer. (Kurtz, 1989, pp. 27–28)

This situation is open to massive exploitation, as Claude Steiner confesses:

> As a successful psychotherapist ... I used my power to the hilt— and not always to my client's advantage ... I interrupted, over-rode, ignored, judged, evaluated, insulted, attacked, patronized, discounted and lied to the people I worked for ... assuming that they needed my gentle, authoritative, sometimes devious, parental attitude, in order to get better. (1981, p. 214)

Steiner is not confessing to malice or bad faith, but simply to compulsive helping combined with belief in his own expert knowledge.

The profession of psychotherapy unfortunately does include those who believe that they know what other people really think and feel. We all make this mistake, of course, we do it all the time, but it becomes particularly dangerous when it is given the benediction of the status of expert. (Sands, 2000, p. 190)

This uncannily echoes a criticism put to Freud by his friend Fliess in the earliest days of psychoanalysis: "The reader of thoughts merely reads his own thoughts into other people" (Masson, 1985, p. 447). Clearly, the more unresolved issues the therapist has (and only psychopaths believe themselves free of unresolved issues) the more danger there is that these "thoughts" will be positively misleading—that, as Cecchin puts it in the context of family therapy, the therapist will try "to instruct the family on his own pattern" of neurosis (1987, p. 411).

And if the client protests, the therapist has a number of finely honed tools for putting them back in their place. The greatest of these is interpretation. I remember once hearing a presentation (similar things are said every day) where a therapist described a difficult relationship with a client who argued against many of his interpretations of her words and behaviour. One day she came in and told him she had bought a new bath, which turned out not to fit properly, so that she had to bash it around to get it unto the available space. His immediate interpretation was that this represented her distortion of her own material in order to accommodate her version of its meaning. But might it not have been the therapist himself who was portrayed as bashing the client's material into his own preferred shape?

Readers who are psychotherapists or counsellors may be starting to feel anxious and defensive. Me too. After all, we know we are (fairly) good people! We know that we are (consciously) well intentioned. Yet therapy can often feel to the client like a "no win" situation, where someone else always holds the better cards. (For an extended analysis along these lines of a case history of Patrick Casement's, see Totton, 2000, pp. 144–146). Sometimes this is recognisably a matter of "bad" therapy, where the practitioner is unskilful, arrogant, or in bad faith. But is there such a thing as "good" therapy, free from problems of uneven power? Jeffrey Masson believes that there is not:

Psychotherapy cannot be reformed in its parts, because the activity, by its nature, is harmful. Recognizing the lies, the flaws, the harm, the potential for harm, the imbalance in power, the arrogance, the condescension, the pretensions may be the first step to the eventual abolition of psychotherapy that I believe is, one day in the future, inevitable and desirable. (1990, p. 297)

As I will explain later, I disagree with Masson that psychotherapy should be abolished. But I think he is right to suggest that it is not only the "bad" therapist who imposes her own judgements and understandings on her clients. Masson's discussion (1990, p. 229 ff.) of Carl Rogers—by general agreement a highly skilled, empathic, and conscientious practitioner, whom Masson nonetheless shows exercising a "benevolent despotism" over his clients—must lead us to ask whether *something about the practice itself*, rather than about particular practitioners, creates problems around power.

This goes beyond the issue of the individual power relationship between client and therapist and raises questions about how therapy works to support and endorse the power relations of society as a whole. Ian Parker draws attention to "the power of the therapist as a ... part of the regime of truth that defines what subjectivity must be like" (1996, p. 459); a "regime of truth" being a discourse that "is effective in organizing and regulating relations of power" (Foucault, 1980, p. 131; cf. Rose, 1990). Therapy that positions the client as powerless in the face of socially sanctioned expertise clearly supports the uneven distribution of power.

Thus Felix Guattari argues that even a radical analyst is repressive through the nature of his work:

> His [sic] whole way of working reproduces the essence of bourgeois subjectivity. A man who sits on his chair listening to what you say, but systematically distances himself from what it is all about, does not even have to try to impose his ideas on you: he is creating a relationship of power which leads you to concentrate your desiring energy outside the social territory. (1984, p. 69)

(That is, it leads you to alienate your subjectivity.)

In one way or another, I suggest, all therapists are carrying out a political programme in their work with clients. Therapists have their own, often highly developed, beliefs about how people should be and live. These beliefs are essentially political in nature; they are also often unconscious and implicit. For us to hold such beliefs is an inevitable part both of our lives as citizens and of our whole approach to interacting with our clients. This is very obvious with therapy styles that think explicitly in terms of cure and adjustment: people *should* be healthy, *should* be well adjusted—and, of course, each school and each practitioner has their own set of small print about what "healthy" or "well adjusted" actually means. "Well adjusted" to what? Each practitioner believes their clients should adjust to whatever aspects of life they themselves see as natural or acceptable.

This programmatic aspect, although more obvious with approaches that explicitly seek cure or adjustment, does not only apply to them. We can see this clearly in relation to sexuality: each therapist has their own ideas about what constitutes normal sexual behaviour and inevitably applies these to their work with clients. It is actually not at all easy even to make our ideas about sex available for conscious consideration. We can spend years in therapy achieving this. Consciously or unconsciously, we seek to move our clients towards a view and a practice of sex that is closer to our own. One position we may take, of course, is that we accept, or try to accept, any sexual behaviour that makes our clients happy. (We may or may not agree unconsciously with this conscious position.) And that itself is a political judgement, a liberal one, that any sexual behaviour is acceptable as long as its participants are happy.

Ideas about how people should be are equally present in more process-oriented approaches, which try to follow and support whatever arises, whether or not this matches the practitioner's expectations. Personally, I see this as a splendid intention, which I try to apply in my own work; but even if we succeed in this quite difficult project, it is still based on a set of beliefs about how people should be. For a process-oriented practitioner, people *should* be spontaneous, *should* follow their unconscious wisdom rather than try to control it, things *should* be left to sort themselves out in their own way—again, an entire political programme.

Many people want to draw a line between a programme for individuals and a programme for society—as if it was possible to have one without the other. But like it or not, our position on how individuals should be necessarily entails a position on how society should be organised. If individuals should be this way, then obviously society should be organised so as to permit and support this way of being—which may or may not already be the case. If our position about individuals is a conservative one, our position on society will also be conservative: that everything should stay more or less as it is or perhaps go back to how it was when we were a bit younger. In that case, our programme can stay more or less invisible: everything is all right as it is. But this is no less a programme than one that wants people and society to change.

In other words, there is no political neutrality, since politics permeates our social experience. Psychotherapy that advocates "adjustment", "realism", or dealing with "the world as it is" arguably damages the client's capacity to tolerate a *difference* between their desire and reality—and to do something about it. As Joel Kovel points out, "Many anxieties can be stilled by fostering acceptance of the established order of things" (1978, p. 316); equally, anxiety can often be lessened by pointing out to a client that their problem is not simply a personal one, but something set up *by* the established order of things (for example, society's arrangements around gender and sexuality).

Let me emphasise that I am not saying there is anything wrong with therapists having beliefs. We are human beings, we have views about how things should be, how people should be. Some of those views, in *my* view, are more compatible with the working of psychotherapy than others; but operating from a set of beliefs is in no way wrong, in fact it is inevitable. What I *do* think is bad practice is to pretend that we are *not* operating from a set of beliefs or that those beliefs are different from what they really are. Then we confuse both our clients and ourselves.

I suggest that it is also bad practice to claim that we are not influencing the client in the direction of our own beliefs or even that we are not *trying* to do so. We do not have to give a lecture in order to communicate our views to our client quite effectively. Our choice of topics and vocabulary, our slightest intonation, pause, or silence, the way that we respond enthusiastically to certain remarks and lackadaisically to others—all these responses tell our clients what we believe and their transference, in all probability, tells them that they should be convinced by us if they want to get better.

What is more, we *want* them to be convinced. This is a bitter pill to swallow, but I think we must do so. The closer an issue is to our own hearts, the more we genuinely feel that one viewpoint is the creative, humane, and *correct* one, the more we hope that everyone we care about, including our clients, will agree with us. Take the example of a woman client who tells us a tale of many years' mistreatment and abuse by men. She clearly has very low self-esteem and seems to feel that women are nothing without the validation and protection of men.

We are likely to harbour a burning wish that she will discover feminism in some shape or form and if she does—through our subtle and tactful guidance—this will certainly (in my view) be very good for her.

We have to accept, however, that this is no less controlling of the client than the 1950s' American analyst who believes this woman is suffering from a lack of adjustment to appropriate sex roles and tries to help her become "better adjusted". The difference is that we, of course, are right, and he is wrong! But so far as power is concerned, we are trying just as much as the 1950s' analyst to impose our view of the world on our client. For her own good (cf. Lees & Freshwater, in Totton, 2006).

I am simplifying wildly here and most therapeutic situations are much more subtle and complicated than this. The values towards which we are trying to steer our clients may be a lot harder to define. But if we accept that such steering is always in some fashion going on, then I do not see how it can make a difference to our judgement of the therapeutic power relationships *which* position the therapist is inculcating in the client. And this means that therapy is faced with a fundamental political problem at its heart.

Attempted solutions

There have been many attempts to deal with this fundamental problem. One of the most radical happened very early on: Sandor Ferenczi's experiments with "mutual analysis", where he tried to address certain patients' suspicion about his motivations by splitting the session into two halves, one in which he analysed the patient and one in which they analysed him (Fortune, 1993). The patients were survivors of massive abuse, who would now no doubt be called "borderline personalities". Probably everyone who has worked with such people can see the point of Ferenczi's experiment but also its pitfalls: for the therapist to stick their arm in the fire like the Roman soldier in order to "prove" their genuineness does not ultimately help the client to bear and explore their mistrust.

Communicative psychoanalysis (Langs, 1982; Smith, 1999) is a more recent approach that takes seriously the client's sense of mistreatment. For the communicative analyst, the core task is to hear and interpret the analysand's unconscious messages about breaches of the analytic frame: only if they experience the analyst's capacity to acknowledge such breaches undefensively can the analysand go deeper into the work.

Otherwise, "… we can identify which person is introducing the most confusion, conflict and defensiveness … the designated therapist … is the functional patient and the designated patient … is the functional analyst" (Smith, 1999, p. 117). Two problems arise here: the first is that there is no clear account of what constitutes the analytic work beyond the interpretation of boundary violations. More seriously, the specific, historically contingent details of Freud's clinical parameters—couch, fifty-minute hour, and all—are somehow hypostasised into the necessary conditions of psychotherapy (Smith, 1999, p. 174 ff.).

Many other innovative methods have been inspired by the desire to resolve stubborn issues of power: for example co-counselling, which dispenses entirely with the expert role of therapist and uses a set of simple techniques to let two people swap sessions (Kauffman, 2004); and any number of experiments with leaderless groups (Ernst & Goodison, 1981). Rogerian person-centred therapy had as a founding motivation addressing power issues in the therapeutic relationship; as already mentioned, there are reasons to think it has not wholly succeeded (Masson, 1990). Perhaps, in fact, it *could not* succeed: the core situation of two people in a room, each with their own view of what is real and what is not and one of them being paid to meet the other, inevitably makes issues of power central to what is going on. The idea that the purpose of therapy is basically to correct the client's understanding, much as an optician might aim to correct their vision, is still pervasive. But all methods of attempting this amount, ultimately, to coercion.

Working with power issues in therapy

The only way to tackle this adequately, I suggest, is that instead of trying hopelessly to eliminate the power struggle from the therapeutic relationship, we place it dead centre, highlighting the battle between therapist and client over the definition of reality, baring it to the naked gaze, and making it a core theme of our work.

In a dyad where each member has exactly one vote on what constitutes "reality"—and can use a wide range of techniques to influence how the other person uses their vote—very early hurts around power, autonomy, and validation can be re-experienced and transformed; if mishandled, they can also be reinforced. The most obvious way, it seems to me, that as therapists we can mishandle the situation, is to claim that because we are therapists we have more than one vote on the reality of the situation: that my expertise, my specialist knowledge, my insight into the human heart and its foibles, entitles me to an extra vote. Unfortunately, irritatingly, this is no more true of the therapy relationship than it is of a parliamentary election.

In order to move forward from this impasse, we need to acknowledge that the therapeutic situation is nearly as hard for us as it is for our clients. No one likes to be in a struggle over reality; and for us there are even certain things at stake (our status, our income) that are not at stake for the client. Hence the temptations to cheat are enormous; especially when, as we have said, a large part of the client wants us to cheat, to assert our authority as expert healer.

To resist the seductions of expertise is not, however, to claim a different sort of immunity from challenge, as some sort of ego-free guru. It is, instead, to come back to Bion's famous picture (1990, p. 5) of "two frightened people in the room": two people both experiencing a threat to their beliefs on which their identity rests. What our training then hopefully allows us to do is to bring awareness, the magic ingredient, to the situation. Then client and therapist can start to explore all the ways in which we are competing to define reality, through assertion, manipulation, seduction, and deception. And, ultimately, we do what is best done in every such situation: we negotiate. This negotiation of realities (where "negotiation" also has the meaning of crossing tricky and dangerous terrain), I would argue, constitutes an authentic and viable psycho-political practice. And as we start to unknot the reality and fantasy of power relations in the room, so we discover threads leading back to power relations in the client's wider world. This does not propose any radical change in psychotherapy practice, but a reconceptualisation, bringing out the political aspect of transference and countertransference that is always already present.

As an analogy for a successful therapeutic interaction, consider two language groups encountering each other (see, for example, Hymes, 1977; McWhorter, 2000). If the members of one language group are considerably more powerful than the other—for example, if they have guns and the others don't—then the second group simply learns the first group's language. But if they are roughly equal in power or if each wants something the other can provide, a new form of communication develops between them: what is known as *pidgin*, an artificial medium using a simple syntax and a vocabulary drawn from both languages. A pidgin is not a natural language: it cannot develop, generate new words and concepts, become a medium for poetry. However, once children are born who grow up speaking it, a pidgin is transformed in an extraordinary way: it becomes what is called a *creole*, a new natural language, as creative and infinite in potential as any other language on earth.

This, it seems to me, is what happens in successful therapy. First, the client and practitioner create a pidgin, assembled from elements of the language that each person brings with them. But from a fertile exchange between therapist and client, a creative intercourse, a new language is born, a creole, a vessel for new thoughts and feelings that did not pre-exist in either original tongue.

What much more often happens, however, is that the therapist over-awes the client—who may well want to be overawed—into *learning the therapist's language*. And, of course, speaking the therapist's language, the client will only tell us what we know already: as Fliess told Freud, the reader of thoughts will always find only their own thoughts in other people. After the passage about "two rather frightened people in the room", Bion continues: "If they are not one wonders why they are bothering to find out what everyone knows" (1990, p. 5).

Getting the client to speak our language is one of many ways in which, as therapists, we can re-enact clients' early trauma. Children grow up forced to speak their parents' language, both literally and symbolically. Most children have painful experiences of being misunderstood or not listened to in the first place. In this and also in other ways, at some point we will almost certainly repeat our clients' early painful experience; this can be minimised, but not avoided. And it is how we negotiate this painful and difficult situation—our ability, simply put, to identify, acknowledge, and apologise for our mistake—that decides whether the therapeutic encounter will be a reinforcement of early experiences of powerlessness or a site where new experiences of empowerment can occur.

Conclusion

I have argued recently in several contexts that therapy is centrally a *practice of truth*. This has not been a very popular line to take. I think people have sometimes misunderstood me to be saying that therapy is a search for *absolute* truth, which is very different. But what therapy does and must do is to examine everything we can know about the truth of a situation—very much including emotional truth—precisely to establish experientially that *there is no absolute truth*, that truth is not singular but plural and contingent and, therefore, subject to negotiation. This is perhaps the greatest realisation of modernity and of immeasurable political importance: it is the gradual spreading of this realisation that has caused fundamentalism to stir in such destructive ways. Many people are coming to psychotherapy in search of help for anxieties that are ultimately produced by the clash between relativism and fundamentalism, as it affects their own deepest subjectivity. For psychotherapy to respond helpfully, on a clinical and on a social level, it needs to think seriously about the power politics of its own practice.

References

Bion, W. R. (1990). *Brazilian Lectures*. London: Karnac.

Cecchin, B. (1987). Hypothesizing, circularity and neutrality revisited: An invitation to curiosity. *Family Process, 26*: 405–413.

Cecchin, B. (1993). Foreword to L. Hoffman, *Exchanging Voices: A Collaborative Approach to Family Therapy*. London: Karnac.

Dale, P., Allen, J., & Measor, L. (1998). Counselling adults who were abused as children: Clients' perceptions of efficacy, client-counsellor communication, and dissatisfaction. *British Journal of Guidance and Counselling, 26*: 141–158.

Ernst, S., & Goodison, L. (1981). *In Our Own Hands: A Book of Self-Help Therapy*. London: Women's Press.

Fortune, C. (1993). Sandor Ferenczi's analysis of "R.N.": A critically important case in the history of psychoanalysis. *British Journal of Psychotherapy, 9*(4): 436–443.

Foucault, M. (1980). *Power/Knowledge: Selected Interviews and Other Writings. 1972–1979*. C. Gordon (Ed.). New York: Pantheon.

Garnets, L., Hancock, K. A., Cochran, S. D., Goodchilds, J., & Peplau, L. A. (1991). Issues in psychotherapy with lesbians and gay men. *American Psychologist, 46*: 964–972.

Guattari, F. (1984). *Molecular Revolution: Psychiatry and Politics*. London: Penguin.

Hinshelwood, R. D. (1997). *Therapy or Coercion?* London: Karnac.

Hymes, D. (Ed.) (1977). *Pidginization and Creolization of Languages*. Cambridge: Cambridge University Press.

Kauffman, K. (2004). *Co-Counselling*. London: Taylor & Francis.

Kovel, J. (1978). *A Complete Guide to Therapy*. London: Penguin.

Krause, I. (1998). *Therapy Across Culture*. London: Sage.

Kurtz, S. (1989). *The Art of Unknowing: Dimensions of Openness in Analytic Therapy*. Northvale, NJ: Jason Aronson.

Langs, R. J. (1982). *The Psychotherapeutic Conspiracy*. Northvale, NJ: Aronson.

Masson, J. (Ed.) (1985). *The Complete Letters of Sigmund Freud to Wilhelm Fliess*. Harvard, MA: Belknap.

Masson, J. (1990). *Against Therapy*. London: Fontana.

McWhorter, J. (Ed.) (2000). *Language Change and Language Contact in Pidgins and Creoles*. Amsterdam, the Netherlands: John Betjamins.

Mearns, D., & Thorne, B. (1988). *Person-Centred Counselling in Action*. London: Sage.

Noel, B., & Watterson, K. (1992). *You Must Be Dreaming*. New York: Poseidon Press.

Parker, I. (1996). Postmodernism and its discontents: Psychotherapeutic discourse. *British Journal of Psychotherapy*, 12(4): 447–460.

Pearson, G. (1983). *Hooligan: A History of Respectable Fears*. London: Macmillan.

POPAN (2004). *Ten Years is Too Long: Proposals for Interim Public Protection Measures in the Talking Therapies*. London: POPAN.

Pope, K. S. (2001). Sex between therapists and clients. In: J. Worrell (Ed.), *Encyclopedia of Women and Gender: Sex Similarities and Differences and the Impact of Society on Gender*. Burlington, MA: Academic Press.

Pope, K. S., Keith-Spiegel, P., & Tabachnik, B. G. (1986). Sexual attraction to clients: the human therapist and the (sometimes) inhuman training system. *American Psychologist*, 41: 147–158.

Prozan, C. K. (1993). *The Technique of Feminist Psychoanalytic Psychotherapy*. Northvale, NJ: Jason Aronson.

Rose, N. (1990). *Governing the Soul: The Shaping of the Private Self*. London: Routledge.

Sands, A. (2000). *Falling for Therapy: Psychotherapy from a Client's Point of View*. London: Macmillan.

Sands, A. (2003). Seeking professional help. In: Y. Bates & R. House (Eds.), *Ethically Challenged Professions: Enabling Innovation and Diversity in Psychotherapy and Counselling*. Hay-on-Wye, UK: PCCS.

Smail, D. (2003). Psychotherapy, society and the individual. In: Y. Bates & R. House (Eds.), *Ethically Challenged Professions: Enabling Innovation and Diversity in Psychotherapy and Counselling*. Hay-on-Wye, UK: PCCS.

Smith, D. (1999). *Hidden Conversations: An Introduction to Communicative Psychoanalysis, 2nd edn*. London: Rebnus Press.

Socarides, C. (1996). Major advances in the psychoanalytic theory and therapy of male homosexuality. In: I. Rosen (Ed.), *Sexual Deviation, 3rd edn*. Oxford: Oxford University Press.

Steiner, C. (1981). *The Other Side of Power*. New York: Grove Press.

Totton, N. (2000). *Psychotherapy and Politics*. London: Sage.

Totton, N. (Ed.) (2006). *The Politics of Psychotherapy: New Perspectives*. London: Open University Press.

CHAPTER THREE

Therapy in late capitalism*

Joel Kovel

Introduction

A radical approaching the institution of psychotherapy often feels inclined to impale it with a barb updated from Marx's judgment on religion: where once was the opium of the people, here stands their heroin, a new, synthetic addiction, concocted out of the brew of late capitalist culture. The hostility is understandable, since therapy has in some respects been even more successful than religion in deflecting energy from the need for radical social change. Religion at least threatened capital with its immanent critique; like a superannuated retainer it reminded its master of a time when his power had not yet come to be, and therefore of one when it would pass away. Therapy, on the other hand, appears seamless: even when pretending to be transcendent, the reward it dangles is no eschatological grappling with ultimates but an ultimately mundane, "sensible" happiness, quite eligible for commodification. What is needed is a concrete and precise analysis of the

*"Therapy in Late Capitalism" originally appeared in *The Radical Spirit: Essays on Psychoanalysis and Society* by Joel Kovel (© 1988, Free Association Books) and is reproduced by kind permission of the author and publisher.

many-sidedness of the phenomenon, situating it within the totality of its society and drawing attention to its liberating elements. In short, we must unearth the latent critical content of therapy, and set it against its more obvious conformism.

Therapy, however, does not exist apart from the neurosis it is supposed to remedy. The relationship is dialectical, for just as the variants of psychotherapy arise in response to the actually existing forms of neurosis, so do they serve to label, identify, and ground neurotic experience in their own terms. Further, neither therapy nor neurosis should be seen as remote from the entire flux of capitalist relations in everyday life, within the family, or in mass culture. Despite the reciprocal relation of neurosis and therapy, it is necessary to begin our analysis from the standpoint of the disorder, neurosis, rather than of the remedy, therapy. We do not choose to be neurotic, but we choose to do something about our neuroses—to ignore them, to subsume them in some kind of activity, to seek therapeutic help for them—or some combination of all these. Thus although neuroses enter the realm of political activity— usually, as we shall discuss below, in a negative way—therapy (or no therapy) is in itself a political act and can only be grasped in relation to the material conditions it seeks to alter.

Neurosis and therapy

Objectively we understand a neurotic person to be failing in tasks of adaptation to the environment through the compulsive repetition of inappropriate behaviors. But what makes the behaviors inappropriate is another, subjective dimension of compulsion: the intrusion of incompletely repressed fantasy. Every neurosis then can be considered a structure grounded on a nodal point in subjectivity and extending beyond the individual to encompass the entirety of his social relations. And at the subjective point of origin, a state of desire, hatred, and fear emerges that is intolerable to the self and against which the most elaborate measures have to be taken. These measures, whose nature is socially determined, form the behavioral surface of the neurosis.

It might be helpful at this point to distinguish between two categories of neurotic experience, the normal and the clinical. *Normal neurosis* may be roughly identified with the neurotic character; it is the standard pattern of neurotic experience imposed by the established conflicts of everyday life, and adapted to them. The normal neurotic pays little attention to his characteristic rigidity and irrationality, for this is the way one is supposed to be. Thus his or her inner subjective compulsion becomes cloaked in the veil of common sense. Neurosis becomes *clinical*, by which is meant potentially treatable, when the individual becomes aware of a certain intolerable degree of suffering and/or is made to feel that his or her disturbance lies outside the perimeter of what is socially acceptable. These two functions—the felt suffering and the label of deviance—are tightly but not necessarily coupled. When we feel clinically neurotic (by becoming grossly depressed, suffering through some repetitive pattern of failure in love, or developing some classical symptom such as a phobia), we are generally experiencing more of the subjective imbalance and compulsiveness that is the essence of neurosis. At the same time we are judging this worsened state of affairs in accordance with standards of well-being internalized from our culture. These factors, each culturally rooted, develop along separate paths that meet on the field of neurosis. One may be severely neurotic yet be considered normal so long as one lives within the parameters of what is acceptable. Similarly, a person may be labeled neurotic—and accept the labeling as valid—when the degree of subjective neurosis is actually outweighed by distress stemming from objective social forces. In this society at least, virtually everybody suffers to some degree from normal neurosis. Indeed, just as capitalism universalizes the commodity relationship, so does it impose, in a quite necessarily related way, a universalized neurotic experience among those who must live according to its terms.

In order to ground this insight we need to demonstrate, first, that conditions of life under capitalism necessarily lead to neurosis; second, that the forms of neurosis bear a definite relationship to the historically evolving relations of capitalist production; and finally, that the presence of neurotic structures in the population plays an actual role in the evolution of capitalism itself. Note that it is not being argued that capitalism creates neurosis as such. Such a thesis would be just as one-sided and inadequate as its vulgar Freudian converse, that neurosis is generated out of fixed biological dispositions. It is necessary to recognize that inherent dispositions exist which, if not strictly biological, are at least transhistorical and thus universal: infantile helplessness, the need for attachment and separation, the unstructuredness of instinctual drives, and the potential for ambivalence. These characteristics are, after all, what makes us human: They give rise to fantasy, symbolism, and subjectivity and value itself; and they put the human in a state of tension with nature, leading to that transformation of the natural, given order which comprises the basic dialectic of civilization. Moreover, they give rise to neurosis as well—but never in themselves, only as they are twisted against a definite social order and turned inwards, bearing the imprint on its particular forms. Neurosis is living proof of the tension between the human subject and the objective social order; it only comes into existence so far as these are incongruent, which is to say, within history.

The social conditions in which neurotic development can flourish are those of domination, of a social fabric composed of conflicting groups organized along lines of class, sex, race, and so on, and where the division of labor reflects the power of one group over others. In such a setting, in so far as the production of a surplus allows a passage beyond brute necessity, the contradictions between what the social order is and what it can be will eventually settle within the self as one form of neurotic distortion or another. The description just given can, of course, fit nearly every form of social order, and if capitalism is only one among all other social orders so far as generating madness goes, it has none the less managed to produce a rather unique form of neurosis, one which reflects the peculiarities of its history.

A most striking feature of neurosis within capitalism is its ubiquity. The reason for this lies in the particular form of reality principle developed by capital—the fetishism of commodities. The commodity relation is, of course, predicated on the creation of objects of exchange, and of a universal standard, money, by means of which their value may be compared. As Marx consistently pointed out, to place something into a system of exchange means that it has to be abstracted and objectified—that is, placed within a rationalized and calculable context. But this necessarily implies that the commodity relation must also include the creation and sustenance of a *subject* who performs the exchanging—a subject who, first, possesses a universal standard of objective rationality by means of which he can attend to the existence and exchange of objective commodities; and second, who is unable to perceive that these commodities are other than what they seem to be—that is, who is prepared to accept their fetishization within the dominant system of value and exchange.

The neurotic individual, normal or clinical, fits the bill exactly by virtue of the split between the deeper layers of his subjectivity and his internalization of the rationalized reality principle of abstract commodity logic. What makes a person neurotic is not hate or fear *per se*, but intrasubjective conflict between the demands of reason and those of desire. A social order, like capitalism, that imposes a universal imperative or rationalization will therefore universalize neurosis, for the simple reason that desire cannot go its own way to work out idiosyncratic solutions, but must be forever hurled against rationalization. In pre-capitalist society, people were amply crazy—the degree of brutal traumatization and privation saw to that. But there was no category of neurosis in which they all had to be inserted, precisely because there was no universal standard of reason in terms of which their madness appeared as negativity.

It would, however, greatly flatten out the historical process to confine capital's role in neurosis to the mere imposition of instrumental rationality. For one thing, we must always bear in mind that what capital has imposed in the way of reason contains the severest contradictions even on an objective level. And for another, we would miss much of what capitalism is about if we overlook its role in restructuring and marketing desire and impulse themselves. The contradictions within reason as well as the new forms of desire (new needs) each enter into the history of neurosis. More, they become elements in the development of capitalist society. In order to grasp this flux, however, it is necessary to consider two moments within capitalist development which represent the early and contemporary phases of its trajectory and which reveal themselves in developments in personal life having to do with the altered nature of work and consumption.

In the early phase of capitalism, most of its energy went into the production and accumulation of commodities. This process required the transformation of productive activity into abstractable labor power. The alienation which resulted cost the individual control of his vital activity and made his productive capacity into a commodity that not only could be bought and sold, but was also subject to an inexorable process of domination by capital. Yet, alienation stopped short of the subjective world itself, except in so far as this became stunted through separation from the means of existence. And this was not due to any grace on capital's part, but simply to the fact that the inner sphere had only been partially developed as an organ of capitalist relations. It mattered little what subjective variations obtained within the time of labor's activity. From the standpoint of capital what counted was the simple reproduction of the workforce and its controlled delivery, like so many draught animals, to the workplace. Around this need there arose a religion and culture of asceticism, submission, and a crude, severe rationalization.

To assist the reproduction of labor, a family structure was emphasized that would generate an ample supply of fresh children to take up the slack of increased commodity production and which would moreover keep these children under control. For this latter function a line had to be maintained between the patriarchal dominators at the top of the social pyramid and their symbolic representative, the father within the family; this line passed through the individual conscience and bound each man and woman of society to church, state, and, ultimately, capital.

The basic work relation of early capitalism, the abstraction and expropriation of labor-time, becomes even more expansive within the social world of late capitalist relations. Its forms become greatly complicated by subsequent developments in the relations of production. As capital proceeds down the self-ordained path of growth for its own sake and not for humanity's, it necessarily expands its productive power past the point at which simple accumulation serves its purposes. We may summarize these developments as the addition of a moment of disaccumulation—that is, of the liquidation of surplus—occurring *pari passu* with the continuing expansion of the productive process (see Aronowitz, 1962).

This occurs at a point of transition, developing in an uneven manner across the Western world towards the close of the nineteenth century and the beginning of the twentieth, a phase during which machinery and the technical apparatus in general—fixed capital—outstrips the productive role of human labor—living capital. And as the machine takes over, writes Marx, "Labor no longer appears so much to be included within the production process, rather the human being comes to relate more as a watchman and regulator to the production process itself. (*What holds for machinery holds likewise for the combination of human activities and the development of human intercourse)"* (1859, p. 705; my italics). And again, "In this transformation, it is ... the appropriation of his own general productive power ... in a word, *the development of the social individual* [my italics] which appears as the great foundation-stone of production and of wealth. The *theft of alien labor-time, on which the present wealth is based*, appears a miserable foundation in face of this new one, created by large-scale industry itself" (1859, p. 705).

Two dialectically intertwined trends are intensified by the development of the social individual as a prime instrument of capitalist relations. Appearing in the unitary moments of production and consumption, they eventually come to reside within the subject, defining a "human nature" which is neurotic in capitalist terms.

From the side of production the social individual is a creature whose work becomes increasingly differentiated and remote from any comprehensible productive process. These trends are manifest in the rise of technocracy, the bureaucratization of work, and, of particular concern for our analysis, the immense development of service occupations. Increasingly, work becomes the cultivation and delivery of human relations themselves. And from these qualities it follows that human relations become technical, swaddled in instrumental logic and prepared for commodification. Rather than being freed by the development of science and productivity, labor becomes degraded owing to the entrapment of productive reason within capitalist imperatives (Braverman, 1974). The "watchman and regulator" of the production process becomes just another instrument within it: The human becomes mechanical and accordingly assumes a machine-like form of reason to the terms of which all living relations become subsumed.

Meanwhile the pace of production and the hunger for profit impose equally far-reaching alterations in consumption. What could be assumed automatically in an age of scarcity and accumulation becomes both more problematic and more compelling in the light of disaccumulation. Now there is a surplus to be sold, though it is not to be simply disposed of, but simultaneously wasted and revalued so that capital keeps moving. The consumerist imperative in late capitalism demands the cultivation of new forms of desire, and this desire is to develop intertwined with the equally contradictory moment of rationality.

Capital no longer regards the social individual as a *mere* means, but rather as a means to be actively controlled with all the forces at its disposal. Indeed the contestation for the soul of the social individual— whether fought out on the field of daily life, in mass culture, or, as we shall touch upon shortly, therapy—has become a principal political struggle of advanced industrial society. It is a contest which complicates, perhaps decisively, all previous forms of class struggle. The measures capital has undertaken in order to undercut the immanent threat from the very reason it itself has brought forth into the world define in a broad sense these new forms of struggle. The twisting of reason into instrumental logic and the fetishization of desire are only the most general ways of viewing these "remediations." Their effect has been to create new kinds of social battlegrounds. The fracturing of modern society demands a series of analyses of the specific forms taken by the contest for the social individual, whether these be advertising, education, bureaucratic rationalization—or, as we shall now consider, the subjective life itself.

The Oedipus complex under capitalism

The changes we have been describing take place within the historical development of the institutions of everyday life, the most critical of which is the family. The family becomes crucial because, in its attempt to fulfill its assigned function of reproducing the individual demanded by the social order, it succeeds mainly by transmitting the contradictions developed within that order into the spheres of personal life (Zaretsky, 1973; also, Ewen, 1976). The need of capital for a "social individual" is another way of saying that capital must intensify and enter into the terms of family life. The space for this was cleared out by the productive surge of late capitalism. As the moment of disaccumulation was reached, the demand for labor-time began to drop below the level at which child labor was needed. Meanwhile the practice had come to seem odious, owing to the progressive development of the reformist impulse during the nineteenth century. The combination of these factors led to the abolition of child labor in late capitalism and the freeing up of childhood as a separate period. This was essential, for only a child can develop differentiated desire, and only a child can be trained for rationality, an enterprise which was undertaken by general public education.

Alongside this occurred a rapid decline in infant mortality as the result of advances in sanitation and public health. Thus, children came to stay around long enough to be valued and cultivated; and, as their labor was no longer necessary as it was in peasant or early industrial society, they emerged into the disaccumulation phase as a whole new class of consumers, the satisfaction of whom became a new task for the family. A related development was the dissociation of sexuality from reproduction, which freed the former as a source of pleasure and desire. Meanwhile, family life was being buffeted about as a result of the increasing erosion of traditional sources of legitimacy. With the advance of alienation the family became a personal refuge for great masses of people who could otherwise not find meaning, gratification or power within community life. Yet, the cultural ties between the individual

family and the larger community were becoming ever more attenu-
ated, thus depriving personal relations of a coherent social framework.
Authority itself became more and more impersonal and decreasingly
mediated by kinship or community.

As a result, people looked for something within the family only to be
frustrated. For the father, promised authority by virtue of his cultural
heritage, yet denied it everywhere, family life became not the simple
dreams of a *paterfamilias*, but a hoax. For the mother, denied authority
by phallic culture, she now unwittingly acquired the burden of becoming Mum—inculcating the categories of childhood, assuaging the hurts
of her increasingly impotent husband, and passively transmitting the
values of consumerism as though they were instilled into her very
milk. At the same time, the split of sex from reproduction opened up
for her—even more than for the male—the possibility for gratification
that had long been concealed beneath the triple burdens of domestic
toil, childbearing, and the ascetic femininity of patriarchal lore. With
the masculine monopoly of sexual power becoming seriously eroded
from one side, and feminine masochistic submission cracking from the
other, the result could only be the release of hostility and guilt into the
matrix of the "social individual". And it is the incoming children who
inherit this cauldron of emergent hope, pent-up rage, confused longing,
and incoherent values.

In this context we can appreciate the achievement of Freud, who did
no more than map out a subjective terrain that history had brought into
view. And it is quite significant that the most prominent features of this
landscape were the neuroses—no less significant than Freud's insight
that neurotic development was entirely continuous with the normal. The
nucleus of Freud's discovery was no mere residual category—an excre-
tion of bourgeois relations, as Marxists have often claimed. Consider that
Freud's first appreciation of the causes of neuroses lay in the practice of
coitus interruptus, an economically necessary yet technically inefficient
form of birth control widely practised at the time; or that one of his
first cases was the adolescent hysteric, Dora, who was enmeshed in a
covert erotic situation involving, among other things, rebellion against
her father (Freud, 1905e). In these and other instances, the neurosis
can be seen as the binding of a potentially liberatory impulse through
entrapment in infantile conflict—structures universalized by virtue of
the growth of the notion of childhood, and of the contradictory reason
and desire embedded within it.

Neurosis is the self-alienation of a subject who has been readied for freedom but runs afoul of personal history—a personal history whose particular terms from childhood on are both individually unique and determined by the general historical process. Neurosis therefore is an auxiliary form of inner domination which reproduces external domination on the realm of the unconscious. It was on this territory that Freud made his authentic achievement: the discovery of the lost infantile body revealed in the qualities of deep subjectivity itself—an infinitely fluid yet irreconcilable language of desire, terror, and hatred which peels the boundary of consciousness away from the registration of the material object and drapes it over phantoms of objects lost. To account for repression, Freud needed the hypothesis of instinctual drive, or *Trieb*— the dialectical non-identity between unconscious fantasy and official, waking thought. And to sustain his realization that repression was a radical process, Freud had to ground the concept of *Trieb* materially— that is, the body had to be granted a real and disjunctive input with respect to the demands of culture. While he largely succeeded, Freud remained to some extent trapped in the terminology of the positivist neuropsychiatry whose assumptions he was demolishing. As a result, he left a legacy of difficulty in mediating psychoanalytic concepts with a genuinely historical social theory.

Every system of domination ensures that potential subjective conflict becomes actual—and maddening—through the class imposition of real suffering and deprivation. Capital's distinctive contribution to this schema was the binding of time through the regimentation of labor-power into an exchangeable commodity. The binding of real time and its eventual translation into the mediating categories of infantile life set forth the principal dichotomy within modern subjectivity: time bound versus Promethean desire. Add domination and the patriarchal family, and we have the forms of the Oedipus complex under capitalism, which Freud read in his consulting room.

The administration of Eros

Thus capital ensured the universalization of a normal neurotic structure. Quantitative variations—too much infantile trauma, biological variations in resistance, and so forth—would suffice, as had always been the case, to bring out one or another clinical variety of "mental illness." To the extent that such afflicted individuals became unsuited for the social process, they would have to be dealt with in one way or another; and although we know that for centuries the fate of the mad had concerned society, it was also the case that only in the early phases of capital and the Enlightenment, as Foucault (1965) pointed out, was there any general differentiation between the "mentally disturbed" and the other assorted misfits who had eternally collected around the base of society.

Early capital may have set the stage for neurosis as a category through its industrial binding of time and universalization of reason, but otherwise it had little use for the problem. And this was because its control of the human world was mainly applied at the point of the quantification of labor itself. With the development of the "social individual," however, the essentially qualitative subjective world becomes necessarily an additional object of control, and neurosis finds itself increasingly at the center of culture. In the new order, dominated by technology, service work, and the commodification of the human relationship, the *way* a person behaves on and off the job becomes an essential aspect of the economic process. Thus the presence of neurosis takes on a significance unthinkable in the days of yore, when sturdy backs, sobriety, faith, and thrift would fit the bill. But of deeper interest yet is the fact that the structure of the neurotic experience itself is decisively affected by the ways of advanced capital.

In the early phase of capital, neurotic discord can be ideal-typically regarded as between an external, directly dominative force that attempts to bind time and an impulse which resists such binding. Since neurotic conflict is never simply between objective and subjective forces, but involves subjective representations of what is real, there must be an inner registration, or internalization, of the external, directly dominative force. Put simply, the individual has to believe that father is there, backed up by God and state, to ward off impulse; and it is his belief in the image of such authority that enters into the neurotic conflict by becoming linked with infantile representations of the same. To continue the model, then, we would say that the suppressing force in early capitalist normal neurosis consists of a more or less direct representation of an actual authority.

In late capitalist neurosis this picture becomes altered by the diminution of direct, immediate authority, whether religious or secular, and its replacement by the instruments for the control of the social individual. This means the installation of an internalized administration of one's own reason and desire. It is essential, however, that the reason which performs this function be of the kind that is instrumental and that fetishizes desire. Otherwise these agencies would go over to the side of impulse and freedom—that is, they would lose their legitimating tie to the external administration of capitalist relations.

It is important to note parenthetically that the above argument, while heavily indebted to Marcuse's "obsolescence of the Freudian view of Man," departs from it in a significant direction (1970, pp. 44–62). By converting the regulating systems of the psyche to internalized repro-ductions of the prevailing administration, Marcuse made one powerful point but lost another, and with it a fully dialectical analysis: He sev-ered too completely the social and the personal orders. By abandoning the concrete mediations of everyday life, the family and psychology, Marcuse unintentionally returns Marxist dialectics towards the econo-mism from which critical theory had tried to rescue it.

In contrast, the analysis developed here seeks to encompass the very non-identity between psyche and society which reflects Adorno's obser-vation of the actual fracturing of advanced capitalist society (1967). Because of non-identity a space has to be cleared away within the self for a phenomenologically determinable core of self-experience which is mediated by actual social relations, yet which contains the capacity to resist them. In short, the sixth thesis on Feuerbach needs to be amended if it is to become worthy of Marxism: the self is not a simple, Lockean "ensemble of social relations" (Marx, in Marx & Engels, 1968, p. 29), but reveals as well the entire Freudian dialectic. The model that emerges is complex yet capable of registering the actual state of contradictori-ness. It includes the fact that essential choices in life have passed into the alienated hands of an impersonal administrative apparatus which attempts to impose unidimensionality upon the human world, but also that the same administration needs to consume the time of a social individual whose personality has been cultivated via the mediations of the family and childhood—a personality locked ineluctably in conflict with the impersonality of the whole.

When one factors out the invariant or trivial elements and arrives at the ultimate historical basis of conflict, it may be seen as the strug-gle between the inviolable space within the subject and the intrusions of administered necessity. These terms can be mapped into Freud's formulation of the clash between the sexual instincts and civilization, since it is infantile sexuality, viewed in its fullest sense as Eros, timeless and uncommodifiable, which constitutes the core of subjectivity left over after all the taming measures have had their due. None the less, the conflict is still experienced by the subject in terms of the actual people—lovers, bosses, co-workers, teachers, and toll-takers—who have come to play the crucial mediating roles between Eros and the administration. Without the concrete mediations of everyday life, there can be no symbolic scaffolding upon which the structures of consciousness, whether false or true, can be built.

Reason and desire under late capitalism

The non-reducibility of self-experience to either social demands or biological need is the precondition of neurotic conflict. The conflict itself, then, is always conducted through mental representations of real people which become split and tossed hither and yon as the subject vainly tries to synthesize the opposed trends within him or her. But for this to be so, the social world has to provide fundamental contradictions of its own such that an inner synthesis cannot be achieved. Thus from the standpoint of whether neurotic development occurs it is all the same if the father exists as an actual suppressing authority or whether he is functionally absent and his power usurped. The *form* that the neurosis takes may be different of course—in the first instance we might, for example, expect a hysterical flight, while in the second the picture is more likely to be some kind of narcissistic or schizoid disturbance—but neurosis will take root in both cases because real objects see to it that desire is both unfulfillable and dangerous.

A person growing up under late capitalism will be materially cared for and educated into instrumental reason regardless of whether he or she be working or middle class. Prolonged and nurtured childhood will have succeeded in stimulating desire well beyond the possibilities of any controlling structure to discharge or bind. Indeed, the very weakness of immediate parental authority, its steady usurpation by remoter expertise, guarantees that desire is both unchecked and ungratifiable. The parent can neither stop children nor be adequate to their yearning. And, the non-provision of a worthy object becomes just as potent a repressing force as the actual threat of castration. In both instances the subject is left helplessly suffused with hate, at the mercy of desire, and driven to falsify consciousness.

In late capitalism, as throughout the history of the human species, the deeper body of alienated infantile feeling is relegated to the unconscious. However, certain auxiliary measures have been added to channel the highly developed surplus desire which flows into contemporary culture via the social individual. The principal structure which accommodates this process is instrumental reason itself. For all the circumstances which tend to stimulate desire do so under the sign of the reasonable imperative. The little children who learn to be creative in their progressive school learn too that the school is an administered entity in which one gets ahead by being creative (within limits, of course). And if the child is not privileged enough to get the point in such a setting, he will when he goes home and is told by some television ad to "feel free" in the interests of a soft drink.

Advanced capital has worked diligently at colonizing the new subjective territory its advance unearthed. The very usurpation of parental authority which plays so large a role in introducing alienation within the subject is itself a measure of this colonial administration. The parent either joins up—becoming, so to speak, a civil servant in the regime of mass culture—or is swept aside to be left screaming in impotent rage, an object of scorn no less than covert yearning.

And like any proper colony, instrumentalized subjectivity provides raw material for the metropolitan region: commodifiable desire. The inchoate longing of childhood bubbles up out of the primary region of self-experience. From earliest infancy it passes through the refinery of instrumental logic as it enters the human world. And there it is named, sorted out, categorized, told—in the fundamental operation of instrumental reason—that it is not part of the subject, that it exists "out there" in abstractable, quantifiable, ultimately commodifiable terms. If, by definition, we term the forms of experience that have been instrumentally severed from subjectivity the secondary symbolic values, and correlatively we term that from which they have been severed primary symbolic values, then it may be that secondary symbolic value becomes valued over the primary. Otherwise the figure will become drawn back into the subjective world and out of the clutches of commodity relations—for *only secondary symbolic values can be exchanged*. It may be that this kind of operation is at the heart of reification.

The simplest notion of the secondary objectification of fantasy in everyday life is the daydream: a controlled exercise in wish-fulfillment whose energy derives from unfulfillable unconscious desire and the objects of which are given by the dominant culture. In this sense capital entails the commodification of daydreams. Such conceptions develop a truth if they are believed in; at least they remain stable enough to enter the marketplace where they acquire a more material grounding. And the developing person comes to believe in them because repression of infantile terror is made the easier thereby; and because, simply, to reify desire makes fulfillment seem nearer, since that which is materializable is also possessable, even on the instalment plan.

The same configuration that serves the neurotic character structure becomes increasingly essential for the disposition of the surplus. From this standpoint it would seem that neurotic alienation is necessary in order to develop a primary subjective core which turns out fantasies suitable for skimming by the instruments of capital. The neurosis is the irritant, like the grain of sand to the oyster, that keeps a natural process in a state of chronic disequilibrium and so sustains another dislocation at a different point. Similarly the sludge of secondary symbols accumulated as a result of the endless reification of mass culture obscures the basic disequilibrium even as it irritates it and keeps it going. Thus the various rationalizations which have come to surround neurotic experience in the post-Freudian era have only served to secure the basic neurotic disposition of the times. Were it otherwise, were people either happy or clear about what they wanted, then capital's ceaseless expansion would be endangered.

In addition to churning out saleable desire for the age of consumerism, neurosis has a number of other basic functions under late capitalism. Neurosis is perhaps the only way one can develop a rationalized subject suitable for doing the work of the social individual, who at the same time does not know what he or she wants, that is, whose capacities to resist are compromised. The simultaneous efflorescence of infantile impulse and fear of a non-instrumental expression of the same makes it that much harder for the neurotic to experience outrage over oppression without lapsing into crippling self-doubt. Similarly, though the parricidal nucleus of the Oedipus complex persists as a spur to rebellion, so long as it remains under the aegis of a preponderantly neurotic organization the rebellion will almost surely be self-destructive and lead to a new round of submission. All in all, normal-neurotic character structures are one of the best ways for an oppressive order to maintain its domination without an embarrassing and economically stultifying overt authoritarianism. Further, designating the normal neurosis as one or another category of clinical neurosis serves the labeling process so dear to instrumental reason and preoccupies people with reified or individualistic explanations for their unhappiness. And when one adds to this highly abbreviated presentation the reflection of how ruinous neurotic bickering and subjectivism (Jacoby, 1971) have been to Left politics, it will not be hard to see how loyal a servant neurosis has been to its master, capital.

But slaves have been known to turn on their masters. The labeling of "psychopathology" represents, to be sure, one way of forestalling awareness of a fuller truth. But the opportunity to do so only exists because of the actual presence of a colossal burden of neurotic misery in the population, a weight that continually and palpably betrays the capitalist ideology, which maintains that commodity civilization promotes human happiness. If, given all this rationalization, comfort, fun, and choice, people are still wretched, unable to love, believe, or feel some integrity to their lives, they might also begin to draw the conclusion that something was seriously wrong with their social order. Moreover, the threat posed by neurosis is not limited to the betrayal of ideology. For impulse is antithetical to administration, while neurosis represents a kind of synthesis between the two. But it is a false and uneasy synthesis, owing to the partial breakthrough of impulse and its inherently sluggish educability. Thus the hidden unconscious forms of impulse become ever more threatening, not just to the individual in neurotic distress, but to the social order whose fundamental irrationality has to be cloaked in a film of rationalization. Neurosis is not only unfreedom; it also contains within itself a thrust towards freedom. Clinical neurosis should be regarded as a twisted effort at cure, yet one which still contains somewhere more hope for freedom than the normal neurosis it replaces.

Consequently, the various forms of therapy have arisen as new forms of mediation—re-mediations or *remedies*—to be inserted into the increasingly uneasy neurotic syntheses. The therapies are in this sense like a kind of mental Keynesianism resorted to by capital to iron out another type of endemic crisis; and like the economic analogue, they suffer from a tendency to inflation, now manifest in the running riot of a whole Babel of schools.

The value of therapy

The concept of what psychotherapy can be has come a long way from Freud's initial insight that making the unconscious conscious may relieve neurotic suffering. It has both retrieved its pre-Freudian roots in suggestion, religious healing, and, indeed, shamanism, and branched forward in countless novel directions. In all of these methods, however, one common condition obtains: The individual whose personal distress has been defined as neurosis undergoes an experience in which certain elements of his or her neurotic structure are reproduced, and as a result he or she becomes reunited with some portion of an existence that had been denied by neurotic splitting. This disequilibrium proceeds to re-equilibration; disunity to unification, always under the sign of self-appropriation. The therapies speak then of developing "insight," or of learning "appropriate behaviour," of discovering one's "true self," or, as in family therapy, of re-establishing broken and chaotic family communications. The modes under which self-appropriation may occur are exceptionally varied but always involve some element of subjective belief or goal that the therapeutic method validates, as well as some objectification of this in the person of the therapist.

The therapy, then, is the dialogue within which these elements are related to each other. The belief, or value system, of the therapy establishes the vector of self-appropriation, while the actual therapist offers a concrete model for incorporation, a framework around which the self-appropriation can take place. Thus in Freud's method the analyst imposes the value of reflective truth-telling and offers his accepting yet disengaged attention to break the neurotic cycle; while in Jung's version, belief in a transcendent unconscious force is held out and the analyst becomes an active guide promoting symbolic reunification; or in Gestalt therapy, immediate contact with current awareness becomes the goal; or in behavioral treatment, altering learned, objectifiable behavior; in transactional analysis, appropriation of a reasonable standard for self-esteem in a group setting; and so forth.

Note that anything can work, at least for a while, in the therapy of a neurosis, so long as it is believed in and backed up with a real therapeutic presence that succeeds in objectively establishing some kind of dialogue with the inner structure of neurosis. The objective factor makes it impossible airily to dismiss the value of some supposed cures as bubbles destined to burst upon disillusionment. Illusions they might be, but no more so than the false consciousness imposed by class domination. While it is true that neurotic contradictions will not be ushered out of existence by therapeutic mumbo jumbo, this is not the same as claiming that a person will not be *convinced* that they have subsided.

Of course, the two dialectics—the therapeutic and the societal—run together. Indeed, it is just the social dimension which provides an essential framework of objectification around which therapeutic goals can crystallize (for example, Jungian treatment works best for those whose life has prepared them to accept a religious worldview). Because of the non-identity between individual and society, however, no absolute fit between personal *telos* and an objectified social framework can be obtained and a great range of practical solutions, each with its own ideology, is possible.

We are thus in a position to attempt a critique of the differing possibilities for therapy according to two criteria: (1) the degree to which they objectively address themselves to the neurosis, as against blurring the realities or indulging in illusions; and (2) the values inherent in the kind of change they offer, both with respect to their respective methods and goals. Are the resistant powers within the subject employed for this end, or does the therapy attempt its unification on terrain that has already been colonized by capital? In other words, does the therapy become an immanent critique or a new form of fetish? Let us now turn to a few examples for clarification.

Critiques of inner and outer worlds have to be made in the language of each sphere. Thus therapies which attempt to apply advanced political insights to emotional disturbances are only imposing another form of false consciousness. This is precisely the problem with so-called "radical therapy," with its naïve illusion that neurosis and oppression are directly connected so that, for example, a woman becoming conscious of her actual oppression as a woman would also be adequately dealing with neurotic distortions of her sexuality. The spontaneous activity of the subject generates a consciousness that is false by the standards of class consciousness. Yet it is also anchored in definite unconscious fantasies, which, though they may stem from a real childhood generated out of late capitalist contradictions, have been cut off by repression from political categories. Thus there is a false consciousness of both the objective and subjective dimensions, and it is deceptive to blend them together.

This is a dangerous question to overlook. It is not a mere intellectual failure to apply political categories to a therapeutic situation. For therapy mobilizes the neurosis in order to resolve it; but while mobilized, neurotic thinking, with its transference wishes of submission to therapeutic authority, will drag the most advanced political ideology back into domination and compulsivity.

Similarly, though mental patients are blatantly abused by society, they do not cease thereby to be troubled on their own. The labeling which defines a career for them as psychotic has a real and deleterious effect on their inner subjective life, but does not occupy the whole ground of subjectivity. To regard people as defined by their oppression flattens the humanity—and the ultimate powers of resistance—out of them, and is not better than the crude categorization that passes for a medical model.

In this regard it should be pointed out that the subjectivity of psychotic people is radically isolated; both world and self are petrified into an objectification of far greater extent than the prevailing degree of capitalist reification. Thus they are lost even to the given state of unfreedom and correspondingly objective measures, such as drugs and restraint, may at times (although far less often than prevailing medical orthodoxy would have it) be necessary as a humane expedient. Here we may be able to appreciate the weakness of Laing's synthesis of the Sixties, which fell short on both criteria. By minimizing the crippling objectification of the psychotic, Laing imposed a deep subjective therapy on them that they could ill tolerate, much less use. At the same time, as Russell Jacoby (1975) has observed, Laing tended to flatten the social dialectic by subsuming the alienation of labor into that of the subject.

Thus a politically advanced position—one mediated through objective societal categories—is therapeutically backward; while a therapeutically advanced position—one that seeks to reclaim alienated subjective territory—is in itself politically inert. And yet, given the historical relationship between neurosis and capitalism, therapy cannot be ignored as a possible element in any overall political strategy. Our analysis tells us, however, that therapeutic practice should be bracketed from objective political goals. Concretely put, a person should be free to unburden him- or herself in a therapeutic setting without regard for the objective consequences.

In a practical sense, for a therapy to flourish in the world of capitalist relations, it has to generate exchange value. This can be done in two ways (which may be combined in the real setting): The therapy can offer something that is perceived to be of genuine value because it is rare and in danger of being extinguished, like fine handicraft; or it can promise power by promoting unification with the main dynamic of capitalist expansion. With respect to the first type, we have therapy which offers the chance for deep subjective reflectivity and/or an intense, caring personal relationship. Time bought for these purposes will continue to have a premium value in a culture that works to obliterate both of them.

To be sure, it is a value reserved for the privileged class. For the rest, therapeutic help will have to come either through a cut-rate compromise or via the second pathway—an already fetishized route. By being fetishized, therapy is able to help the subject defend against his or her deeper anxieties, thus feel less neurotic, indeed, full of "mental health."

In today's world the therapist has become a technologist of behavior and value. Everything there is to know about sex is known. The dialectic of ineffability is abolished by behavioral technology. Masters and Johnson, fresh from their conquest of the orgasm, dance on Reich's grave as the reigning experts on the ways of Eros. Spread out around them are a host of behavioral and cognitive therapists dedicated to the Skinnerian dogma that behavior is determined by its consequences—that is, purely objectively, undialectically, positivistically, and instrumentally. Systems analysts abound with a somewhat more subtle but equally instrumental vision of people caught hopelessly in a net of communication. And of course the tide of drug treatment continues unabated. Indeed, the ultimate is already with us: therapy by computer—and anybody who doubts that subjects have been found who like getting treated by a machine is out of touch with the pace of reification.

Fetishized therapy

Similarly, commodifiable desire—the same that sells deodorants—has been amply mobilized in the interests of therapy. Here a glimmer of the hope set going by capital's democratization—that everyone is entitled to happiness—has become fused with the equation, happiness equals stimulation, into a powerful instrument upon which the neurotically troubled and alienated can seize. The basic thesis of this dimension of therapy is that the neurotic impulse should not be tinged with the hatefulness which is in fact its distinguishing feature. In order to promote this illusion, repression of the hateful side of impulse—the side which wants to possess, devour, castrate, and so forth—is necessary; and this is secured by magnifying the image of the non-hateful side—that which just wants to enjoy—out of proportion. Here consumer culture stands at the ready with its cornucopia to back up therapeutic ideology. The Human Potential Movement, with its Joy Therapy and maximization of encountering, spontaneity, and impulse, bears witness to the fetishization of this dimension. In the place of an authentic desire which might emerge through overcoming the historically induced split, Human Potential, or post-Freudian psychology dredges up an internalized Manifest Destiny: nothing should be too much for these Americans who compulsively gobble up experience as though it were choice mineral rights. Instead of genuine freedom, then, which would mean an honest confrontation of hatred, evil, and madness, fetishized therapy offers us a Disneyland of the mind. And it should be noted that the therapy of an unreflective spontaneity bears more than a haphazard resemblance to the politics of spontaneity. The infantilism that afflicted Left politics of the 1960s—the "gimme-now" variety—becomes swiftly retooled into the therapist of instant breakthrough (namely Jerry Rubin).

All of the strands of bourgeois reification get rewoven in fetishized therapy. Its mystification returns through the adoration of the latest guru or in the cultivation of "pure" consciousness through meditation. Its idealistic naïvety crops up cloaked in the preachings of a Carl Rogers or an Erik Erikson. And its latent puritanical authoritarianism marches again dressed up, coyly enough, as the Reality (*sic*) Therapy of William Glasser. In sum, any ideological stance which preserves the split in bourgeois culture can be used to promote unification between the neurotically split subject and the alienated world. Thus it can be inserted into the neurotic disequilibrium where it will serve repression and reconvert a clinical into a normal neurosis.

Given the increasing alienation of bourgeois culture and its steady commodification of the subjective world, even this tenuous balance is hard to sustain; and the half-life of therapies now comes to resemble that of schools of art or rock groups. With progress in alienation, therapies have had to shout louder and promise more to get a rise out of their increasingly jaded subjects. As a result of these trends—which match on the cultural scale the development in the individual of forms of neurosis which lack clear lines of internal repression and hence lack classical symptoms—there has come to be a gradual coalescence of therapy with other forms of mass culture. Consider the case of transactional analysis, one of the most successful of the new therapies, and the first to be clearly modeled on the soap opera or situation comedy, with its apparatus of games, scripts, and so on. TA is unabashed about its congruity with consumerist culture—neurotic patterns, for example, are said to earn "trading stamps." This not only helps to account for its success as a therapy but also for its lead in the assimilation of the categories of therapy to those of social control on other levels—namely, its widespread use, along with other group therapies, in corporations, the military, and other arms of bureaucracy as an instrument to help people get along with each other and the order of things. Thus work, therapy, and everyday life each become suffused with the ethos of "human relations"—the model of a "social individual" suitable as a means of production and consumption and disinclined to resist the order of capital.

It should be emphasized that in actual practice, especially as it evolves over time, no therapy fits any category of fetishization in a neat fashion. Nor, except in rare instances, can any practice be assigned wholly to the camp of domination. A brief glance at the tangled path of psychoanalysis may show why.

The main theme of the history of psychoanalysis—a history, it should be added, not yet adequately written—is that of the absorption of critique by the dominant culture. The heart of psychoanalytic therapy is restoration of integrity through the appropriation of reflective powers lost by neurotic splitting. But this is an attack at one of the points where neurosis buttresses the reification demanded by capitalist culture. Self-reflection counters the instrumentalization of reason so essential to capital. A reflective subject is a critical, resistant subject. Moreover, psychoanalysis in its critical form reveals both the existence of Eros and the actual shambles of erotic prospects for human liberation by the bourgeois world. To be sure, it also plunges into the twisted hate which is the subjective tracing of outer domination, and so tends to discourage ready-made solutions to the human dilemma. But at its heart is a search for the truth, which necessarily serves the quest for freedom, as Marxists from Reich and Trotsky to Adorno, Marcuse, and Jacoby have observed.

Consequently, in its initial phase (up to 1920), psychoanalysis was a fundamentally revolutionary doctrine, although Freud's ambivalence toward the critical potential of what he had discovered left the way open for a number of courses. After 1920 the battle for the future of psychoanalysis began, with Marxists, Surrealists, and so on, on the one side and bourgeois culture on the other. We cannot recount these struggles except to note that they took a decisive turn towards the bourgeois side when Stalinism forced anything critical out of Marxism and Nazism uprooted the psychoanalytic movement *en masse* and drove most of it to America. Before the emigration, the way had been cleared for the "bourgeoisification" of psychoanalysis with the realization by mass culture that in the new science a weapon had been handed to them for the exploitation of their new subjective domain. Significantly enough, it was Edward Bernays, Freud's nephew and the founder of public relations, who spearheaded the appropriation of psychodynamics by advertising and the mass media in general. Meanwhile, the first among neo-Freudians, Alfred Adler, was disseminating his consciousness-bound version of psychoanalysis among the educational and social-work establishments.

In general, in order to catch hold in American culture, a psycho-analytic idea had to be stripped of its dialectical thrust, as with the neo-Freudian de-emphasis on the unconscious. By the same token orthodox Freudianism held on to the unconscious but grounded it in an unmediated id psychology safe for bourgeois culture. In this guise psychoanalysis portrayed people as Hobbesian animals needing to be trained, an ideology compatible with historical formulations such as "capitalism exists because of anal-sadistic instincts" or "the police exist because of the masochism of the masses."

Then in the 1930s the ego psychology of Heinz Hartmann (1939) began to hold sway. As Adorno (1967) pointed out, Hartmann's work was in a basically correct theoretical direction in so far as it restored the principle of non-identity within the subject (ego reflecting reality and id reflecting desire) and so tended to rescue psychoanalysis from the undialectic morass into which it had fallen. But the same deadly biolo-gistic flaw inhered in Hartmann's ego, which was handed the job of "deinstinctualizing psychic energy." Given the class position of psycho-analysts and the need of the Second World War and postwar culture to justify the ways of the bourgeois god to man, it was an inevitable path to yet another flattening of the critical dialectic, this time the enshrinement of ego-reality over id-desire. Co-ordinated with this was the absorption of psychoanalysis into medical orthodoxy and psychiatric education as an avatar of truth about mental illness. The result was its transfor-mation into an adjustment psychology that found itself trussed up in conformist thinking and upper-middle-class mores when the crises of the 1960s reopened the question of Marxist liberation.

Psychoanalytic practice—a term which embraces a goodly variety of pursuits—reflects the history of the doctrine. Thus psychoanalysis may be used as a mode of therapy in which the instrumental reason-ing of ego psychology can be imposed as an ethos of intellectualized self-administration; or the conformism inherent in any undialectical psychology can appear as moralization, with all unconventional and protest activity being dismissed as "neurotic acting-out"; or a caricature of its original, unmediated depth-psychology can persist as rampant subjectivism, the old idealist myth that passive contemplation is praxis enough for life's problems. All of these forms may be expected to crop up in one guise or another, simply because the therapy has been rooted in bourgeois culture as long as it has.

But just as that culture continually creates possibilities for its own overcoming, so can psychoanalytic practice touch from time to time its critical origins. Several conditions remain indispensable for this. One is the eschewing of any liberatory, radically curative, or transcendent goal which is to emerge from the therapy itself—that is, there should be no superordinate value to what is going on, no pretence that a shortcut through history has been found, nor that a "true self" will emerge at the end of the treatment. Another, related condition is the bracketing out of objective and political considerations during sessions, in the interests of permitting the emergence of even the most violent and forbidden thoughts (since, as in a dream, there would then be no realistic consequences). Yet another is the recognition that, under the sway of neurotic subjectivity, political thinking will degenerate towards domination, since it is the child-mind which is mobilized by the therapeutic situation.[1] And finally, a certain respect for the integrity and worth of the person is necessary, no matter how far short of universality this may be—along, however, with the insistence that this individual be truthful concerning his or her warts and blemishes.

Therapy so construed—be it psychoanalytic or otherwise—retains the possibility of critique by refusing to present itself as more than what it is. Its very modesty is its strength. Its refusal to provide the Big Answer opens for the subject the possibility of looking outward. And by moving negatively, refusing to give answers, and drawing in the limits of its judgment, a critical therapy draws a line against the colonization of the subjective world which defines late capitalism, and thereby works towards the restoration of the dialectical mode of resistance. In concrete terms, the person who emerges from therapy conducted as critique is no True Self, nor even free of normal neurosis. But he or she has widened the scope of the choices that can be made, while a certain part of locked-in subjectivity has been freed to make real demands upon the world. In sum, they are more ready for love and the politics of liberation.[2]

Notes

1. Our child-mind is a creature of the age of surplus: commodified desire is part of consumerist society; and instrumental reason requires delay, leisure, and an elaborate educational process. The terms of our subjectivity were forged within a capitalism undergoing more or less incessant expansion.

2. This essay was prepared in collaboration with Carol Lopate, Stuart Ewen, Stanley Aronowitz, Rosalyn Baxandall, Elizabeth Ewen, and David Nasaw. Without their input, it could never have come to be. I am also grateful to Russell Jacoby, Brigid Marcuse, Bell Chevigny, and Jean Elshtain for their editorial advice.

References

Adorno, T. W. (1967). Sociology and psychology. *New Left Review, 46*: 67–97.

Aronowitz, S. (1962). The end of political economy [unpublished MS].

Braverman, H. (1974). *Labor and Monopoly Capital.* New York: Monthly Review.

Ewen, S. (1976). *Captains of Consciousness.* New York: McGraw-Hill.

Foucault, M. (1965). *Madness and Civilization.* New York: Random House.

Freud, S. (1905e). Fragment of an analysis of a case of hysteria. *S. E., 7*: 1–123. London: Hogarth.

Hartmann, H. (1939). *Ego-Psychology and the Problem of Adaptation.* New York: International Universities Press.

Jacoby, R. (1971). The politics of subjectivity. *Telos, 9*: 116–126.

Jacoby, R. (1975). *Social Amnesia: A Critique of Conformist Psychology from Adler to Laing.* Boston, MA: Beacon.

Kovel, J. (1988). *The Radical Spirit: Essays on Psychoanalysis and Society.* London: Free Association.

Marcuse, H. (1970). Obsolescence of the Freudian concept of man. *Five Lectures.* Boston, MA: Beacon.

Marx, K. (1859). *Grundrisse.* M. Nicolaus (Trans.). London: Pelican, 1973.

Marx, K., & Engels, F. (1968). *Selected Works.* New York: International Publishers.

Zaretsky, E. (1973). Capitalism, the family and personal life. *Socialist Revolution, 22*: 13–15.

CHAPTER FOUR

The selfish society: the current state of things*

Sue Gerhardt

Introduction

Right from the start we are all responsive to other human beings. Even newborn babies have a basic capacity to imitate others and to resonate with other people's feelings through their brain's mirror neurons. If you copy a smile, you often feel happier, and if you copy a yawn, you are likely to feel more tired. We need this ability to be social creatures. To the brain, self and other are part of the same process. In fact, it's the same area of the brain—the right frontal insula, in particular—which lights up whether we are being aware of our own body states or other people's.

Many years ago, my studies in early childhood observation under the auspices of the Tavistock Clinic in London gave me my first insights into babies' mental development. Although already a mother twice over, watching babies on a weekly basis for over two years enabled me to see the process of development more objectively. It stimulated my interest in the impact of those early experiences on the baby's brain, so

*This chapter is an edited version of *The Selfish Society: How We All Forgot to Love One Another and Made Money Instead* by Sue Gerhardt (Simon & Schuster: London, 2010), and is reproduced by kind permission of Simon & Schuster and the author.

I immersed myself in reading widely in the literature of neurobiology. I found myself in an Aladdin's cave of fascinating material which confirmed that the brain is not a machine which operates in glorious isolation, but a nervous system which is designed to respond to the environment in which we find ourselves, and to help us predict what will happen in that environment. Brains are shaped by experience, and the quality of care and attention we receive as babies affects the neurobiology of our brains. Early brain development, in particular, is very rapid and sets up many biochemical systems and neural pathways that we will continue to use for the rest of our lives.

This view contrasts with the popular notion that our genes are all-powerful directors of our behaviour. Although it is true that we are born with a genetic make-up which may determine the colour of our eyes, our basic temperament, or our susceptibility to various mental and physical health conditions, it is vital to understand that the genes involved in social behaviour don't turn themselves on or off, but—according to recent epigenetic studies—are triggered into activity by the environment. This opens the possibility that it is not only parenting which affects our psychological development and our brain structure, but also the society and culture in which we live.

When I wrote *Why Love Matters: How Affection Shapes a Baby's Brain*, my purpose was to explain what I had learned about the importance of babyhood as the foundation of individual well-being, mental health, and good character. I demonstrated the links between the quality of early care and later incidence of depression, personality disorders, and antisocial behaviour—issues that specifically concerned me as a psychotherapist working with individuals who were struggling with their relationships, their unfulfilled potentials, or their destructive and self-destructive behaviours, as well as reflecting my work as a parent–infant psychotherapist helping families to bond with their babies. My goal was to encourage parents and policymakers to become more aware of the importance and significance of early child-rearing, in order to prevent further individual suffering and poor emotional development. Since then I have become more interested in the way that these babyhood experiences are not just an issue for individuals, but also matter to society. Particularly in the current economic crisis, when we are beginning to question many assumptions about ethical standards, I believe that it is important to understand these connections between our infancies and the kind of world we create. In my work with individuals, understanding someone's early developmental history is central to understanding the person. In this chapter I want to apply a similar developmental perspective to the bigger social picture, to discover whether psychology could help throw light on our social and historical processes and the problem of how to achieve a more empathic society.

The social brain

Many people living in Western culture today assume that it is simply "true" that we will put our own interest ahead of those of other people, and these beliefs underpin their acceptance of industrial capitalism as an economic system. However, the eighteenth-century theorists who advanced the "self-interested" view of human motivation did not have access to the information that we now have, especially the great advances in psychological knowledge that have taken place. Their theories rested on Enlightenment ideas of rationality, uninformed by modern awareness of unconscious processes, group behaviour, or emotional development. These old forms of thinking tend to be based on assumptions that people respond to rational argument and can change their behaviour by using logic or willpower. Yet time and time again, experience proves this pervasive belief wrong. For example, in 2005 there was a rise in teenage pregnancies despite a government campaign for better sex education and information about contraception. The British minister for children at the time, Beverley Hughes, made a comment that conveyed her bewilderment. "We've reached a sticking point," she said. "People for one reason or another don't think through the consequences" (cited in Ward, 2005, p. 9). The implication is that teenage pregnancy was a failure of rationality on the girls' part, as if their need to be loved, or to find meaning in a life that was devoid of other opportunities, could not be taken seriously as salient factors. Our economic and political thinking is still locked into these old belief systems, unaware of many of the core factors that drive our behaviour—in particular, the crucial role that early experience plays in setting up our emotional behaviours, and the importance of the inner life of feelings and implicit beliefs in our decision-making.

In practice, our "moral values" are often not so much the conscious ideas that we express when we reason with our children, although that may be an important aspect of parenting, but the unconscious assumptions that we all live by in our everyday relationships.

Of course, it is hard to see these things clearly. They take us out of the realm of verbal knowledge to the invisible realm of emotional experience, the more mysterious, unseen aspects of reality that guide us and drive our behaviour. Although it is largely parents who convey many of these unconscious messages and practices to their children, our moral behaviour—selfish or unselfish—is not just about the values of individual parents. Parents themselves are heavily influenced by their social relationships. Without necessarily being aware of it, they pass on the culture in which they are immersed. Just as children don't choose the family they are born into, so too parents don't choose their society. They respond to it and adapt to its norms, often unwittingly. If everyone around you is behaving selfishly, it is difficult not to join in. Each society is a sort of mega-family which transmits many underlying beliefs and attitudes, simply through the way things are done and the way things are.

This "social unconscious" mostly arises from the current power structures, which shape our values and expectations without our being aware of it. Many of our social structures and practices—such as the allocation and control of resources—are difficult to discuss or question because they seem to be inevitable. We experience them as a given "reality", not as a social context that we create together. In the West, our "reality" has been a culture focused on material and technical progress; we take it for granted that human relationships will in many ways be subordinated to our concern with expanding productivity and growth. So ingrained is this attitude that it is hard to perceive the underlying assumptions we make that material well-being should take precedence over emotional well-being.

Even those who have the most power to define our social reality are not necessarily aware of it. The early pioneers of industrial capitalism did not foresee the potential impact of their economic system and its "self-interestedness" on people's relationships. They were simply excited by the creative energies that were being released and their potential for greater material benefits, and took it for granted that relationships would continue as they always had. The early philosopher of capitalism Adam Smith still lived in an age when he could assume that humans had a natural "sympathy" for each other which was beyond question. As he said, even the "greatest ruffian" can "feel for the misery of others" as well as finding pleasure in others' happiness (1979, p. 4). He could not have imagined the extent to which his concept of a *"Homo economicus"*, driven by self-interest in his dealings, would come to stand for the whole of human nature and convince many people that a selfish way of life is the only way of life.

These notions of the inevitability of self-interest have prevailed for more than two centuries. However, even before the recent economic crisis, such ideas were beginning to look a little worn and threadbare. There was a gathering consensus that our materialism and our self-centredness had become a problem because those values had taken over in every sphere of our lives. I was alerted to this emerging view a few years ago when I read an opinion piece by the *New Statesman* columnist and academic Martin Jacques deploring the sad decline of family, community, and caring. We are living, Jacques said, in "the age of selfishness": "The credo of self, inextricably entwined with the gospel of the market, has hijacked the fabric of our lives." His thesis was: "Our social world has come to mirror and mimic the rhythms and characteristics of the market, contractual in nature. Meanwhile, the family—the site of virtually the only life-long relationships we enjoy—has become an ever-weaker institution: extended families are increasingly marginal, nuclear families are getting smaller and more short-lived, almost half of all marriages end in divorce, and most parents spend less time with their pre-school children" (2004, p. 14). Yet although I found myself endorsing much of what he said, Jacques offered little sense of what should replace these trends, other than, implicitly, a return to more traditional forms of the family. His conclusion was hopeless and pessimistic: "What is to be done, I hear the policy-wonks say. Nothing much, I guess" (ibid., p. 15).

We have become used to hearing that we are living in a "broken society". In 2008 the Conservative leader David Cameron described the United Kingdom as a society characterised by knife crime, poverty, ill health, family breakdown, and worklessness. He called it "a de-moralised society" where "children grow up without boundaries, thinking they can do as they please". Seeing the problem as a disciplinary one, he bemoaned a society where there has been "a decades-long erosion of responsibility, of social virtue, of self-discipline, respect for others, deferring gratification instead of instant gratifications" (Cameron, 2008, p. 7). In his view, this was the result of a national culture in which people saw themselves as "victims" of drug addiction, obesity, or family breakdown, instead of recognising that they had choices and should take responsibility for themselves. According to a representative poll of 1,832 adults taken shortly after this speech, the vast majority of people agreed with him (Oliver & Oakeshott, 2008).

Cameron identified something which, regardless of their political persuasion, people could recognise in the world around them: a carelessness about child-rearing, and a lack of responsibility for long-term well-being. However, both Martin Jacques and David Cameron diagnose the causes of these ills in terms of a lack of individual discipline or commitment. This is only half the story. *Why* are people like this? If they are, it is not just because they are weak and selfish, but also because they live in a society which does not help them to flourish and to care for each other. The heart of the matter is that we are living in an impoverished emotional culture, the end product of decades of individualism and consumerism, which have eroded our social bonds. This emotional impoverishment may look very different at different ends of the social scale—for the poorest socio-economic groups, it can result in being caught up in violent crime or in the benefits culture, whilst for the rich, it is more likely to result in being caught up in excessive consumption or fraudulent financial dealings—but whatever form it takes, I see materialism and social breakdown as the culmination of a value system which by definition does not take other people into account. This is manifest at every level, from the individual to prevailing social policy.

I would define selfishness as the pursuit of self-interest without regard for others' needs or interests. Of course, we all act like this at times. As individuals, our ability to hold other people's needs and interests in mind is a capacity that wobbles and wavers depending on our own state of mind and current circumstances, as well as on our emotional maturity. I am sure my own tendencies to selfishness are as great, if not greater, than anyone else's. I suspect that each of us tends to think that selfishness is our own guilty secret, not a social issue. But selfishness is not just an individual failing. It is equally possible to have a selfish society, a society which sustains individualism, greed, and materialism at the expense of collective interests and the needs of the social group as a whole. For me, all these issues are intertwined, and will be discussed as aspects of selfishness, because they all involve an element of disregard of others' needs and others' claims.

Although I would endorse Jacques's view of our times as an "age of selfishness", I would, however, question whether the way forward is to strengthen the traditional family, as Jacques and Cameron suggest. Nor do I think it is a matter of attempting to be "better" people by voluntarily adopting new moral values. Instead of reaching for familiar moral guidelines from the past, a more helpful starting point might be first to reach a thorough understanding of how and why self-ishness arises. By looking at both social and family contexts, using all the current knowledge at our disposal across the various disciplines of history, neuroscience, sociology, and psychology, we might arrive somewhere new.

Capitalism and the erosion of empathy

Unlike Martin Jacques, I believe that there is much to be optimistic about. Major scientific advances in recent years can help us to understand how we develop both as individuals and as societies. Neuroscientific understanding may even be able to explain how the wider culture has an effect not just on our ideas, but also on our very brain structure and function. The evidence is now stacking up that among industrial capitalism's unintended side effects is the way that it has shaped our brains as well as our moral attitudes. As Fred Previc, a former US government research scientist, observed: "Just as it was once thought that human activity could not dramatically alter the world's climate, so would it have once seemed unlikely that modern societies and lifestyles could produce widespread and serious neurochemical imbalances and associated impairments in brain function" (2009, p. 149).

According to Previc—now no longer carrying out research for the government and perhaps freer to say what he thinks is really going on—the highly stressful competitive environments which we have allowed to prevail in Western societies have reshaped certain aspects of our brain development. He argues that our pressurised way of life alters the behaviour of the brain's neurotransmitters—the vital substances which are like a variety of biochemical lubricating fluids that help the different parts of the brain to connect. When humans are stressed, the calming neurotransmitter serotonin gets used up and as its level sinks, the level of the motivational neurotransmitter dopamine tends to rise, producing more "active coping", driven, and self-willed behaviour. Previc believes that many of these effects are passed on pre-natally. In societies where mothers are under stress, their babies' brain biochemistry—either in the womb or in the delicate post-natal period of development—can be affected. The more stressed she is, the more sensitive to stress the baby's brain may become.[1]

Whilst scientists can illuminate the damage we cause ourselves by living in a competitive and emotionally unsupportive environment, and can demonstrate the effects of poor relationships on our bodies and brains, philosophers can illuminate new ways of thinking which may help us to achieve a more caring and co-operative society. Looking towards the future, I found profound inspiration not amongst politicians, but amongst feminist thinkers who have put forward their ideas for a new "ethic of care".[2] Their vision is not a sentimental ideal of a caring world, but a more down-to-earth analysis of what care means in practice. They emphasise that care is an *activity* not a set of principles or feelings. It is an activity that all human beings are involved with because we all receive care and give care in different ways. Yet although it is very much about how we relate to other people and how well we pay attention to them, it does not have to be based on personal emotion but "includes everything that we do to maintain, continue, and repair our 'world' so that we can live in it as well as possible" (Tronto, 1993, p. 102). It is highly practical.

This doesn't mean that it is easy to meet everyone's needs. Thinkers like Joan Tronto, professor of political science and women's studies at the City University of New York (CUNY), are realistically aware that "[T]here will inevitably be more care needs than can be met" (ibid., p. 103). There will always be difficult issues to face about which needs should take priority. For Tronto, these must be decided through collective political debate, not by relying on the "false security" of abstract individual rights and idealistic moral universalism—views which originated with the Enlightenment in the seventeenth century, but which fail to recognise the reality of unequal social power and our differing needs for care at any one time. Instead, she advocates a more pragmatic ethic based on paying attention to actual people living specific lives and striving to take their needs as seriously as we take our own.

In this sense, the "ethic of care" is closely related to the influential concept of "mentalization" developed by the British psychoanalyst and academic Peter Fonagy.[3] This is a concept that is gaining many adherents amongst psychotherapists, because it helps to understand how good relationships with other people work. In essence, mentalization is about the ability to grasp that other people have minds and feelings of their own which motivate their behaviour, just as our own do, and to understand that other people may experience things very differently from ourselves. It's a capacity which depends on openness to one's own experience, since it is difficult to be open to other people's emotions and to respect their different points of view if one cannot tolerate and fully experience one's own emotions. In many ways, the success of an ethic of care depends on people being able to "mentalize". Developing a new politics based on practical caring and mentalizing is an urgent task.

The politics of mentalization

The challenge now is to integrate the scientific knowledge that psychology and neuroscience offer us, information about how people develop and how their emotions are played out in the public sphere, with action: only then will we have a chance of moving towards the right solutions. Psychological discoveries have more often been used, however, to manipulate customers, and to increase our consumption through advertising, with its empty promises of sexual fulfilment. In other words, like so much else in this phase of human history, psychology has been subordinated to material pleasure and comforts. We have been mesmerised by the ease and enjoyment offered by the technological feats of the last century—electricity, telecommunications, health care, entertainment, rapid transport, and domestic conveniences—yet our consumer sophistication has not yet been matched by our psychological maturity or understanding.

Nor have the conveniences themselves—whilst pleasurable and superbly clever—helped us to become more human or enhanced our relationships in any way. Even though dishwashing machines, DVD players, or iPods—to name just a few—demand complex social organisation and sophisticated technology to bring them into being, no active participation in the production process is required from us, the users. Mentally they engage only the most basic programmes of the brain—those set to achieve immediate and short-term pleasures and to avoid painful experiences which are neurologically speaking our most "selfish" instincts.

Lately, however, there has been a growing interest in the value of relationships as well as things. It is tempting to hope that this shift is driven by a newly found concern and responsibility for others, but the evidence suggests that it is more likely to be a new form of self-concern. In affluent societies, people now expect capitalism to deliver on the promises of its advertising and provide happiness as well as material comforts. We yearn for the real satisfactions that relationships of various kinds bring. Yet the richer we get, and the more apparent it is that capitalism cannot deliver this kind of fulfilment, the more dissatisfied and preoccupied with our own increasing psychological ill health we become. Some recent studies, notably by the psychologist Daniel Kahneman, have shown that people in the wealthiest consumer societies have become no more happy or fulfilled over the last fifty years, despite their increased wealth. Kahneman won the Nobel Prize for Economics for his work in "behavioural economics", which demonstrated that there was a "weak relationship between income and global life satisfaction" (Kahneman & Tversky, 2000; see also Kahneman, Krueger, Schkade, Schwarz, & Stone, 2006). According to his research, if we really wanted to be happy, we would sleep more and spend more time with friends, not pursue greater income and buy more consumer goods.

Despite all the immediate gratifications that have been on offer—the sexual freedom, easy credit, labour-saving devices, and on-tap personal entertainment, all of which are still only aspirations for those in less developed economies—we have not got happier. In fact, depression is now classified as one of the world's most prevalent illnesses. As Richard Layard, an economist at the London School of Economics, put it: "Depression has actually increased as our incomes have risen" (2005, p. 25). In the USA, statistics reveal that over a quarter of the population suffers from a diagnosable mental disorder in a given year.[4]

Such figures are shockingly high. However, there are valid questions about whether this is an objective change or the result of changed perceptions in a medicalised, therapeutic culture which tends to define everyday problems of living, such as feeling unhappy, as aspects of mental "disease". The psychiatrist Derek Summerfield, the sociologist Frank Furedi, and others linked to the Institute of Ideas have argued that labelling problems in this way undermines people's natural coping resources. Summerfield is outraged at the World Health Organization's claim that depression "is a worldwide epidemic that within twenty years will be second only to cardiovascular disease as the world's most debilitating disease". He sees this as "a serious distortion, which could serve to deflect attention away from what millions of people might cite as the basis of their misery, like poverty and lack of rights" (2006, p. 161).

Poverty is of course a source of acute misery for those people who live and suffer in the undeveloped areas of the world where they have yet to reach adequate fulfilment of even their most basic needs, but in the richer nations, it is a relative concept. The poor in the USA have cars and air conditioning. In practice, poverty in the affluent nations often has less to do with physical conditions such as extreme hunger, disease, or lack of shelter, and more to do with psychological hopelessness. Although I don't want to downplay the despair of living in the worst communities which are blighted by unemployment, crime, and a lack of purpose, recent evidence emerging from a large study of 8,000 children in Britain is finding that socio-economic circumstances are not the key determinant of a child's mental or physical health; what is more crucial is their mother's and father's own mental health and ability to be an effective parent (see Waylen, Stallard, & Steward-Brown, 2008).

Nor is poverty—though it restricts life and can cause unhappiness—the only source of mental illness. Depression and psychological illness frequently affect those who are better off, too. Very often, poor mental health is due to early life experiences that have undermined the sense of self and ability to manage feelings and relationships well. In affluent countries, it can also be exacerbated by our tendency to compare ourselves with others, and to find happiness or satisfaction in our social standing and material wealth relative to others.

In the West, we are trapped in these cycles of endless striving and dissatisfaction, trying to keep up with the ever more elaborate displays of consumption we see on television and on the internet. This drive to accumulate material goods and services appears to have addictive qualities: it is a powerful appetite which has no inbuilt mechanism to alert us when we have had enough; we want more and more—especially, it seems, just that little bit more than everyone else. This is partly a natural aspect of the human brain's dopamine reward systems, which are more active in response to unexpected gains than to getting the same old things (they are primarily designed to help us to adapt to new experiences). However, this human tendency has also been exploited by our economic system, which delights in stimulating new needs and in creating a momentum for the development of new products. After all, it would not be helpful to capitalism if we were satisfied with what we had.

What is less natural is the addictive quality of so much of our current behaviour. Even in the midst of material comfort and physical security that our forebears could only dream of, we continue to act as if we were deprived and must compete with others to get as much as we can. The reason for this may be that although we have relative material abundance, we do not in fact have emotional abundance. Many people are deprived of what really matters. Lacking emotional security, they seek security in material things.

This psychological message has been elaborated by Tim Kasser, a professor at a liberal arts college in the USA who himself espouses an anti-consumerist lifestyle of "voluntary simplicity". He lives in the countryside, grows his own vegetables, produces his own milk and eggs, and has no television (a tempting way to avoid the mind pollution of advertising, yet in my view a somewhat dubious strategy since television is the source of so much of our shared culture). Kasser is building up a body of research which begins to show that there is a link between the materialistic attitudes of the younger generations and their mental health. He has found that the more materialistic young people were, the less satisfying their relationships. This confirmed previous research by his colleague Ken Sheldon, professor of psychology at the University of Missouri, showing that those teenagers with the most materialistic attitudes had the most conflict and aggression in their dating relationships, and demonstrated the least empathy and satisfaction in close relationships of all kinds. Kasser's research also showed that this was related to the early care they received in their families: "Individuals who have not had their needs met in the past will come to think that wealth and possessions will bring them happiness and a good life" (2002, p. 28).

In other words, they confuse material well-being with psychological well-being. The way this may have come about is illustrated by the story of some very young, sick children with tuberculosis observed by James Robertson, a social worker linked to John Bowlby, over a period of two years in the late 1940s. The treatment of tuberculosis at that time demanded that the children must endure prolonged separations from their parents whilst they were in hospital. Robertson described how the toddlers went though stages of adapting to their emotional deprivation—first protesting and looking for their lost mother, then becoming despairing and listless, and finally becoming emotionally detached. As Robertson described it, once they had reached this stage, the children seemed indifferent to their parents when they visited on Sundays: "They were more interested in what their parents had brought them than in the parents themselves. They searched bags and stuffed chocolate into their mouths." His impression was that the children had numbed their feelings because of their repeated disappointment at not being taken home, and had replaced those longings with a "hunger for sweet things which did not disappoint" (James and Joyce Robertson, quoted in Karen, 1998, p. 75).

So many of us are now like those children. Billion-dollar industries exist to provide us with the comforts we crave when people let us down, whether that is sweet things, alcohol, or the latest consumer toys and fashions. All too easily, these sources of satisfaction become more desirable than unreliable close relationships. Experimental research on monkeys and rats suggests that the key once again lies in very early childhood. This research has shown that social isolation, emotional deprivation, or stress in infancy alters the dopamine pathways, particularly in the "social brain". This can increase impulsive, "grabby" behaviour, and can create a predisposition to addiction. The current research of Dr Gene-Jack Wang, at the University of Florida, is finding that compulsive overeaters and compulsive drug-takers both have decreased dopamine D2 receptors (Wang, Volkow, Thanos, & Fowler, 2004).

Not everyone is hooked on particular substances, yet "things" still seem to provide real psychological benefits for many people. In the absence of a feeling of confidence about the social world, it is easy to become selfishly preoccupied with acquiring things and ignoring the relationship between your own desires and the needs of the wider society. Things can provide security of various kinds: owning your own home enables you to feel confident that it will not be taken away, owning a car means you don't have to depend on unreliable public transport. Things can even become a source of individual identity, since "brands" sometimes appear to deliver a sense of self that people have not been able to derive from their family relationships. Equally, "retail therapy" can sometimes provide a sense of power and choice that is lacking in everyday life—often, the only power many people will ever experience is purchasing power.

Whatever the psychological drivers are, consumerism has become a kind of "mania", as the psychiatrist Peter Whybrow calls it (2005). Massive overconsumption has become the norm—most notably in the USA, where the majority of sixth-grade children have a television in their bedrooms, and where huge portions of high calorie food have led to an obesity crisis. The powerful and successful seem just as driven to acquire more, no matter how much they already have. The overpayment of chief executives and the overspending of the poor are the twin poles of the same phenomenon. In fact, the mania has been at its most extreme in the corporations. In the UK, between 2000 and 2007, top chief executives' pay rose by 150 per cent (Toynbee & Walker, 2008), whilst in the USA in the same period, it rose around 313 per cent (Hennigan, 2007; see also Mintzberg, 2002). By 2007, a typical chief executive officer earned more in one working day "than the typical worker earned all year", according to the American politician Joe Biden.[5] These kinds of behaviour have almost come to seem natural—just another demonstration of good old opportunistic human nature. But this is the explanation we fall back on when we can't make sense of our behaviour.

As a psychotherapist, I argue that we must bring a deeper understanding of the role of emotional development into our political awareness, and recognise that political behaviour in general is not something separate from other forms of human relationship and is influenced by the same emotional dynamics. For example, the way that our public figures behave in positions of leadership, as well as the policies they espouse, are influenced by the moral framework they themselves acquired in infancy. I want to make it clear that family life is not just a private sphere but is centrally important in passing on and sustaining our public emotional and moral culture. Parents, whether they are aware of it or not, reproduce current cultural values and shape their offspring for a particular way of life. Infancy, it turns out, is the hub of cultural transmission; unselfishness is not just an individual achievement (which it is), but at the same time is a *cultural* achievement.

The culture of narcissism

The American historian Christopher Lasch identified what he termed a "culture of narcissism" in the USA as early as the 1970s. In his groundbreaking analysis (1979), he described how the individual self had become weakened and infantilised by the consumer society. Ironically, whilst capitalism pushed us towards independence and self-sufficiency, in many ways the rise of consumerism had the opposite effect. It prolonged the experience of dependence into adult life, surrounding us with "fantasies of total gratification", a trend which has accelerated in the last thirty years, epitomised by the Hollywood actress Carrie Fisher's witticism: "Instant gratification takes too long" (1987). Yet Lasch noted that without self-control and deferred gratification, it becomes much harder to develop the real satisfactions of learning skills, competencies, and care for others. In Lasch's view, people were becoming less well-equipped to deal with the difficult aspects of life, such as the need for self-sacrifice or the pain of loss. Stuck in an infantilised state, grown-up people imagined that they would be cushioned from reality, from what Bly called "a complicated web of griefs, postponed pleasures, unwelcome labour, responsibilities and unpaid debts to gods and human beings" (1997, p. 50). Long-term goals that required effort and sustained commitment became increasingly unattractive.

Lasch believed that modern capitalist society reinforced narcissistic traits in everyone, and allowed "celebrities" with narcissistic personalities to set the tone of public and private life. However, his analysis was unusual because, unlike many social critics before and since, it did not assume that people's selfishness or superficiality was the natural state of humankind. Instead, for Lasch, narcissism is actually the psychological outcome of our *lack* of power: "In its pathological form, narcissism originates as a defense against feelings of helpless dependency in early life, which it tries to counter with 'blind optimism' and grandiose illusions of personal self-sufficiency" (op. cit., p. 231).

In the last few decades the US and the UK, in particular, have given a free reign to narcissistic illusions and addictive materialism. As a result, the gap between the rich and poor has widened. Those at the top of the social scale, such as the senior bankers and lawyers interviewed by the liberal journalists Polly Toynbee and David Walker for their book *Unjust Rewards* (op. cit.), revealed a strong sense of entitlement to their luxurious lifestyles and a staggering ignorance about the amount of money most people have to live on. These interviewees fiercely resisted the prospect of redistributing income, calling such measures "bullshit crap which doesn't help the people" themselves, describing them for the most part as "lazy" and undeserving (ibid., p. 36). Clearly, when there are extremes of wealth and privilege, within one nation or between nations, the stage is set for resentment and fear, not for empathy and mutual understanding. For this community of the rich, the claims and concerns of other—poorer—people did not have equal weight and value. The global poor are unlikely to merit much of their sympathy either.

The self-advancement of those at the top of the social scale turned out to come at a huge cost to others. We now know that the risk-taking that bolstered the exaggerated salaries and bonuses of the world's top financiers and chief executives has had a major impact on both their own societies as well as globally, threatening the collapse of the banking system and the well-being of millions. In less dramatic and obvious ways, their wealth has also been achieved at the cost of spending on public, social goods, both at home and abroad. For example, when poorer nations are in relationship with the richer, narcissistically self-centred countries, they are often prevented from spending money on social goods and welfare support for their own desperately needy peasantry or urban poor by economic policies dictated by rich nations. When loaning money to developing countries, the international financial organisations, led by the US, demand "structural adjustment programmes" which insist that poor countries pursue policies such as privatisation, deregulation, or reducing trade barriers—policies which reflect Western ways of operating and which often benefit the donor countries more than the recipients (Davies, 2006).

Narcissistic societies often behave in much the same way as narcissistic individuals. There is no neat divide between "private life" and "public life", since the people who lead the banks, governments, or corporations bring their psychological attitudes and values to their public tasks. They shape the culture in their own image, often demonstrating the same problems in facing difficult realities as do narcissistic individuals. As a psychotherapist I am often struck, when observing the behaviour of those in power, by their remarkable similarity to those less powerful people who are designated as "patients". Whether people are depressed, unhappy, or could even be diagnosed as having borderline, narcissistic, or antisocial personality psychopathology, the bottom line is that they have difficulties with the quality of their attachments to other people and often find it a struggle to think of others' needs. The same lack of emotional connection to other people is often seen on the public stage.

Yet we rarely address the underlying psychological and emotional dynamics of our public figures, or our culture as a whole. Public commentary is usually restricted to economic or political analysis—together with a sprinkling of gossip. I believe this undermines our attempts to understand the forces that are at work in our lives. At a time when we need to adjust our values and expectations away from a world economy based on growth and the exploitation of fossil fuels towards a world based on greater empathy for others and care for our natural resources, we will need to understand why we behave as we do and what drives us. I would suggest that we need the more collective values of empathy, care, and thoughtful collaboration if we are going to solve the problems that face us.

Notes

1. A useful overview of research can be found in Emma Adam, Bonnie Klimnes-Dougan, and Megan Gunnar, "Social regulation of the adrenocortical response to stress in infants, children and adolescents", in Coch, Dawson, and Fischer, 2007. See also Wismer Fries, Shirtcliff, and Pollak, 2008.
2. In particular, I am thinking of Robinson, 1999; Sevenhuijsen, 1998; and Tronto, 1993.
3. Usefully summarised in Slade, 2005.
4. National Institute of Mental Health, *The Numbers Count*, NIMH factsheet, 2008.
5. Joe Biden, speech at Miami Beach, Florida, 5 March 2009.

References

Biden, J. (2009). Speech at Miami Beach, Florida, 5 March 2009.

Bly, R. (1997). *The Sibling Society*. London: Penguin.

Cameron, D. (2008). Speech at Glasgow East by-election, 7 July 2008. www.telegraph.co.uk.

Coch, D., Dawson, G., & Fischer, K. (Eds.) (2007). *Human Behavior, Learning and the Developing Brain*. New York: Guilford Press.

Davies, D. (2006). *Planet of Slums*. London: Verso.

Fisher, C. (1987). *Postcards from the Edge*. New York: Pocket Books/Simon & Schuster.

Gerhardt, S. (2004). *Why Love Matters: How Affection Shapes a Baby's Brain*. London: Routledge.

Gerhardt, S. (2010). *The Selfish Society: How We All Forgot to Love One Another and Made Money Instead*. London: Simon & Schuster.

Hennigan, M. (2007). Executive pay and inequality in the winner-take-all society, 2007. www.finfacts.com.

Jacques, M. (2004). The death of intimacy. *Guardian*, 18 September.

Kahneman, D., & Tversky, A. (Eds.) (2000). *Choices, Values and Frames*. Cambridge: Cambridge University Press.

Kahneman, D., Krueger, A. B., Schkade, D., Schwarz, N., & Stone, A. A. (2006). Would you be happier if you were richer? *Science, 312*: 1908–1910.

Karen, R. (1998). *Becoming Attached: First Relationships*. Oxford: Oxford University Press.

Kasser, T. (2002). *The High Price of Materialism*. Cambridge, MA: MIT Press.

Lasch, C. (1979). *The Culture of Narcissism: American Life in an Age of Diminishing Expectations*. London: Abacus.

Layard, R. (2005). *Happiness: Lessons from a New Science.* London: Penguin.

Mintzberg, H. (2002). Beyond selfishness. *MIT Sloan Management Review,* *44*: 1.

National Institute of Mental Health (2008). *The Numbers Count,* NIMH factsheet.

Oliver, J., & Oakeshott, I. (2008). Ethics Boy. YouGov survey. *Sunday Times,* 13 July.

Previc, F. (2009). *The Dopaminergic Mind in Human Evolution and History.* Cambridge: Cambridge University Press.

Robinson, F. (1999). *Globalising Care: Ethics, Feminist Theory, and International Relations.* Boulder, CO: Westview Press.

Sevenhuijsen, S. (1998). *Citizenship and the Ethics of Care: Feminist Considerations on Justice, Morality and Politics.* London: Taylor & Francis.

Slade, A. (2005). Parental reflective functioning: an introduction. *Attachment and Human Development,* *7*(3): 269–281.

Smith, A. (1979). *The Theory of Moral Sentiments.* Edinburgh: Kincaid & Bell.

Summerfield, D. (2006). Depression: epidemic or pseudo-epidemic? *Journal of the Royal Society of Medicine,* *99*: 3.

Toynbee, P., & Walker, D. (2008). *Unjust Rewards: Ending the Greed that is Bankrupting Britain.* London: Granta.

Tronto, J. (1993). *Moral Boundaries: A Political Argument for an Ethic of Care.* New York: Routledge.

Wang, J.-G., Volkow, N. D., Thanos, P. K., & Fowler, J. S. (2004). Similarity between obesity and drug addictions as assessed by neurofunctional imaging. *Journal of Addictive Diseases,* *23*(3): 39–53.

Ward, L. (2005). Appeal to parents on teenage births. *Guardian,* 26 May.

Waylen, A., Stallard, N., & Steward-Brown, S. (2008). Parenting and health in mid-childhood: a longitudinal study. *European Journal of Public Health,* *18*(3): 300–305.

Whybrow, P. (2005). *American Mania: When More is Not Enough.* New York: W. W. Norton.

Wismer Fries, A. B., Shirtcliff, E. A., & Pollak, S. D. (2008). Neuro-endocrine dysregulation following early social deprivation in children. *Developmental Psychobiology,* *50*: 588–599.

CHAPTER FIVE

Divided brain, divided world*

Jonathan Rowson and Iain McGilchrist

Introduction

JR: The notion that we are rational individuals who respond to information by making decisions consciously, consistently, and independently is, at best, a very partial account of who we are. A wide body of scientific knowledge is now telling us what many have long intuitively sensed—humans are a fundamentally social species, formed through and for social interaction, and most of our behaviour is habitual. The discussion and reflections that follow feature an inquiry into a singularly profound, complex and fascinating thesis about the relationship between our brains and the world. Through this inquiry, I attempt to illustrate what a mature discussion about the social and political relevance of neuroscience might look like.

Rather than thinking about the link between brain and behaviour as if it always has to be direct and reductive, and then proceeding to argue about the significance of the link, the discussion that follows takes a

*This chapter is an edited version of "Divided Brain, Divided World: Why the Best Part of Us Struggles to be Heard", a discussion workshop that launched the RSA's Social Brain Centre (RSA, 2013), and is reproduced by kind permission of the RSA and the authors.

different route. Iain McGilchrist's work provides a fresh and powerful perspective because the route from brain to behaviour is mediated by phenomenology and values. *The Master and His Emissary*, the book that informs the following discussion, is about the profound significance of the fact that the left and right hemispheres of our brains have radically different "world views" (McGilchrist, 2009). The hidden story of Western culture, as told by the author, is about how the abstract, instrumental, articulate, and assured left hemisphere has gradually usurped the more contextual, humane, systemic, holistic, but relatively tentative and inarticulate right hemisphere.

The divided brain

JR: Iain, let me begin by stating the argument as I have come to understand it, and you can tell me how you might express it differently or more fully. You seem to be saying that the left hemisphere of the brain is gradually colonising our experience. While the brain hemispheres are connected by the corpus callosum, and both are involved in everything we do, if we cease to ask what the hemispheres do, for example, language, reasoning, creativity, forecasting, and instead ask how they do it, we find very significant differences in the two hemispheres. For instance the left hemisphere tends to decontextualise issues while the right contextualises, the left tends to abstract while the right makes vivid and concrete, the left seeks instrumental feedback while the right prefers affectively nuanced responses, and the right hemisphere appears to be much more receptive to evidence that challenges its own position. Both of these "hows" are important and necessary, and the evidence for these differences is meticulously unpacked in your book in a cautious but extensive inductive argument.

You are clear that there is insufficient evolutionary time in Western cultural history for left or right hemisphere dominance to manifest at the structural level of the brain. So you are not saying the left hemisphere is getting bigger or denser or better connected than the right. The point is that the left hemisphere's "way of being" is more culturally contagious than the "way of being" of the right hemisphere. The suggestion is that, slowly but surely, the left hemisphere's perspective shapes our culture in such a way that the culture begins to respond to it as the dominant one.

Your thesis matters because there is a very real danger that we may reach what you call "a hall of mirrors" in which the explicit, instrumental, defined, confident, abstract voice (not unlike the current voice of the materialistic orthodoxy in neuroscience or the neoliberal voice placing unqualified faith in markets) becomes the only one we appreciate, while the relatively implicit, intrinsic, fluid, visceral perspective of the right hemisphere begins to sound diminished and irrelevant. Is that about right? If so, can you give some practical examples to illustrate the nature of this change?

IM: I think that is a good initial formulation. As you say, it is not about *what* each hemisphere *does*, as we used to think, because it is clear that each is involved with literally everything. It is about *how* it is *done*—an approach, a stance, a disposition towards things. Above all, this is not about "thinking versus feeling". It is—as Mary Midgley perceived in her review in *The Guardian* (2010)—about two kinds of thinking. And, contrary to popular belief, it is the right hemisphere's, not the left hemisphere's, thinking that is more accurate, more down to earth—in a word, "truer" to what is.

Practical examples

IM: But you ask if there are practical examples of what I see as us drifting ever more into the left hemisphere's version of the world. That's not hard. Let's begin with the financial crash. It was fuelled by a belief that human behaviour can be confidently predicted by algorithms, whereas in fact we not only don't know—but in principle can never know—enough for this sort of prediction to be valid. This false belief also allowed people to feel that their wise intuitions about the differences between individual borrowers, or individual economies, should be overridden, because such context-dependent uniqueness was nowhere to be found in the model. The situation was compounded by an absorption in the virtual—complex self-referring systems of numbers—to the extent that we lost track of what these figures represented in the real world. Financial institutions disregarded the importance of trust, and instead traded in a war of all-against-all, inducing an atmosphere of paranoia, deception, and chicanery. All these are features of the way the left hemisphere conceives the world, not the way the whole brain would have seen it.

Equally I could point to the mass of petty legislation, and the obsession with accountability and audit in all walks of life, designed to fill the vacuum left by trustworthiness and merely serving further to erode trust; a litigious culture, which imposes a heavy burden on the economy and saps morale; the bureaucracy and micromanagement that stifles originality in research and ensures mediocrity; the narrow-minded obsession with economic gain here and now that attacks educational institutions and the world of scholarship; the managerial culture that is destroying professionalism in medicine, and substituting machine-like "decision trees" for skill and judgment; the neglect of practical hands-on, embodied experience and common sense, that turns nurses and policemen into office-based paper-pushers with degrees; the exploitation of the natural world as if it were just so much resource to "go get"; and so on.

Sometimes people seem to think that when I talk about the hemispheres this is "just" metaphorical. But it is not. There is evidence that autistic spectrum disorders and anorexia nervosa, both of which mimic, and almost certainly involve, right hemisphere deficit states, are on the increase. But it goes much further than that. It affects us all. After a talk I gave recently in Toronto, a member of the audience came up to the microphone. What she said struck me forcibly. "I am a teacher of seven to eleven year olds," she began. "My colleagues and I have noticed in the last three or four years that we have started having to teach children how to read the human face."

Of course, in itself it's alarming that a proportion of our children are no longer able to understand implicit communication, not even so much as to respond appropriately to the face of their fellow human beings. In the past such problems would have been confined to children on the autistic spectrum. But more than that—it fell into place with other messages I had been getting from teachers since the publication of the book. These teachers reported that in just the last few years their children had become unable to carry out tasks involving sustained attention, tasks that ten years ago almost every child would have been able to do easily. When you put that together with research suggesting that children are now less empathic than they used to be, you get a startling picture. Because each of these faculties—the ability to read faces, to sustain attention, and to empathise—as well as being essential to the human world, is particularly reliant on the right hemisphere of the brain. So their relative demise is precisely what you would expect if my hypothesis is correct.

JR: That's a striking example. But it is curious that you mention just "the last few years" rather than the longer time frames that are unpacked in your book. What might be going on there?

IM: Well, these particular faculties are also likely to be impaired by over-reliance on TV and computers, the "virtual" reality that comes through a screen, and which is expanding exponentially. Instead of spending much of his early years engaged with his mother's face (which is how children crucially develop the sense of a secure self, distinct from, but not entirely separate from, others), a child now is likely to spend more time interacting with a piece of equipment. There he will expect to be constantly distracted and overstimulated, and in due course to watch scenes of violence with calm detachment. All that is true. But then this virtuality and emphasis on technology is also in itself a reflection of a world dominated by the left hemisphere.

JR: The impact of technology on our capacity to pay attention, sustain concentration, appreciate implicit communication, and so forth is certainly an important issue, not least because some (Nick Carr, Susan Greenfield, Kenneth Gergen) feel this is an acute and growing problem that we need to address, while others dismiss such fears as reflex technophobia without any evidence to back it up, and are quick to point out that many, though not all (e.g., Jaron Lanier) of those expressing such fears have relatively limited experience of the technologies in question, which are often intensely social and creative in nature, with exacting intellectual content. I think there is an important discussion to be had here, but I would prefer to focus for now on making sure the core argument is as clear as possible.

Is the brain "foundational"?

JR: Your thesis seems to entail an implicit theory of consciousness, in particular how different aspects of the brain relate to mind, and mind to world. You don't wade into the major debates in the philosophy of mind, perhaps wisely, but you do seem to have views on these fundamental ontological matters that underpin your argument. The main thing I want to clarify is that you are not "reducing" everything to the brain, but at the same time you do seem to be saying the brain is a kind of touchstone, and it serves to give the argument a foundational feel: can you help clarify?

IM: I am not one of those people, of whom there appear to be all too many these days, who think that they have said something profound—even perhaps revealed the real, the ultimate truth—about a human experience simply by re-describing it at the neuronal level. That is just naivety. People got terribly excited when they found what was referred to as the "neural circuitry" involved in falling in love—but what exactly did they expect? A blank? *Something* lights up in my brain when I eat a cheese sandwich—it just doesn't taste of cheddar.

The brain: divided and asymmetrical

IM: But it is odd that in recent times science has largely ignored two absolutely fundamental and incontrovertible findings about the brain. First, that it is, literally, profoundly divided. And second, its obvious asymmetry: there are clear observable differences at every level.

JR: And in the book you spend some time detailing those differences.

IM: The two hemispheres are different sizes, shapes, and weights (the right hemisphere is bigger and heavier in all social mammals); have expansions in different areas, different gyral conformations on the surface, and in places different architecture of the underlying cells; have different proportions of grey matter to white, different sensitivity to neuroendocrine influences, and rely on different preponderances of neurotransmitters. And in psychometric testing they consistently yield different results, which is in keeping with something any clinician could tell you: when there is damage to one hemisphere or the other, through injury, tumour, or stroke, there are consistent differences in what happens to the subject and his world depending on which hemisphere suffers the lesion.

JR: So I guess you are saying something like this: if people are getting so excited about the brain in general—as they clearly are—why are they not saying more about perhaps the most obvious feature of it, namely that it is so fundamentally divided in so many different ways, and not just divided, but also profoundly asymmetrical?

IM: Exactly. And the first of these facts is particularly odd, because the power of the brain consists precisely in the number and complexity of its connections. Having it divided, on the face of things, is a massive waste of "computing power". Add to this that the main band of fibres connecting the two hemispheres, the corpus callosum, has got smaller over evolution, rather than larger, and in any case spends much of its time facilitating the blocking or inhibition of action in the other hemisphere, and it looks like quite some investment has gone into keeping the two hemispheres apart. Why?

JR: Why indeed? What is it about the nature of the difference between the hemispheres that, despite their ongoing interaction and interdependence, a considerable degree of separation and neural inhibition is nonetheless somehow "adaptive"? You try to answer this at length in the book, and make the point above that it is not what each hemisphere does that is significant, but rather how they are—their way of being. But I think for lay people, and perhaps even for many scientists, that's really hard! What things do just seems to be the default way that we think about how one thing compares with another, and we reserve the "how", the "way of being" that you mention for people.

Hemispheres: it's not what they do, it's the way that they do it

IM: Well, that is indeed a crucial point, and it's the only conceivable explanation of how we came to neglect these obvious hemisphere differences. Dogma came to obscure facts. Because we thought of the brain as a machine, we were asking "What does it do?" and getting the answer "They both do everything". If instead we had thought of the brain as part of a person, rather than a machine, we might have asked a different question: "What's he or she like?" How, in other words—with what values, goals, interests, in what manner and in what way—did this part of a person do what he or she did? And we would have got quite another answer. For each hemisphere has a quite consistent, but radically different, "take" on the world. This means that, at the core of our thinking about ourselves, the world, and our relationship with it, there are two incompatible but necessary views that we need to try to combine. And things go badly wrong when we do not.

So when people say, what does looking at the brain tell us about the human world that we couldn't have found out some other way? I say—nothing. But that's also true of a map. There's nothing on it you couldn't have found out by wandering aimlessly around in the rain for quite some time. But would you throw away the map for that reason?

JR: Interesting. So you are not giving the brain extra explanatory power because it is the brain as such, but because it is something we now have a fairly large amount of information about, and it would be foolish not to at least try to apply some of that knowledge to making sense of the world?

IM: It's like this. Suppose it could be shown—because it can—that our brains are so constructed as to enable us to bring into being and conceive the experiential world in two quite distinct, complementary, but ultimately incompatible, ways. Suppose each has its uses, and that—here's why the brain view helps—these versions of the world, which have importantly different qualities, are generally so well combined or alternated from moment to moment in everyday experience that individuals are *not aware of this being the case.*

Now suppose also that it could be shown—because indeed it can—that these "takes" on the world are not equally well grounded: the part of the brain that makes one of these views possible (the right hemisphere) takes into account more and better integrated information, over a broader range, than the other (the left hemisphere). One *sees* more, in the broadest sense of the word.

Now further suppose—because this is in fact demonstrably the case—that persons who, by experimental contrivance or through injury or disease, have to rely only on the part of the brain which sees less (the left hemisphere) tend to be unreasonably certain, more rigid and exclusive than those who are, for similar reasons, obliged to rely on the part that sees more (the right hemisphere), who are more tentative and more able to see other points of view. And suppose it could be shown—because, again, it can—that while most people, most of the time, draw on each hemisphere, individuals often show a bias towards drawing on one more than the other, with predictable results for that person's understanding of the world.

The evolution of two types of consciousness

IM: Survival requires the application of two incompatible kinds of attention to the world at once. A bird, for example, needs to pay narrow-beam sharply focussed attention to what it has already prioritised as of significance—a seed against a background of grit or pebbles, or a twig to build a nest. At the same time, it must be able to bring to bear on the world a broad, open, sustained, and uncommitted attention, on the lookout for whatever else may exist. Without this capacity it would soon become someone else's lunch while getting its own. Birds and animals all have divided brains, and regularly use one hemisphere for vigilant attention to the world at large, so as to make sense of it, including to bond with their mates, and the other for the narrow attention that enables them to lock onto whatever it is they need to get. Humans are no different in this respect: we use our left hemisphere to grasp and manipulate, and the right to understand the world at large and how things within it relate to one another, as well as our relationship with it as a whole.

It is the left hemisphere that controls the right hand which for most of us is the one that does the grasping, and provides that aspect of language (not all of language) that enables us to say we have "grasped" something. But it is the right hemisphere that is the basis of our nature as the "social animal", which Aristotle saw as our defining feature.

It is easy to think of attention as just another "cognitive function". But it isn't. It is an aspect of consciousness: a machine can process data but it cannot attend. The nature of the attention we choose to pay alters the nature of the world we experience, and governs what it is we will find. This in turn governs the type of attention we deem it appropriate to pay. Before long we are locked into a certain vision of the world, as we become more and more sure of what it is we see. To a man with a hammer everything begins to look like a nail. And some beautiful research demonstrates that what we do not expect, we just do not see.

Not what but how: the "worlds" of the left and right hemispheres

IM: Because of its narrow focus and emphasis on getting certainty, the left hemisphere sees only bits and pieces, fragments which it attempts to put together to form a whole. The left hemisphere alone encodes tools and machines. In the living world, context is everything, but this is neglected by the left hemisphere. Thus the left hemisphere prefers the explicit, without understanding that rendering things explicit, and isolating them under the spotlight of attention, denatures and ultimately kills them, just as explaining a joke or a poetic metaphor robs it of its meaning and power. The view through the lab window distorts the meaning of everything most precious to us—the natural world, sexual love, art, and spirituality all fare badly when treated in this detached and decontextualised way.

The left hemisphere focuses on detail at the expense of the bigger picture, and on procedures at the expense of their meaning. This loss of proportion and preference for the forms of things over any real world content, lend themselves to a "tick box" mentality, which is also an aspect of its risk-averse nature. Since its purpose is control in the service of grasp or manipulation, rather than understanding of the world, it is anxious and even paranoid if it senses loss of control. This makes it prone to bureaucracy, and indeed one could see the bureaucratic mind as an epitome of the left hemisphere's take on the world, prioritising not just control but procedures that are explicit and that favour abstraction, anonymity, organisability, and predictability over what is individual, unique, embodied, and flexible. In the process justice gets reinterpreted simply as equality.

JR: It's just worth adding here that by highlighting these limitations you are not just cheerleading for the right hemisphere—both hemispheres have important limitations?

IM: I spend a lot of time these days going round the place speaking up for the left hemisphere. Woody Allen said that the brain was his second favourite organ: one might say that the left hemisphere is my second favourite hemisphere. We desperately need both in order to reason properly and to use our imagination creatively. If I seem to have a lot to say in favour of the right hemisphere in the book, it is because there was a balance here that needed to be redressed—and still does. A completely false view prevailed that the right hemisphere was somehow airy-fairy and unreliable and simply added some emotional colour to the perceptions of the "intelligent" left hemisphere. But it is in reality the right hemisphere that sees more, that is more in touch with reality, and is more intellectually sophisticated (incidentally, there is evidence that those of highest intelligence, whatever their discipline, may rely more on the right hemisphere) (McGilchrist, op. cit., p. 92).

The left hemisphere does not understand things, so much as process them: it is the right hemisphere that is the basis of understanding. This has an impact on the way we live now: because the left hemisphere is better than the right hemisphere at manipulating both figures and words, but less good than it at understanding their meaning (or in fact meaning in any sense), information becomes more important for it than knowledge, and knowledge than wisdom, which is implicit, paradoxical, and discoverable only by experience. Similarly, skills and judgment, embodied, implicit, and born of experience, seem merely unreliable versions of a procedure, and have to be "operationalised" by algorithms that a machine could follow. This produces a standard product that is guaranteed to rule out any form of excellence.

Systems become designed to maximise utility, that is to say the efficiency that one would require of a machine: quantity, speed, and reliability of production. The problem here is that while this may apply to making plastic spoons, it does not apply to any human relationship, such as that with a teacher, a doctor, a policeman, a clergyman, a judge, or a social worker, all of whom will do a worse job by doing more, more quickly, and to a standard template. Reasonableness, a highly sophisticated quality that used to be thought a goal of education, as well as a hallmark of civilisation, becomes replaced by mere rationality, and there is a resounding failure of common sense.

Reason and rationality

JR: Perhaps you could say something more about this distinction that you highlight in your book, because at first blush it sounds like a minor semantic quibble, but the distinction has real practical import, and relevance, for instance, for our adherence to what has been called "*zombie economics*" (Quiggin, 2010) in which we continue to use "rational" economic models that we know do not make sense of "reasonable" economic behaviour in the real world.

IM: The difference I am seeking to point up here is one that is recognised in other languages—certainly in Greek, Latin, and German—by having two quite distinct terms. Rationality is the mechanical following of the rules of logic. Reason is the sort of judgment that comes from combining this with the fruits of experience, and leads to wisdom. People who are rational, but not reasonable, are impossible to live with: they can't see, for example, that what might be appropriate in a court of law is not appropriate in the bedroom. And it leads us to imagine that human minds are like computer programmes designed to maximise return on investment: it is amazed to learn that people often forgo their own good for the pleasures of community, or actually become demotivated by some kinds of reward.

Rationality does not understand how the uniqueness of things, especially of contexts, means that general rules can only ever be highly approximate, and are often plain wrong. Uniqueness, the quality of a thing, is not understood by the left hemisphere, and so quantity, what it can measure, alone counts in its world. Because of its need to collapse things to a certainty, false distinctions and dichotomies thrive, with an emphasis on "either/or" rather than "both/and".[1] Matter becomes mere resource to be exploited, and human mental processes are divorced from the body which shapes them, with the consequence that things become both more abstract, and more reified, more merely material, at the same time.

The left hemisphere must conceive of society as an aggregate of individuals, seen as equal, but inert, units. The right hemisphere alone can understand that individuals are unique and reciprocally bound in a network, based on a host of things that could never be rationalised, creating something much greater than the sum of its parts, a society; and that that society has no meaning apart from them, but neither do they apart from it. The left hemisphere's "mis-take" on this tends towards a mechanistic idea of society that does not take into account emergent properties of a system, or complex reciprocal and fundamentally unpredictable interactions. It leads to a loss of social cohesion, and an emphasis on a mass of rules, regulations, and mechanisms of accountability which are supposed to substitute for trust. This has huge financial and social costs, as well as costs in terms of the further erosion of trust and morale.

The left hemisphere is not, as is sometimes thought, unemotional and down to earth. Anger is one of the most clearly lateralised emotions and it lateralises to the left hemisphere. The left hemisphere is manifestly not in touch with reality, and when it does not understand something it simply makes up a story that makes sense in its own terms and tells it with conviction. It prioritises as "truth" the internal consistency of a system rather than its correspondence with the world outside the window. It tends to deny problems, abjure responsibility, and take an unreasonably positive view of itself and its capacities. All of this can be demonstrated by ingenious experiments, detailed in *The Master and His Emissary*. As a result, according to it we are passive victims of the wrongdoing of others, more spectators than actors in the world, yet unwarrantedly optimistic about where we are going. In relation to that last—and very important—point, when individuals are asked to complete self-rating scores with one hemisphere isolated at a time, and these are compared with scores completed by their acquaintances, the left hemisphere reveals itself to have an unwarrantedly high opinion of itself compared with the right hemisphere. People with right hemisphere injuries, thus relying to a greater extent on their left hemisphere, have completely unrealistic ideas about their limitations, and are harder to help. They will even completely deny an obviously paralysed limb, and if ultimately forced to confront it, they will claim it belongs to someone else—say, the person in the next bed.

In a world in which the right hemisphere plays little part you would expect art in general to become conceptual, visual art to lack depth or perspective (both of which are provided largely by the right hemisphere), and music to be reduced to little more than rhythm, since in the normal course of things this is all the left hemisphere provides, melody and harmony being heavily dependent on the right hemisphere in most people. Language would become diffuse, excessive, and lacking in concrete referents. There would be a deliberate undercutting of the sense of awe or wonder, which suggest the existence of something beyond what the left hemisphere can conceive: and the left hemisphere would be unreasonable and intemperate in rejecting the idea of a transcendent or spiritual realm.

The questionable "success" of the left hemisphere

IM: The left hemisphere's purpose is to use the world. It sees everything—education, art, morality, the natural world—in terms of a utilitarian calculus only. If decisions are to be made about the value of a university faculty, of teaching the humanities in schools, or of what research project to fund, arguments are mounted, often with considerable ingenuity, but in the only permissible language, that of a financial balance sheet. If a quarry is planned that will destroy a wilderness, pollute a landscape, and violate the holy place of a native people, the arguments will be only about how much "value" (money) can be extracted, and what the value of tourism or the "leisure industry" might otherwise have been to the local economy. If it can't be measured it apparently doesn't exist. Yet everything most valuable defies measurement in this way.

JR: That's a pretty important claim for anybody trying to act constructively in the world. Why exactly do things that are most valuable evade measurement?

IM: There's a famous saying attributed to Einstein: "Not everything that counts can be counted, and not everything that can be counted counts." But why is this? One obvious factor is that the most valuable things are not tangible and are therefore not entities to be numbered. But they could be measured in other ways—subjective scoring based on self-report, for example, or asking what money or tangible goods one would be prepared to give up in exchange. These methods have their uses but also have inherent limitations; and they miss the point that the worth of truly valuable things changes with context, and may not increase as we have more of them.

It seems hard for many people to believe this, but once you have the basics of food and shelter, the rest does not correlate with an increase in happiness. And we should not neglect the fact that there are huge costs to industrialisation—for example, the break-up of stable communities, the loss of practical skills, and the disruption of ancient ways of life that are closer to the earth, things that we know do give life meaning and contribute to happiness and fulfilment.

Just as we don't live to eat, but eat to live (however much we may enjoy the business of eating), we don't live to make money but make money in order to live better lives. The culture of a people does not serve as a decorative addition to life, there to help one relax after one is tired from the real business of amassing wealth, but is what gives meaning to life, and wealth is only good in so much as it enables a richer culture to flourish. This is not done by immersing ourselves more and more in technological gadgetry that removes us from the business of embodied existence.

JR: "The business of embodied existence" is an arresting way of putting it. Is alienation from the body part of what left-hemisphere dominance brings about?

IM: Yes, and it is more important than it sounds. At the literal level, the right hemisphere is more in touch with the body: for instance it is the right hemisphere that has the "body image", which is much more than just a visual image. It's more of a "multimodal" image, a sense of the body as a coherent, living (and lived) whole, that is part of us, not a container *in* which we happen to live. By contrast the left hemisphere sees the body as an assemblage of parts, more like a machine. And the right hemisphere has richer connections with the body via the limbic system, an ancient part of the brain that we share with animals and which integrates thought with feelings and information from the body, as well as via the hypothalamic–pituitary–adrenal (HPA) axis, which regulates autonomic responses.

But that is not all. In a much more general way it is the right hemisphere that enables us to feel ourselves to be part of the living web of experience, not detached observers seeing the world pass on a screen: embodied beings in a concrete, incarnate world. It is the one, as I say, for which life is present, not represented—literally "re-presented", after the fact.

Political challenges: exploring practical and policy implications

JR: Many people who grasp the essence of your argument, and who have contented themselves with your answers to the challenges above, will no doubt be eager to understand what follows in terms of actions, in terms of the "So what?", or "That's fascinating and inspiring, but what do we do now?" However, thus far you have been fairly reticent about being explicit or prescriptive on this matter. Why is that?

IM: It probably sounds like a cop-out, but I do believe that prescriptions are one of the reasons we are so messed up nowadays. We always have to have a plan, an algorithm, a set of bullet points, and that immediately narrows things down, so we imagine that we just need to put this plan into action. It discounts the creative, the spontaneous, the improvised, the unexpected, the fruits of the imagination of those who take the "plan" forward. What I can see now is limited; what others may see is limitless. Our plans are always at too local, too detailed a level. For example, if you want to educate people, you don't give them a lot of procedures to carry out or just information to spew. You inculcate habits of mind: curiosity, a habit of sceptical questioning, enthusiasm, creativity, patience, self-discipline—the rest comes naturally. Equally you can't go into a country and set up the structures of democracy. That is back to front, and they will inevitably fail. What is needed is a habit of mind that sees the value in democratic institutions; in time they will then emerge naturally, and flourish.

I am more interested in indicating the right questions than giving the right answers. For me to give a list of bullet points—"Eight Things You Should Do to Save the Planet"—would be to enact the left hemisphere's agenda. I am a physician and a psychiatrist, and in my experience getting the diagnosis as accurate as possible is primary. I also know that raising consciousness of what we are doing wrong is the first step on the path to recovery, and that it is often a matter of what *not* to do, rather than what to do, that opens up the field of possibility for change. There is much we should stop doing, in other words, and allow things that are currently crushed almost out of existence—so much so that we no longer even *know what they are*—to flourish.

I certainly believe we will never solve the major global problems we face by tinkering with the current model. My hope is that a better understanding of the limitations of the mechanistic model offered to us by our left hemispheres will lead us to think differently about our situation in ways that I cannot now envisage, but which are available to all of us if we look for them.

JR: By "the current model" do you mean "capitalism", or is it more nuanced or perhaps more fundamental than that?

IM: Capitalism is an aspect of it, and, to paraphrase Churchill, I suppose one might think of capitalism as the worst possible system—apart from all the others. But I mean something much broader than this, a complete shift of perspective.

Economy and government are not ends in themselves

IM: The point about the reference to the story of the master and his emissary is that the emissary, however expert at what he does, serves the master, and cannot himself become the master. We first need to think why we have a society, with a government and a market, at all. We have a society not to serve the government and the market; government and the market are no more than highly necessary evils. They enable the true business of a society to continue without its foundering for lack of life's essentials: enough to eat and drink, adequate shelter from the elements, and as little antisocial behaviour as possible. Free marketeers agree that government is an evil, true, but only because they have an inflated idea of what the market can and should achieve: socialists think the market an evil because they have an inflated idea of what government can and should achieve. But neither can provide a better future. What we need to see with 20/20 clarity is that neither of these is any use in itself.

Our society is worthless unless it serves something higher than itself, higher than the government and the market—therefore the answer can never be better government or a less trammelled economy in themselves. These are only means to an end.

With the Enlightenment came a hardening up of the left-hemisphere point of view. Many of the aims of the Enlightenment were, of course, laudable, and much of what it brought we have to be thankful for. After all, the left hemisphere, the emissary of the story from which my book takes its title, is, at its best, the right hemisphere's—the master's—faithful servant. But its problems are those of hubris: believing itself to be the master, believing that it understands and can control everything, whereas in fact it is ignorant of what the right hemisphere knows. Thus the problem of the Enlightenment was its faith that, as long as we continue to think purely rationally, and prioritise utility, we can understand, and thereby come to control, everything. With the rise of capitalism and the coming of the Industrial Revolution (both children of the Enlightenment), one sees a further cementing—literally—of the left hemisphere's vision. The thinking they both involved is instrumental and competitive and they promote a more atomistic and competitive model of society, a more detached and manipulative stance in relation to one another and the world at large, which comes to be seen as just a heap of resources.[2]

JR: When you mention that tinkering with the current model is not enough, is your point that "reform is the enemy of revolution" in the sense that minor adjustments and improvement just strengthen the root of the problem?

IM: We must step back to see the bigger picture. Living headlong we skim over the surface of the world rather than allowing ourselves to enter into its depth. At the same time, as it might seem paradoxically, our view is too "close up": always in a hurry, we are narrowly focussed on a few salient things and miss the broader picture. We need to find a more natural, a slower, more meditative, tempo. That way too we see more. So although we can think of temporary fixes, the problem is not the sort that can be cured by a tweaking of what we are already up to. It demands a change of mind, a change of heart. We need to think at a much bigger and broader level, and ask the difficult questions.

As to who must do it, we must all, from the ground up be involved with and committed to resolving these problems—not just a government

on its own, and not just isolated groups of individuals without government support. The vested interests that will be against it are commercial, and we cannot do much against them as long as we carry on being
brainwashed by the rhetoric of consumerism. Once again, the solution involves not just a few measures of the kind that we are already
taking, only stronger: it involves a complete rethink of what our lives
are about.

For example, one of the worst aspects of modern life is the divorce
between work and the community where one lives, the image of which
is the packed commuter train. This way of living destroys communities,
takes a huge toll on individual health and happiness, wastes energy on
a massive scale and pollutes the environment. One might be tempted to
think that one part of the solution to that would be the internet, which
allows people to work from home. And that is surely an advantage we
could build on—but only if there is a change of heart about what work
itself is. Because if it carries on being, as it is for so many people, virtual
and mechanical, you end up with a lot of people even more isolated
than they were when they had to go into an office, and no real community reviving around them. Work needs to be more actual, hands-on,
involving the learning and exercise of real skill, and involved with the
lives of those with whom one lives. For professionals, such as doctors,
teachers, and solicitors, it always has been to a large extent, and for too
many others it used to be, but no longer is.

JR: A similar claim is made by Matthew Crawford in *The Case for Working
with your Hands* (2009). I suspect we are becoming increasingly alienated
from the world around us. But again I wonder whether the hemispheric
perspective really adds to your argument?

IM: The alienation you speak of is ultimately not because of something
we have done, such as build large cities, but because of an attitude of
mind that lies even deeper. It is the one that makes virtual work more
important—better paid and of higher status—than the practical job that
is done with one's hands in the real world. That is the left hemisphere's
point of view.

Working too hard

JR: And it's not just the kind of work we do, but the amount of it too? (And
by "we" here I mean people in post-industrial, developed societies.)

IM: We work too hard. We are hooked by the greedy machines of capitalism. I have seen the toll this takes among my patients. Many of us lack employment altogether, but those who are lucky enough to be employed have to work ever harder, faster, and longer—for what? The logic of the left hemisphere is that if something is good, more of it must be better. It is also concerned with amassing goods for use, and expert at seeing us as disconnected from the world we are engaged in exploiting.

Now we find that the retirement age is being put back. The working day is extended. Though the average labourer's hours have decreased, most of the rest of us work longer than people in similar jobs used to do forty or fifty years ago. Moreover, at that time a single person's wages were enough for a family to live on: now two people often struggle to meet their needs working longer hours. The machinery of the market used the legitimate arguments for women's equality to its own ends. It was a way to get twice as many people into the workforce. But now we are no better off, just both parents in a family now have to work, whether they want to or not. It is a case of what I call the football match paradox. One person stands up to get a better view, the person behind stands up to see beyond his neighbour, and soon everyone is standing—but the view is no better than when everyone was able to sit down. It's just that, like it or not, no one can now sit down any more.

JR: The New Economics Foundation has been arguing for some time for a shorter working week, even as little as twenty-one hours per person.[3] The claim is that this will be good for well-being, balance out employment opportunities, and rapidly reduce carbon emissions, without diminishing living standards. I am guessing that this kind of perspective—though the devil is of course in the detail of the macroeconomic models—is the sort of thing you might mean by a more fundamental shift in our attitude?

IM: Well, it's an example of a step in the right direction. I was very struck by the experience of going to stay with a former teacher of mine who went to live on a self-sufficient smallholding in Wales in the 1970s. He and his family bred or grew all their own food. I expected to find the days packed with labour, and was astonished at how much leisure time there was. He explained that there were a couple of times in the year when they were very busy—lambing and harvest—but even those were fun because the local farmers all mucked in and helped one another. Otherwise there was a great deal of leisure time. A Langland scholar, he pointed out that Langland twitted the peasants of his day for their habits of lying around drinking and refusing all but bread made with the finest flour. He helped me see that it was only when, in the eighteenth century (the age of "Enlightenment" and the rise of capitalism), people started to realise that they could grow far more than they needed, sell it, and get rich, that the farm labourers' lives became intolerably hard. Once more the problem of the narrow left hemisphere "logic" that seeks power but impoverishes a community. Also—a vital point—the left hemisphere view is narrow not only in space, but in time. It is effectively the short-term view—what's good for me here and now, not what's good for us all in the longer run. Now we have no leisure to enjoy what we earn. A civilisation depends on leisure. But that is not just absence of work. It involves something so hard that many people would rather fill their lives with "busy-ness": learning to be still. In the absence of this, leisure is just an unwanted space where boredom must be driven out by constant stimulation of one kind or another. Leisure is pointless without knowing what to do with it—otherwise it just gets filled up with "noise". In any system that is full of noise the true message will be lost. As Josef Pieper observed over half a century ago in *Leisure, the Basis of Culture*, true idleness is being *unnecessarily busy*, not opening oneself to that stillness out of which all spiritual and artistic, as well as scholarly, achievements, and the sense of oneness with nature, must come.

JR: When you say "learn to be still", I think of the famous Pascal quotation—that all our miseries stem from not being able to sit quietly alone in a room—but you seem to mean something else here—that we should—what—buy less, be less "driven to distraction", meditate more?

IM: Obviously stillness is particularly hard to achieve if we are constantly uneasy, craving something more, something new, as advertising and the media constantly exhort us to do, at the beck and call of our phones, our computers, busy getting money and getting goods—never getting to know ourselves, who we really are. This was the ultimate goal of human life that was carved over the entrance to the Oracle at Delphi: "Know thyself". In terms of the hemispheres, it is the left hemisphere that is acquisitive, competitive, distractible, and ultimately unable to perceive the meaning of life, or of ourselves. We are over-busy, busy a lot of the time doing—ultimately—nothing that counts "all day long".

JR: That makes good sense to me, and is a tangible example of why the hemispheric perspective might be relevant, in this case for our arguably perverse attitude to work. From the left-hemispheric perspective—the one you believe is increasingly dominant—work becomes something we use to acquire things and to gain various forms of power. While these goals might be legitimate ones for working people they should be in the service of something other than the goals themselves. The balancing perspective that asks: "Are the things that I am gaining important? What does my contribution mean? How does it link to wider sources of value?" These questions that you suggest are posed by the right hemisphere—are not heard as they once were, and will increasingly go unbidden if we continue on our current course.

IM: I believe so. And I am not saying that work is not often intrinsically valuable—it gives worth and purpose. But in that case, precisely, it is being valued for something other than its utility in amassing wealth. It is hugely important that we break out of the purely utilitarian calculus according to which financial considerations are the only ones that count. So many important issues these days are argued on the wrong grounds—those of immediate benefit (or not) to the economy. One has only to listen to the *Today* programme—time and again one hears opposing factions in any debate root around for economic grounds on which to argue a case that has far deeper and broader foundations, and often misrepresent their own cause in doing so, because it is assumed that no other criterion will cut any ice these days.

Mental health

JR: On mental health—there seems to be some equivocation about how levels of well-being have changed, and how best to characterise the relationship between income and well-being. My impression is that your view, broadly, is that if nothing else we are much less happy than we might be. Why do you think that, and what might we begin to do about it?

IM: In as much as happiness can be measured, the evidence is clear. We are certainly no happier, and almost certainly less happy, than when we were materially enormously much less well off.

JR: Are you sure? My impression is that the evidence is a bit more equivocal?

IM: It is clear, and applies to Britain, the rest of Europe, the US, Japan … everywhere it is the same story. Which should make us stop in our tracks and ask what we are trying to achieve in despoiling the planet, making ourselves ill, and degrading social trust in the effort simply to amass wealth.

JR: Assuming that's right, bizarrely it doesn't seem to make us stop in our tracks. Again it looks like a kind of denial?

IM: That's true, but it is also a failure to be able to take on board something so contrary to the beliefs that the left hemisphere holds—getting more goods in the material realm must equate with greater well-being. One distinguished elderly colleague of mine could not accept that people were less happy, because, as he pointed out, "They have washing machines now—they must be happier." At some level material well-being was, for him, well-being, so the information "did not compute". What's less certain is whether *depression* is actually on the increase. The figures suggest that 25 per cent, even up to as much as 50 per cent of us, will experience a diagnosable mental illness during our lives. There are many possible confounding factors, including raised awareness (both in the public and the medical profession), reduced stigma (leading to more readiness to seek help), the need to establish illness in the context of personal injury claims, or in order to get hold of scarce resources for a child, diagnostic fashions, and the readiness of Big Pharma to capitalise on the fuzziness of diagnosis.

Having said all of that, there is evidence that our way of life does make us sick, and it seems fairly certain that depression is on the increase. One way to look at this is to study the trends across immigrant generations at a moment in time: Mexican immigrants to the USA start with a low level of mental illness, but increase in proportion to the time spent in the US. The lifetime prevalence of any mental disorder in one large study was 18 per cent for Mexican immigrants with less than thirteen years in the US, 32 per cent for those with more than thirteen years, but only for those born in the US did it approximate, at 49 per cent, to the national rate for the whole US (Vega et al., 1998).

When one considers that we have got better and better at manipulating the world, yet less and less able to discern any meaning in our lives—the topic of an e-book I released earlier this year (McGilchrist, 2012)—this is perhaps not surprising. The stability of social networks outside work, a sense of being trusted by, and able to trust, one's work colleagues, a sense of belonging, a sense of mastery of a skill, are all important to human happiness and are less common now than they were before. The secret to happiness, known to every CBT therapist, never mind to generations of the spiritually wise, is to appreciate and be grateful for what one has, not constantly comparing oneself and what one has with other people, or some imagined ideal. Yet our society is founded precisely on propagating this unhealthily comparative attitude of mind.

JR: Which is at least partly about advertising, but also the political emphasis on consumption-filled economic growth, and I imagine you can link this to the left hemisphere's tendencies in certain ways. Tim Jackson even speaks of "the social logic of consumption" in that we increasingly use what we buy to project status and identity, which we then compare with others who are doing the same thing. But I just want to tease the implications out a bit. Does it follow from your argument that advertising should be curbed and economic growth should be less of a priority? It feels slightly absurd to have ended up here, after starting with hemispheric differences, but is there a sense in which it follows?

IM: Yes. Chasing the phantom of endless economic growth is destructive of the world and of our happiness, and the ever-presence of advertising is a terrible blight on modern cities. But far worse, in such places, it requires a constant effort to block it out: it's a sort of awful mental pollution that drifts into one's consciousness whatever one may be doing, like the plastic bottles that till the end of time will drift onto the remotest and most beautiful beaches of the world.

But we were talking about health and happiness, so let's leave that to look again at the bigger picture. Let's return to first principles—not the left hemisphere considerations of what we can have and control, but the right hemisphere ones of who we are and how we relate to others that live alongside us and that came before and will come after us. If we do so we can see right away that there are a couple of things we must address.

We are too isolated, most of us don't have a sense of connectedness with a community in the way we used to—and we need to do something about that. We need to have a broader context in which to see ourselves and our lives—and we need to do something about that. Some of that comes through education, and I am sure we will discuss that, but some comes from access to what we would have to call a realm of spiritual value. That doesn't mean signing up to a religion. In a way, spirituality is simply a question of having an open enough mind to see that there are things in the world at large that transcend what we can know and fully comprehend, that are not fully accounted for in a reductionist, materialist account. Rationally this is extremely likely: it would be extraordinary if we just happened to have arrived at such a summit of evolution that our brains allow us to understand and be aware of all that exists. The fact that it may look that way to us now does not prove anything, except the impossibility of conceiving what it is that one cannot conceive. If a squirrel could reflect, it would imagine that it understood everything, too—it couldn't conceive of the kind of understanding it didn't have.

Children should not grow up ignorant of the fact that other peoples in all parts of the world at all times and in all places have had religions. It should not be implied that this is just a sign of foolishness and ignorance. It might well be our own lack of insight. After all, what we don't expect we simply won't find. It's in any case a good discipline to keep an open mind, not to think one knows it all, and to respect and to some extent feel in awe of what is greater than ourselves. By the same token, it's a disastrous belief that we understand everything and have it all under control.

Education

JR: When you spoke at the RSA (McGilchrist, 2010) you said that education was a big part of the answer, and I recently read a review that said your book was the best defence of the arts and humanities ever written in the English language (Read, 2012). What would an education for health and well-being entail that it doesn't currently?

IM: Education is the perfect example of how we get things wrong by not taking a broad enough, or long enough, view. The emphasis now being called for on technical training—business, admin, computing, science—is precisely the opposite of what we need. So is the emphasis on "relevance", on the here and now and the contemporary—that's the very last thing we need. It seems to me that one of the main purposes of an education is to broaden minds, not narrow them further. That means not learning more and more about what we are already familiar with, and hardening up the sort of thinking we have anyway, but understanding other points of view, the ways people would have thought about the problems we confront in other times and other places. It cannot be strongly enough emphasised that scholarly learning is in and of itself valuable, regardless of any functional application of immediate interest to the economy. We will perish if we do not explore avenues we have no way of knowing now will be fruitful. Once we want to see only more of what we already know about, we have fossilised. However, it is a characteristic of the left hemisphere "take" on life that it sees only what it predicts it will see, focusses narrowly on the issue in front of it, is overconfident in assessment of what it understands and knows, and has one driving value—utility.

At the same time we need to understand the values and mores of those who forged the foundations of our own culture and civilisation. Too often when these things are brought into the curriculum it is with a sense of ironic, knowing superiority to the ways of other times. It has become politically incorrect to laugh at the ways and manners of other cultures, but not at those of past ages. So the chance of learning from them is lost. Even the great works of literature of the past are not met on their own terms, but judged by our own narrow ones, and found to be examples of colonialism, racism, sexism, class struggle, or whatever. But we must meet art on its own terms, if we are to appreciate it, understand it, and grow from the experience—not with our agenda already set. If we do not think in this broader and more long-term way, we will try just to patch up the current morally bankrupt system of competitive capitalism by training narrower and narrower technicians so that we can out-compete other economies.

Quite apart from conveying information—knowledge, at any rate, is important—schools should be places where children are taught to use their imagination, ask difficult questions, think flexibly, concentrate effectively, sustain attention, and learn self-discipline. If we are honest, they are all too rarely any of these. Children need to be encouraged to question the accepted views of our own age, not just the things their teacher doesn't like. No person should leave school so ignorant as to believe that he or she really knows much at all. Good teachers should be trusted, not micromanaged and over-controlled. There is too much constraint of the syllabus and too much monitoring of staff and pupils alike.

In closing

JR: Gramsci famously said that we should have "pessimism of the intellect, but optimism of the will". Is that where we are now?

IM: I call myself a hopeful pessimist. In respect of where we are currently headed, yes, I am a pessimist. In respect of our potential to adapt and change quickly, I am hopeful. I sense that people are sick of the current worldview in the West (alas, all too quickly being espoused by the East that used to know better). In response to my book, people of all walks of life all over the world have written to me. They are looking for a change in direction, and I think all I have done is to give them courage to believe in what they already really know at some level—something which has not been articulated in quite the same terms before. In many ways my message is a very positive one. We have been sold a sadly limiting version of who we as human beings are, and how we relate to the world. Inside each one of us there is an intelligence, in fact a superior intelligence, that sees things differently from the way we have been sold—if we would only listen to it. Let's hope that we can.

Notes

1. Interestingly this also reflects the relationship between these two kinds of thinking, that of the left hemisphere and of the right: the left hemisphere cannot understand the value of what the right contributes, whereas the right does understand the value of what the left contributes. This is the basis of the story behind the title *The Master and his Emissary*.
2. The case that the left hemisphere has gradually become more dominant at a cultural level over historical time is taken as a given on the basis of the evidence unpacked in the historical analysis that forms the second part of *The Master and his Emissary*.
3. www.neweconomics.org/publications/21-hours.

References

Crawford, M. B. (2009). *The Case for Working with Your Hands: Or Why Office Work Is Bad for Us and Fixing Things Feels Good*. London: Penguin.

Jackson, T. (2011). *Prosperity without Growth: Economics for a Finite Planet*. New York: Routledge.

McGilchrist, I. (2009). *The Master and his Emissary: The Divided Brain and the Making of the Western World*. New Haven, CT: Yale University Press.

McGilchrist, I. (2010). The Divided Brain and the Making of the Western World [RSA event, online]. Available at: https://www.youtube.com/watch?v=SbUHxC4wiWk.

McGilchrist, I. (2012). *The Divided Brain and the Search for Meaning*. Kindle Books.

Midgley, M. (2010). Mary Midgley enjoys an exploration of the left-brain/right-brain divide. *Guardian* [online]. Available at: http://www.theguardian.com/books/2010/jan/02/1.

Pieper, J. (1958). *Leisure: The Basis of Culture*. London: Faber & Faber.

Quiggin, J. (2010). *Zombie Economics: How Dead Ideas Still Walk among Us*. Princeton, NJ: Princeton University Press.

Read, R. (2012). The Master and his Emissary book review. *Phenomenology and The Cognitive Sciences*, Springer Science, DOI 10.1007/s11097-011-9235-x.

Rowson, J., & McGilchrist, I. (2013). Divided Brain, Divided World: Why the Best Part of Us Struggles to be Heard. RSA Action and Research Centre. https://www.thersa.org/globalassets/pdfs/blogs/rsa-divided-brain-divided-world.pdf (last accessed 4 July 2016).

Vega, W. A., Kolody, B., Aguilar-Gaxiola, S., Alderete, E., Catalano, R., & Caraveo Anduaga, J. (1998). Lifetime prevalence of DSM-III-R psychiatric disorders among urban and rural Mexican Americans in California. *Archives of General Psychiatry, 55*(9): 771–778.

PART II

OUTSIGHT

CHAPTER SIX

Born to run: wounded leaders and boarding school survivors*

Nick Duffell

Introduction

This chapter provides a psychological profile for what I have termed the "Wounded Leader" and a brief psychohistorical overview of the genesis of the attitudes that underlie this type.

Despite the complexities involved in explaining it fully and the controversy that it inspires, the chief point of this chapter is simple enough. Because our elite are raised in boarding schools—away from their families, out of the reach of love, far from the influence of any feminine values and so on—we have been perpetuating a situation in which a grave disservice is done to individuals and the whole of our society. For we have been replicating, by means of a perfected, "industrialised" process, a type of *Wounded Leader*, no longer knowing why we are doing it or even that we are doing it. Notwithstanding the costly privileges of such an education, it consistently turns out people who appear much more competent than they actually are, especially in terms of non-rational

---

*This originally appeared in *Wounded Leaders: British Elitism and the Entitlement Illusion—A Psychohistory* by Nick Duffell (© 2014, Lone Arrow Press) and is reprinted by kind permission of the author. All rights reserved.

skills, such as those needed to sustain relationships. This is the principal reason I use the surprising word "wounded".

This woundedness is compounded because these people are unaware of their own defects and carry on regardless. British public life, especially politics, is overflowing with such types, and they are a familiar breed—more than half the 2010–12 cabinet, for example, went through this hothousing process. Their dominant position in the second decade of the twenty-first century shows how resistant Britain is to real change.

Since the major path to power in our society—via public school and the glories of "Oxbridge"—is still desirable and well trodden, it has been easy for us to normalise this tradition and remain seamlessly accustomed to the entitlement it affords. For the most part, our elite fail to recognise the degree and manner of their entitlement; some of today's politicians appear to suggest—even to believe—that they have got where they are by means of hard work alone. This is one reason I introduce the notion of the *Entitlement Illusion*. We are used to it: it goes largely unrecognised, in the way that fish do not notice water.

The Entitlement Illusion is not an isolated phenomenon but a systemic problem that affects the whole of our society: the place and self-esteem of the British working classes is directly conditioned by it, as well as the whole nation's political apathy. We joke about it but we find it hard to take seriously the notion that our elite may be wounded and that our cherished private education may be perpetuating those wounds. It then becomes very complex; even many of those who see themselves as being against the Establishment or against bullying, are tragically subject to these themselves.

The Entitlement Illusion has a long history in Britain. It is a very successful mental conjuring trick that accounts for how we managed our colonial and imperial project without being troubled by much of a conscience. Later in the text, I will show how this was done by describing the psychohistorical context in which it occurred and explaining the psychodynamics of the dissociative "defence mechanisms" by which such mental feats were accomplished. I will show that the latter are still being taught to young boarders today, masquerading as values.

In its heyday in the nineteenth century, the Entitlement Illusion meant that when we abolished slavery we paid compensation to slave owners, but not to slaves, and then felt good about ourselves. The process of what psychotherapists call *dissociation* and *objectification* made slavery possible. This process is at the heart of the boarding culture, and conditions many aspects of our society to this day. We still enjoy the wealth accrued by the Empire, run by ex-boarder gentlemen. Colonialism's enduring legacy is that it pioneered the model for globalised capitalism, which shapes the current age. The Entitlement Illusion is alive and well: it ensures we cannot feel we belong to a communal project like Europe without imagining ourselves as its leader; and its deceptive familiarity means that we go on blindly investing in an education system that produces wounded leaders and in a politics that no longer serves us.

My earlier book *The Making of Them: The British Attitude to Children and the Boarding School System* (2000) revealed the price paid for the ex-boarder's passport to elitism: a defensively organised personality that is durable, if brittle. I am now able to add findings from other disciplines, chiefly neuroscience, to obtain a much broader sense of the problems, particularly the long-term effects on the brain. The notion of the *Entitled Brain* is introduced to denote one that is over-trained in rationality, has turned away from empathy, and has mastered and normalised dissociation in its most severe dimensions; it is consequently incapable of recognising the fault in its own system.

Schooled in the development of such a brittle mindset, British elitism supports an outdated leadership style that is unable to rise above its own interests, perceive the bigger picture, and go beyond a familiar, entrenched, and unhealthy system of adversarial politics. Such a leadership style is not to be recommended—it may well be dangerous. It is manifestly unfit for purpose, given the demands of the current world in which, increasingly, problems are communal—indeed global—and in which solutions urgently demand non-polarised cooperation and clear focus on the common good, in order to take effect on a worldwide scale.

Back to the simple point I started with. Socially privileged boarding children are forced into a deal they have not chosen. They trade access to a normal family-based childhood for the institutionalised hothousing of entitlement. Paradoxically, because they have to speedily reinvent themselves as self-reliant pseudo-adults, they struggle to mature. The child who has not been able to grow up organically, whom ex-boarders are unwilling to identify with, gets stranded, as it were, inside them. As a psychological consequence, an abandoned child complex inside these leaders ends up running the show. The political implications of this are huge, for it means that it's the children inside the men running the country who are effectively in charge.

Boarding school survivors

Before we return to politics we need to establish a psychological profile for the Wounded Leader. This will involve introducing the complex psychodynamics of *Boarding School Syndrome*, which I hope to do in plain language. By the end of this analysis I hope that readers will be able to recognise the boys in the men who run things.

Perhaps the most deceptive feature of the syndrome is that ex-boarders tend to hide their emotional and relational dysfunction behind a façade that projects confident functioning and indeed resembles a classic national character ideal. Attempts to approach the subject therefore demand an added delicacy, as if they were attempts to deconstruct the beloved British national psyche. The character ideal is one that is well known and regularly celebrated in our letters, theatre, and film. Mostly, it appears as the self-effacing, conflict-avoiding, intimacy-shy, gentlemanly type so classically represented in the late twentieth century by the actor Hugh Grant. Its other face—the hostile, sarcastic bullying type—is also known, usually in the form of a "Flashman" sort of character. In England, the efficient bully with his smooth, sarcastic humour is either normalised or too cloaked in innocence to be named as such. We make do with words like "robust", which describes for us admirable aggression. As far as identification goes, we prefer the niceness. But common sense reveals that there are two sides to any coin, and D. H. Lawrence's poem, "The English Are So Nice", makes the other side of our famous niceness very clear.

> The English are so nice
> so awfully nice
> they're the nicest people in the world.
> Americans and French and Germans and so on
> they're all very well
> but they're not really nice, you know.
> That's why one doesn't have to take them seriously.
> But it doesn't really matter what you say to them,
> they don't really understand—
> you can just say anything to them:
> be nice, you know, just be nice—
> but you must never take them seriously, they wouldn't
> understand

> just be nice, you know! Oh, fairly nice,
> but not too nice of course, they take advantage—
> but nice enough, just nice enough
> to let them feel they're not quite as nice as they might be.[1]

Hostility and niceness are hand in hand here. You can be bullied in Britain and not even notice it if you are not alert to all the cues in the language.

Psychologically thinking, a bully is only ever one facet of a character, for bullying inevitably arises out of fear, and there is plenty of fear around whenever children are herded together over long periods without anyone to love them. The key to understanding ex-boarders is to understand the institutional conditions in which they grew up and the fear that is engendered there. In my research, I came to realise that boarding produces a specific personality type, or style of *False Self* (in the terminology of the famous British expert on childhood D. W. Winnicott), which I named the *Strategic Survival Personality*.[2] Living in rule-bound institutions where they are unable to show their feelings, constantly surrounded by their peers who are scared and on the lookout to scapegoat any signs of vulnerability in others, boarders, needing to survive, quickly develop a strategic way of life. This means becoming Machiavellian, trying to stay one step ahead, staying out of trouble, anticipating danger, promoting the false selves they are selling, sometimes self-effacing, sometimes bullying. They develop a personality that is born to rule but also "Born to Run."[3]

The plethora of incomprehensible rules in the boarding system and the ease with which they can be broken is retained in the memory of all ex-boarders. I now think that the obsession with rules was far more deliberate than first appears and I see three reasons for it. First, it was to give a sense of a miniature society bound by internal self-referring codes, as if society itself was an institution, which was the British model, as Alexander Herzen has pointed out so vividly (Herzen, 1924).[4] Second, and more darkly, it was to break the loyalty of the child to any prior rules about conduct learned in earlier belonging groups—family, culture, or class. This was especially important since boarding school is the highway that opens up the hierarchy to the classes below, whose inferior cultural ties, according to the grim logic that prevails, must be severed. In the colonies, boarding schools would be the prime tool for breaking the ties to native languages and religions. A third reason may have been to protect boys against the "depravity"—in other words, homosexuality, or sexuality in general. Thus, the sociologist Alisdare Hickson has suggested that rule obsession was a deliberate policy of the disciplinarian movement to reform the public schools that kicked off in the puritanical 1860s. The chief motive was to counteract the boys' tendency towards "beastliness". The extraordinary idea ran like this: the less the boys met each other—especially those of different age groups—the less they would be tempted to have sex with each other. This left only the vice of "self-abuse" to be policed (Hickson, 1995). In consequence, every second of the day was regimented with volumes of pointless tasks, codes, rules, and regulations invented to limit the boarder's freedom—always something on the timetable. The result of this was not wholly successful. Unsurprisingly, breaking rules for the sake of it appealed to teenagers, while sexual experimentation during adolescence in single sex institutions was given the extra flavour of forbidden fruit, serving freedom as a realisable vote of protest against institutionalisation. However, the process did have some long-lasting effects: most ex-boarders find it difficult not to be self-scheduled on a permanent timetable; many are still tormented about their sexuality.

Raised in the overcharged atmosphere of multiple rules and the consequent hunting down of transgressors means that boarders strategically develop one of two obsessions, depending on their individual proclivity: either keeping their heads down, or breaking the rules without getting caught. How might this affect them psychologically? It is clearly a dangerous cocktail. Adding the rule issue to the double bind about being wrong ("If they love me, why do they send me away? And if it is so important to them and I don't like it, there must be something wrong with me"), plus the need to maintain a brave face without any emotion, plus the inner shame of privilege, it is not difficult to see how evasive secrecy becomes a way of life at school and extremely hard to shed in later life, because the ex-boarder is unaware of doing it. Furthermore, the strategic habit has a very dark side because in the strategic way of life, anything—or more pertinently anyone—may get sacrificed through a variety of face-saving behaviours, including betrayal, bullying, or simply being dropped. The latter is very prevalent in intimate relationship situations and causes enormous hurt, even if unintentionally done. It is extremely difficult both for the victim to name it and for the ex-boarder to recognise it, let alone lose the habit, precisely because the self he formed is not used to being in situations of loving mutuality. He has had to look after Number One for as long as he can remember.

Over the years, many things confirmed the strategic hypothesis. For example, boarding school survivors in psychotherapy frequently recounted dreams with similar elements: they are on the run from something or someone, or about to get caught and be unmasked, or are up for trial and facing the death penalty. The novels of John Le Carré, the famous spy author, repeatedly and accurately feature dilemmas of ex-public school men caught between belonging to and being against the establishment, living lives full of duplicity, subject to repeated acts of betrayal. I had therefore to discover a way of working with ex-boarders that could give them the confidence to stop "surviving", without them fearing that they were being unmasked, stripped naked, as it were. Originally, I was influenced by the sexual abuse recovery work that I was professionally engaged with at the time. The appellation "survivor" derives from this but it has an additional and crucial dimension, one that even some therapists, who recognised the trauma of children away from home for very long periods, found very difficult to see.

Any psychotherapist's daily practice includes work around early deprivation and family of origin, so the client with what is known as "attachment problems" is familiar—especially as attachment theory regains popularity.[5] Less understood, and needing emphasis when introducing the syndrome, is the sophistication of the ex-boarder's strategic survival self and the widespread devastation it can bring to individuals, couples, and families over generations. It starts with the loss of connection to parents. It may never be recovered, the distance never repaired, as emotional repression often turns into what could best be described as amputation, especially for those starting to board at the six- to nine-years-old age range. Children are not able to make informed choices; they trust their parents to know what is best for them and don't want to disappoint them. Being sent away, they learn expertly to put on their brave faces, unaware of the problems this will cause them later in life. Then the normalisation really begins to bite, for, the syndrome being barely recognised, adult ex-boarders take their experience to be normal and easily discount problems in intimate relationships and family life. They frequently retreat into workaholism, ill-equipped to heal from something they don't know they suffer from.

Dissociation

All boarders have to learn to survive by means of dissociation or *splitting*, the therapist's everyday word for this defence mechanism and the foundation stone of self-protective personality structures. Dissociation begins as a self-saving mental trick that any of us may instinctively perform when we are ashamed or embarrassed to make something known, to accept or integrate something. We put it to one side, think of something else; we use forgetting, not referring to, compartmentalising, or denial in order to assist us in maintaining our internal composure. Dissociation is the original "divide and rule" strategy in its individual and pre-political form.

Technically, dissociation's function is to protect the individual from realities too difficult to identify with or to integrate, and thereby avoid the problem of a kind of a meltdown in the brain known as cognitive dissonance. Here is the very readable Stephen Grosz's elegant explanation:

> Splitting is an unconscious strategy that aims to keep us ignorant of feelings in ourselves that we're unable to tolerate. Typically, we want to see ourselves as good, and put those aspects of ourselves that we find shameful into another person or group. Splitting is one way we have of getting rid of self-knowledge. (2013)

Psychoanalytic scholars regard dissociation as a primitive defence mechanism, and their bible, the American Psychiatric Association's *Diagnostic and Statistical Manual of Mental Disorders* (DSM), classifies it as an indicator of pathology. We now know that dissociation involves highly compartmentalised mental processes depending on the activities of the left hemisphere of the brain in its function of inhibiting the right hemisphere, which has a greater aptitude for larger contexts and relational realities (McGilchrist, 2009).[6]

Where dissociation becomes habitual, as when it is used to maintain identity and combat perceived threats of annihilation, such as when a child has to fend for himself over long periods without protecting parents, it can become a chronic mental state. This extreme degree is *unconscious* dissociation, which employs the psychological mechanisms of *disowning* and *projection*. Splitting as a defence of the fragile or invaded self is well known in psychoanalysis. The most severe cases involve people whose consciousness seems to be utterly detached from their bodies and *in extremis* results in cases of *multiple personality disorder*. Much less is known about dissociation in better functioning individuals, since the focus has been on what has been considered pathological, and, as we saw above, ex-boarders put on a good show of conforming to the national character ideal.[7]

When a child, needing to survive long periods without love, touch, or parental guidance, is encouraged to cut off from his primary emotions and bodily reality and taught instead a form of emotional *un*-intelligence (to paraphrase Daniel Stern's famous term), he will need to employ dissociation extensively (Stern, 1985). The resulting adult cannot avoid being in deep psychic trouble, for he will have developed a defensively organised psyche built on disowning and projection. This means his stance in the world will be quite rigid and precarious, despite what it looks like from the outside. He will have difficulties distinguishing between friend or foe and therefore in maintaining authentic relationships. Remaining sexually immature and severely challenged by the demands of emotional intimacy and parenting, he will be eternally on guard.

In the context of an elitist education, the awareness of privilege instils an additional and rather unique problem: an unrealistic and unconscious dose of either entitlement or shame, and sometimes a combination of the two. Entitlement can be understood as a compensation for the emotional deprivation of boarding, but it acts in a mischievous way. It inflates the brittle veneer of confidence that functions as a smokescreen to such an adult's pathology, and a society that values hyper-rational competition over authenticity colludes. Over time, these attitudes become seamlessly normalised; associated with tradition, they have become co-opted into a British national character ideal, which further conceals their problematic nature.

Running on fear and confidence

I now propose the briefest psychohistorical overview of origins of these particular attitudes in which I will attempt a summary of the psychodynamics of British entitlement. This is necessary, I believe, in order to understand how and why such educational practices, and their consequent psychological problems, have become such a distinct and unique feature of these islands.

Neither the French Revolution nor the Industrial Revolution would have been possible without a previous revolution that had begun more than a hundred years earlier. This one was not political: it was a revolution of thought. The Enlightenment introduced a major new way of thinking about the world that favoured the rise and pre-eminence of rationality over experience, of concept over matter. In *The Making of Them*, I discussed how the worldview that privileged reason (or rationality) over all other approaches to life inspired and created the conditions in which British public schools were conceived, and made possible the standardised production of rational gentlemen. I suggested that this way of thinking still underlies the boarding schools' championing of independence and competition at the expense of feeling, relating, and all forms of perceived dependence. I argued that this way of thinking is out of date and puts intolerable strain on individuals. I now propose to take things further and examine how Victorian hyper-conservatism and its public school ethos—the former rather widespread but the latter unique to us and our colonies—have been supported by what I like to call the *Rational Man Project*. My thesis is that Britain is still singularly in its grip, and therefore stuck in an outdated past, and that the addiction to the public school educated elite is an addiction to an outworn Rational Man Project. Let me explain.

In nineteenth-century Britain, rationality had a unique spin, I believe, and became identified with a specifically British way of dealing with the world because of two contradictory overarching psychological pulls. First, there was an *internal contraction* due to fear of revolution and chaos generated by the revolution in France; secondly, there was an *external expansion* of Empire, propelled by the dynamism of the age of industry and its unstoppable confidence and appetite for new resources and markets. This dynamism was fuelled by greed and resulted in grandiosity. These two contrary forces—fearful internal contraction and grandiose external expansion—gave British society its particular character. Despite vastly different world situations, we are still trying to regulate and balance these deep unconscious emotional drivers, I suggest. In our current world, therefore, I think it makes sense to argue that the fallout from the British Rational Man Project is still with us. It causes our society grave problems in the following way:

- It maintains the inherited class structure with its entitlement-rich male elitism intact and is still strangely confident, despite a changing world.

- It impedes the maturation of the British political scene because of its outdated and self-referring character.
- It prevents the emerging new paradigm of thinking globally from finding fallow ground among our leaders—particularly the notion of thinking about the world as a communal issue—due to fear of foreigners and fear of losing the status quo.
- It continues to support the fee-paying, hyper-rational, love-free institutionalisation of the elite's children.
- We do not notice the Rational Man Project's grip on us because we are too close to it, like the fish who do not know the water; identified with it, we believe it to be our hallowed tradition.

To appreciate the extent of this problem, we must continue the story of its origin and heyday. Specifically, we must consider how "Rational Man"—the generic specimen of the Rational Man Project—functioned internally. To that end, we must examine how Enlightenment thinking developed in the British case.

The foundations of the extraordinary expansive movements of the Enlightenment were dug by great pioneers, such as Galileo and Copernicus, at the end of the Middle Ages. The Renaissance had marvellously set Westerners free from the Church's traditional stranglehold on thinking. It allowed European men to sally forth in boats and "discover" the "New World" and was the preparation, we can now say in hindsight, for the overturning of all previous conventions of thinking. Descartes and his colleagues created the next step towards mental freedom: the Enlightenment would change everything. With the new ability to be curious about the natural world as an objective phenomenon that could be measured and predicted, with laws that could be ascertained, natural science flowered and rational ingenuity blossomed. This revolution in curiosity built up a head of steam that boiled over into the invention of countless machines, devices, instruments, and tools—the beginning of what today we would call "technology".

This technological and scientific revolution was the proud engine of the new god, Progress. Progress was to the Rational Man as reliable a divinity as Providence had been to the Puritans. Progress brought enormous wealth and fuelled the potential to analyse and classify the entire range of creation, hitherto considered the business only of God and his earthly representatives. According to this new logic, the non-European world was now destined to be fully harnessed, colonised, and exploited (what today we would call "developed") simply because it was there.

In Britain, the visible benefits of this expansionism can clearly be seen. A short walk around the Clifton district of Bristol, with its oversized stone buildings, raised from the accrued wealth of colonies run by slavery, confirms the pragmatic advantages of the rational colonial project. By the latter half of the nineteenth century, feasting on the wealth created by the biggest import-export business ever known, British grandiosity hardly knew any bounds. Now Darwin's theory of natural selection, rationalised as inbuilt competition, established the superiority of man—specifically white British man—according to the laws of nature. For, in his ability to cognitively map the world and dominate it, Rational Man's role as subjugator of existing indigenous populations was theoretically legitimised. This was masterfully achieved by means of a very convenient—but devious—logical process, which I shall explain. Once again, I will attempt this by analysing its psychological mechanisms.

The logic of Rational Man's Entitlement Illusion

Deprived, apparently, of the gift of abstract thought or the ability to form recognisable civilisations, the world's indigenous people and their lands were clearly there for the taking. In the eyes of Europeans, those faraway foreigners started to become more like things than persons. Symbolically, they stood for the direct opposite of the grand ideal— Rational Man—and thereby made him even more prestigious. By this inverse psychological principle, indigenous people fulfilled an inhuman role—mere objects—sometimes colourful, sometimes loathsome.

Rational Man, on the other hand, operated by measuring, classifying, and compartmentalising the world. He was therefore identified with the *measurer*, not the measured. In order to keep his identity distinct and separate, he needed to employ various mental processes. The chief of these were *dissociation* and *compartmentalisation*, the central components of what I refer to as the "Strategic Survival Personality".[8] From the mid-eighteenth century onwards, we can observe dissociation operating on a massive, global scale. Dissociation became the unconscious driveshaft of the engine of colonialism. It becomes visible throughout the Rational Man Project the moment one develops the eyes to see it. In fact, it soon becomes evident that dissociation is the project's most prominent feature.

Rational Man's logic starts out fairly simply but soon becomes extremely complex. It runs as follows: the indigenous people encountered in the New World provided labour and servant material in abundance but could also be very useful in other subconscious ways. Not being white Europeans, they represented that which was "Not-Rational Man". As such they fulfilled a symbolic role, ranking as subhuman vessels that embodied all those qualities that Rational Man would not identify with and was therefore busy disowning. These qualities were all enemies of the great god Progress: laziness, childishness, vulnerability, ignorance, promiscuity, and so on.

In his fervent wish to dissociate from anything that was not rational progress, the idea that in some cultures people might work during one season and then rest or conduct religious ceremonies during another was not considered significant to Rational Man. It simply meant that they were "lazy savages" not wedded to the notion of *industry* or the Protestant work ethic, Rational Man's favourite themes. Britannia was well on the road to riches because of the New World. Economically, Rational Man needed natives to do the manual work; but he needed them psychologically, too—to stand beneath him.

Indigenous life was neither seen nor appreciated in its own context but entirely interpreted through the emergent excessively rational mindset. The small minority of Rational Men who were curious about these other worlds had to disguise their interest in satirical fairy tales, as Jonathan Swift did in his *Gulliver's Travels*. Daniel Defoe's *Robinson Crusoe* was a much better depiction of Rational Man's psyche than Swift's novel, for Crusoe was a survivor who organised and developed his desert island, unselfconsciously taking Man Friday—his opposite—as his servant. Crusoe "saves" Friday from being cannibalised and justifies his own superior status by virtue of the mental gymnastics emanating from his rational Protestant intellect and sense of entitlement. He rationalises Friday's unpaid service to him as a step forward in the black man's own betterment. Crusoe's Entitlement Illusion results directly from his widespread use of dissociation and compartmentalisation.[9] This trick became a crucial part of the popular and enduring narrative that allowed the white man's unquestioning motivation—his sense of entitlement, coupled with his charitable duty. For there is one more psychological function for indigenous man to fulfil: psychologically, this second role of Friday's is much more subtle and important than simply being a servant.

In the mid-twentieth century, psychoanalysts identified the principles of *objectification*. In its origin, this is a psychic process whereby an infant uses his mother as a platform for satisfying his own needs for safety and nourishment. In adults, the same psychic process can be used pathologically to promote narcissistic behaviour or as a defence. In short, it is the turning of people into objects so they can be used or exploited, either psychologically or economically. In the case of the early British colonists, both ways fitted miraculously well together.

Next, psychoanalysts recognised that the objectification of people can manifest in two apparently separate but interlocked forms: *denigration* or *idealisation*. In the former, the object is looked down upon, hated, and despised; in the latter it is looked up to and even worshipped. But in both cases, it has little or nothing to do with external reality. The estimation of the object's value is entirely virtual, since all the referents are internal to the objectifier. In other words, they are all about the attitudes of the person who is doing the objectifying. What's more, in the end, denigration and idealisation turn out to be but different sides of the same coin. In clinical practice, psychoanalysts discovered that whenever they were idealised by their narcissistically wounded patients, they were likely to be denigrated quickly thereafter, so that both polarities were, in the end, meaningless.

Through this lens, we can see that the colonial denigration of the indigenous world had further possibilities of transformation into a kind of idealisation. Using other Enlightenment principles, this time libertarianism or utopianism, the savage could be idealised or romanticised. Or, maintaining good Quaker benevolence, one could have pity on these strange figures, deemed so inferior. The wonderful thing about both these options was that the practitioner could feel better about himself, since both fitted his value system and helped him override the otherwise obvious excesses of exploitation.[10] He could emerge with his conscience wiped clean. Not that this psycho-conjuring did much for the indigenous world, since it was but another spin of the virtual merry-go-round.

Pitying the poor Indians

Enlightenment style pity needs a little defining. It is not an outpouring of empathic feeling or the joining in communal grief, as might be depicted in the scene of a medieval *Pieta* sculpture, belonging to a world of reference now abandoned. The Rational Man Project was based in a more Protestant ideal, abstract and yet pragmatic. It translated emotions into ideas or actions—preferably both. With Enlightenment pity bolted onto the worship of Reason—as celebrated in Alexander Pope's pity for the "Poor Indian"—Rational Man could compensate his rank exploitation of the indigenous world with some moral balance.[11] Furthermore, according to Professor Laura M. Stevens of the University of Tulsa, the sentimental side of Protestantism would thrive on finding those "who must be lost in order to be found" (2004). Such a version of pity went to the heart of the redemptive gospel of Protestant evangelism: the natives could become the lost sheep that the colonial shepherd would restore to the flock. It further legitimised an impassioned export drive in the form of the "benefits" of Christianity and European languages.

Over time, this meant that the recipients of pity would have their own beliefs and tongues eradicated as a matter of policy. And here is where the British boarding school system suddenly came into its own as a valuable export item. The eradication of instinctual desires and customs learned at the mother's bosom had been perfected in the public schools at home. The revamped "public" schools of the mid-nineteenth century were able to apply industrial techniques to education and turn out a consistent supply of stoic administrators for the expanding British Empire.[12] Their internalised superiority was a more effective and much cheaper weapon than even their military prowess: a tiny amount of Brits ruled vast areas of the colonies. Here is how Dadabhai Narojii, the first Asian MP elected to Westminster in 1892 described their skills:

> The natives called the system *sakar ki churi*, the knife of sugar. That is to say, there is no suppression, it is all smooth and sweet, but it is the knife, notwithstanding. (cited in McElvoy, 2014)

Applying the same educational techniques in the colonies was a mission especially suited to the British Victorian ideal. The Victorians had learned how to break the will of their own children and they would now practise it abroad. So, towards the end of the nineteenth century, the establishment of native boarding schools in Australia and North America became the new gold rush. Civilising the savages was a project that went hand in hand with taking over their land, while the apparent need for the former would easily obscure the cunning of the latter.

Official records from the time concerning the legacy of these institutions are only now coming to light. In 2008, the Canadian government set up a truth and reconciliation commission, an official independent body, to look into the history and legacy of residential schools for aboriginal peoples in Canada. Initially, this was a response to numerous complaints from former students, represented by the Assembly of First Nations and other aboriginal organisations, against the government and the Church of Canada. The commission had a budget of C$60 million and was to complete its work by June 2015. In the spring of 2012, it published its interim report, *They Came for the Children*, and summarised the first principles of the residential school movement thus:

> First Nation leaders entered into the treaty making process for the purpose of establishing a relationship of respect that included an ongoing set of mutual obligations including land sharing based on kinship and cooperation. For its part, the Canadian government saw the treaties only as land transfer agreements. The government's policy was one of assimilation under which it sought to remove any First Nation's legal interest in the land, while reducing and ignoring its own treaty obligations. Schooling was expected to play a central role in achieving that policy goal. (Truth and Reconciliation Commission of Canada, 2012)

Remember, pitying did not actually mean *identifying* and *empathising* with the aboriginal residents; that was not part of the Rational Man Project. Rather, pity as a conceptual stance became a mechanism for Enlightened society as a whole to rationalise its superiority and take advantage over those who had lost their personhood and become objects. In fact, in the most rational of all languages, French, someone whom we pity or to whom we give charity becomes known as an *objet de pitié*, an *objet de charité*. In the final analysis, pitying meant fixing the "poor Indian" in a subhuman category. Unconsciously, both idealisation and denigration had inevitably come full circle: dissociation, compartmentalisation, and objectification had done their work.

Enlightenment pity and human rights

The withholding of human rights, particularly from Africans, made it possible for Europe to gain extraordinary wealth from the New World, primarily by means of the Atlantic slave trade. From its beginnings in the sixteenth century, it is estimated that about 12 million Africans were transported across the Atlantic to the Americas.[13] Britain gained her enormous wealth and mastery of the oceans through perfecting what became known as the "triangular trade", in which her ships took arms, cloth, and metal goods to West Africa to trade for captured Africans. Those who survived the voyage would be sold into slavery in the Caribbean for sugar and coffee to satisfy emerging tastes at home.

This was not the only trend emerging in the coffee houses of London. The great liberalising movements that had been released by the Enlightenment and had resulted in the American and French revolutions, also meant that some thinkers would take Enlightenment pity a step further—out from dissociation and into the reality of humane political action. Their chief focus was to try to wean Britain from the addiction to slavery that had fuelled the pre-industrial colonial world, first through pamphleteering and eventually through the reform of Parliament. Here is William Cowper, from his poem, "A Pity for Poor Africans", written in 1788 but not published till his death in 1800, ironically resonating on Pope's earlier piece:

> I own I am shocked at the purchase of slaves,
> And fear those who buy them and sell them are knaves;
> What I hear of their hardships, their tortures, and groans
> Is almost enough to draw pity from stones.
>
> I pity them greatly, but I must be mum,
> For how could we do without sugar and rum?
> Especially sugar, so needful we see;
> What, give up our desserts, our coffee, and tea?
>
> Besides, if we do, the French, Dutch, and Danes,
> Will heartily thank us, no doubt, for our pains:
> If we do not buy the poor creatures, they will:
> And tortures and groans will be multiplied still.

As Cowper sweetly hints, the slave trade had an immensely powerful lobby whose argument ran that slavery was indispensable to the success and wealth of Britain. Through their tame MPs, the merchants and planters warned that abolition would mean ruin for Britain, as the whole economy would collapse. If Britain ceased to trade in slaves with Africa, her commercial rivals would soon fill the gap. The Africans, to boot, would apparently be in a much worse situation if they were humiliated by Johnny Foreigner rather than by English gentlemen. As an aside, readers may note how the arguments against abolishing slavery summarised by Cowper are reminiscent of those used by the British government in the twenty-first century to avoid regulating or penalising banking and financial trading: "It's a no-brainer! We have to do everything to save our banks or we will lose our advantage and others will mop up the gains!"

Eventually, a collection of Romantic literary figures, Quaker activists, and political reformers built up a head of steam and, having since 1787 bombarded Parliament with petitions, managed to get both Houses to take the human rights situation seriously. Alarmed by a violent revolt of slaves on the Caribbean island of Saint-Domingue (later Haiti) in which Napoleon lost more men than at Waterloo, Parliament passed the Slave Trade Act in 1807, which was an attempt to ban *slaving* rather than slavery itself. It took exactly fifty years, from the end of the War of American Independence to the Abolition of Slavery Act in 1833, to have the practice banned in the Empire's domain, and even then it excluded those lands governed by the East India Company.

The 1807 Act resulted in a payout of millions of pounds in compensation to some three thousand individuals, including several bishops, who had investments in the lucrative trade (Traub, 2013). Amongst the compensated, as researchers at University College London revealed in 2013, were ancestors of David Cameron (Jones, 2013). Shameful as it clearly was even then, such business was as common as people investing in stocks and shares today, for the objectification of those plucked out of their lives in West Africa had been fully and completely normalised. The slaves and their descendants have never been compensated. And, as Baldwin Spencer, prime minister of Antigua and Barbuda, argued in a Caricom (heads of government of the Caribbean Community) meeting in July 2013, much of the region is still suffering as a direct result of such exploitation.

Important as the outlawing of slavery was for humanity, it was a further step of self-invention for the British. In *Bury the Chains: Prophets and Rebels in the Fight to Free an Empire's Slaves* (2005), award-winning American historian Adam Hochschild suggests that after the 1807 Act, British self-congratulation knew no bounds. In the late 1830s and 1840s, the imperial fleet, staffed mostly by press gang, ruled the waves. At the same time, it saw itself as an international do-gooder—a police force with a duty to enforce a ban that was not yet agreed to by less evolved

Continentals and Americans. For the British felt good about themselves; they were proud to be the world's leaders.

The project was sufficiently advanced that Rational Man was beginning to feel secure about his ordained place at the top of the tree; and so, out of *noblesse oblige*, he could direct his generosity towards those at the bottom. Much more importantly, however, Britain's industrialisation was in full swing. Bit by bit, the profit from the use of machines began to rival the profit from the exploitation of slaves abroad and the feudal classes at home; the latter would eventually—even happily—turn into consumers. Thus, some economic disincentives of slavery were beginning to arise. Drunk with greed and success, Rational Man marched unstoppably on, trying to exploit and control the world in the name of the grand new god, Progress.

Unconsciously, however, the side effects of Enlightenment dissociation remained active, even if they had yet to be recognised. Psychological forces drive behaviour whether they are acknowledged or not; and, by one of the first laws of psychology discovered by its founding fathers, while they are unconscious they do more than drive—they control. In its attempts to reintegrate, or recycle, as it were, the ecological nature of the psyche means that what is disowned eventually begins to oppress he who has disowned it. Rational Man needed to employ the powerful psychological forces of dissociation, compartmentalisation, and objectification to cope with that which was "Not-Rational Man"—women, children, "natives", and, in Britain, foreigners and the working classes. But this meant that he had a serious psychological problem, because in his inability to integrate them as part of his identity, he was building psychological weakness into himself, even as he built himself up.

It is a problem that continues to this day for those raised in British boarding schools, those rational hothouses in which the inmates *are* in fact children, born of mothers; for the logic means they have to rapidly disidentify from and disown those aspects of themselves and are left with but their brittle defensive personalities hidden under rational perfection. It was from these schools, in less than ten years, that exquisitely manufactured Rational Men would emerge—as long as they had learned to practise the arts of dissociation, idealisation, and objectification as tiny children and took these skills as normal. But they would leave with a built-in sense of entitlement that was as natural and unquestioned as anything they had known. It was breathlessly fast and almost perfect—except for one flaw.

What Rational Man had disidentified from was now felt as *outside* him, specifically *below* him. It was threatening to the maintenance of his identity and existence and therefore fearful; at any moment it might rise up. What he dreaded was represented by real live people, so his weakness was unconsciously constantly being excited or provoked. In terms of the psychodynamics of the Strategic Survival Personality, when chronic dissociation is practised, that which is disowned is imagined to be capable of attack. This paranoiac phase of dissociation then legitimises keeping the original defence mechanism in place and supports the entire vicious circle. This, readers may recognise, is the psychological mechanism behind the recent so-called "War on Terror". The concept of "terror" gets created and then has to be fought. The fight then becomes legitimate because it has been psychologically legitimised.

In fact, Rational Man was (and still is) permanently at war. He was at war with himself and with the world he had created. The self he was at war with was his own indigenous self, the natural, emotional, innocent, spontaneous, sometimes lazy, sometimes erotic self—the self the boarding school survivor had to send into exile. The expression of this forbidden self was restricted to secrecy and dreams, waiting for Freud to uncover this truth. The incongruity of Rational Man's outer grandiosity and inner war meant that, by the end of the nineteenth century, he ruled supreme in the outer world but was controlled in his inner world—and was about to enter the folly of ritual self-destruction that was the First World War. By then, the indigenous world, from Australia to India and from Africa to America, had been fully brutalised and subjugated: the natives, now fully objects and not persons, had become unworthy of the fulfilment of any promise made to them. Thus, all promises were duly broken.

Notes

1. Abridged from *The English Are So Nice* by D. H. Lawrence.
2. In his 1960 article, "Ego Distortion in Terms of True and False Self", D. W. Winnicott says that when a "mother's adaptation" is not good enough (he is describing the very early years, but I believe the process continues into latency) "… the process that leads to the capacity for symbol-usage does not get started (or else it becomes broken up, with a corresponding withdrawal on the part of the infant from advantages

gained) … in practice the infant lives, but lives falsely. The protest against being forced into a false existence can be detected from the earliest stages … Through this False Self the infant builds up a false set of relationships, and … even attains a show of being real" (pp. 145–146). In Roberto Assagioli's psychosynthesis, Winnicottís *False Self* is commonly known as the "Survival Personality", and from 1988 I adapted this term to its specific character in ex-boarders.

3. *Born to Run* is a famous song and the third album by the American singer-songwriter Bruce Springsteen, released in 1975.

4. According to Herzen, the relentless inculcation of these internalised "self-referring codes" as part of the educational process is one of the reasons why British society is extraordinarily good at self-policing: we don't need a police state, he suggested, because we police it ourselves. This policing is embedded in the language. Similarly, Michael Goldfarb has recently suggested that the skill people ultimately learn at public schools is not how to *think* but how to *speak* (2012). His analysis indicates that what Oxbridge students learn is not so much ways to understand the world or the various disciplines they are supposed to be studying, but rather to develop their way with *words*. In this sense, perhaps learning to speak cleverly and nuance your bullying is the real training for future leaderships.

5. Attachment theory was principally the work of Dr. John Bowlby (1907–1990). Like Freud, Bowlby believed that mental health and behavioural problems could be attributed to early childhood. After the Second World War, Bowlby developed naturalistic infant observation at the Tavistock Clinic in London within the newly created National Health Service. In the 1940s and 1950s he humanised and systematised objects relations theory, the prevailing psychoanalytic discipline. Born into a prosperous family, the young Bowlby rarely saw his mother, who like many others of her class considered that parental attention and affection would lead to a dangerous spoiling of a child. Bowlby was brought up by his nanny, but lost her when he was four years old. At the age of seven, he was sent off to boarding school. In his 1972 book *Separation: Anxiety and Anger*, he revealed that he had had a terrible time and later said: "I wouldn't send a dog away to boarding school at age seven."

Bowlby's attachment theory suggests that children come into the world biologically preprogrammed to form attachments with others, in order to survive. Bowlby was influenced by the biologist Konrad

Lorenz who, in his 1935 study of imprinting, demonstrated that attachment was innate in young animals and therefore had survival value. In evolutionary terms, it would have been the babies who stayed close to their mothers who would have survived to have children of their own. Bowlby suggested that a child's attachment figure acted as a secure base for exploring the world and that the attachment relationship acts as the prototype for all future relationships.

6. McGilchrist's book, *The Master and his Emissary: The Divided Brain and the Making of the Western World*, is an extraordinary feast of information and conclusions recommended to anyone interested in such topics.

7. In this context, the work of the American psychotherapist Stephen M. Johnson is extremely helpful, since he shows how degrees of dysfunction can be conceived on a continuum between what he calls character style through character neurosis to personality disorder. This level of degree rating is both humanising and illuminating for therapeutic workers and opens up many more possibilities for understanding. See Johnson, 1994.

8. See Chapter 4 of *Wounded Leaders: British Elitism and the Entitlement Illusion* (Duffell, 2014) for a fuller discussion of the psychodynamics of this type of personality.

9. James Joyce noted that the true symbol of the British conquest is Robinson Crusoe: "He is the true prototype of the British colonist … The whole Anglo-Saxon spirit is in Crusoe: the manly independence, the unconscious cruelty, the persistence, the slow yet efficient intelligence, the sexual apathy, the calculating taciturnity" (*Daniel Defoe*, translated from an Italian manuscript and edited by Joseph Prescott, *Buffalo Studies 1*, 1964, pp. 24–25). I am still wondering why this had to be said in Italian, not English.

10. See Emile Zola's wonderful account of this phenomenon as revealed through writing of the time, from the sixteenth to the twentieth century (1973).

11. The classic rational idealised/denigrated eighteenth-century portrayal of the American Indian in literature could be represented by the famous lines from Alexander Pope's 1734 *Essay on Man:*

> Lo, the poor Indian! whose untutor'd mind
> Sees God in clouds, or hears him in the wind.

12. The public schools ("public" as they were open to all who could pay the fees) were soon churning out the requisite young men in droves. I use the phrase "churning out" quite deliberately, for this was a quasi-industrial

process using human factory lines, and the industrial metaphor is not a coincidence. When I first began my study of boarding, I was astonished to discover that by far the most common complaint I heard from ex-boarders about their schooling was not the separation, not the beatings, not the wretched food, but the feeling of being objects put through what several correspondents called a kind of "sausage machine" turning out uniform products in terms of accent, opinions, and codes of behaviour. Remarkably, the objectification process was now operating at the top of the ladder as well as the bottom.

13. Retrieved from www.abolition.e2bn.org/slavery_45.html.

References

Bowlby, J. (1972). *Attachment and Loss, Vol. 2: Separation: Anxiety and Anger*. London: Hogarth.

Duffell, N. (2000). *The Making of Them: The British Attitude to Children and the Boarding School System*. London: Lone Arrow Press.

Duffell, N. (2014). *Wounded Leaders: British Elitism and the Entitlement Illusion—A Psychohistory*. London: Lone Arrow Press.

Duffell, N., & Basset, T. (2016). *Trauma, Abandonment and Privilege: A guide to therapeutic work with boarding school survivors*. London: Routledge.

Goldfarb, M. (2012). *The British Establishment: Who For?* http://downloads.bbc.co.uk/podcasts/worldservice/docarchive/docarchive_20111025–1000a.mp3.

Grosz, S. (2013). *The Examined Life*. London: Chatto & Windus.

Herzen, A. (1924). *My Past and Thoughts: The Memoirs of Alexander Herzen*. Berkeley, CA: University of California Press, 1991.

Hickson, A. (1995). *The Poisoned Bowl: Sex Repression and the Public School System*. London: Constable.

Hochschild, A. (2005). *Bury the Chains: Prophets and Rebels in the Fight to Free an Empire's Slaves*. Boston, MA: Houghton Mifflin Harcourt.

Johnson, S. M. (1994). *Character Styles*. New York: W. W. Norton.

Jones, S. (2013). Follow the Money: Investigators Trace Forgotten Story of Britain's Slave Trade. *Guardian*, 27 August.

Lawrence, D. H. (1986). *D. H. Lawrence: Selected Poetry*. London: Penguin.

McElvoy, A. (2014). What's in a name? It could be Salmond Street next. *Evening Standard*, 17 September.

McGilchrist, I. (2009). *The Master and his Emissary: The Divided Brain and the Making of the Western World*. New Haven, CT: Yale University Press.

Prescott, J. (Ed. & Trans.) (1964). Daniel Defoe by James Joyce, in *Buffalo Studies 1*. Buffalo, NY: State University of New York.

Schaverien, J. (2011). Boarding school syndrome: Broken attachments—a hidden trauma. *British Journal of Psychotherapy*, 27(2): 138–155.

Stern, D. (1985). *The Interpersonal World of the Infant*. New York: Basic Books.

Stevens, L. M. (2004). *The Poor Indians: British Missionaries, Native Americans, and Colonial Sensibility*. Philadelphia, PA: University of Pennsylvania Press.

Traub, R. (2013). *Sieg der Empörung. Das Britische Empire 1600–1947: Als England die Welt regierte. Der Spiegel—Geschichte* 1/January. (Outrage's Victory. The British Empire 1600–1947: When England ruled the world. *Der Spiegel* History Supplement, January).

Truth and Reconciliation Commission of Canada (2012). *Canada, Aboriginal Peoples and Residential Schools: They Came for the Children*, Interim Report, February 24. Available at http://www.myrobust.com/websites/trcinstitution/File/2039_T&R_eng_web[1].pdf.

Winnicott, D. W. (1960). "Ego distortion in terms of true and false self. In: *The Maturational Processes and the Facilitating Environment*. New York: International Universities Press.

Zola, E. (1973). *The Writer and the Shaman: A Morphology of the American Indian*. New York: Harcourt Brace Janovich.

CHAPTER SEVEN

On killing: the psychological cost of learning to kill in war and society*

Lt. Col. Dave Grossman

> *War has always interested me; not war in the sense of maneuvers devised by great generals ... but the reality of war, the actual killing. I was more interested to know in what way and under the influence of what feelings one soldier kills another than to know how the armies were arranged at Austerlitz and Borodino.*
>
> —Leo Tolstoy

Introduction

Why should we study killing? One might just as readily ask, Why study sex? The two questions have much in common. Every society has a blind spot, an area into which it has great difficulty looking. Today that blind spot is killing. A century ago it was sex.

Sex is a natural and essential part of life. A society that has no sex has no society in one generation. Today our society has begun the

---

*This chapter is an edited version of *On Killing: The Psychological Cost of Learning to Kill in War and Society* by Lt. Col. Dave Grossman (© 1995, Back Bay Books) and is reproduced by kind permission of the author. All rights reserved.

slow, painful process of escaping from the pathological dichotomy of simultaneous sexual repression and obsession. But we may have begun our escape from one denial only to fall into a new and possibly even more dangerous one. A new repression, revolving around killing and death, precisely parallels the pattern established by the previous sexual repression.

In this study it is my intention to delve into this taboo subject of killing and to provide insight into the following:

- The existence of a powerful, innate human resistance toward killing one's own species and the psychological mechanisms that have been developed by armies *over the centuries* to overcome that resistance.
- How the American soldier in Vietnam was first psychologically enabled to kill to a far greater degree than any other soldier in previous history, then denied the psychologically essential purification ritual that exists in every warrior society, and finally condemned and accused by his own society to a degree that is unprecedented in Western history. And the terrible, tragic price that America's three million Vietnam veterans, their families, and our society have paid for what we did to our soldiers in Vietnam.
- Finally, and *perhaps most important*, I believe that this study will provide insight into the way that rifts in our society combine with violence in the media and in interactive video games to indiscriminately condition our nation's children to kill. In a fashion very similar to the way the army conditions our soldiers. But without the safeguards. And we will see the terrible, tragic price that out nation is paying for what we are doing to our children.

The Marshall statistic

Our first step in the study of killing is to understand the existence, extent, and nature of the average human being's resistance to killing his fellow human. In this section we will attempt to do that. Prior to World War II it had always been assumed that the average soldier would kill in combat simply because his country and his leaders had told him to do so and because it was essential to defend his own life and the lives of his friends. When the point came that he didn't kill, it was assumed that he panicked and ran. During World War II U.S. Army Brigadier General S. L. A. Marshall asked these soldiers what it was that they did in battle.

His singularly unexpected discovery was that, of every hundred men along the line of fire during the period of an encounter, an average of only fifteen or twenty would take any part with their weapons. This was consistently true whether the action was spread over a day, two days, or three.

Marshall was a U.S. Army historian in the Pacific theater during World War II and later became the official U.S. historian of the European theater of operations. He had a team of historians working for him, and they based their findings on individual and mass interviews with thousands of soldiers in more than 400 infantry companies, in Europe and in the Pacific, immediately after they had been in close combat with German or Japanese troops. The results were consistently the same: only 15 to 20 percent of the American riflemen in combat during World War II would fire at the enemy. Those who would not fire did not run or hide (in many cases they were willing to risk great danger to rescue comrades, get ammunition, or run messages), but they simply would not fire their weapons at the enemy, even when faced with repeated waves of banzai charges.

In Marshall's case, every available parallel scholarly study replicates his basic findings (see *Men Against Fire*, 1978). Ardant du Picq's surveys and observations of the ancients (1946), Holmes's and Keegan's numerous accounts of ineffectual firing, Holmes's assessment of Argentine firing rates in the Falklands War, Griffith's data (1989) on the extraordinarily low killing rates among Napoleonic and American Civil War regiments, the British Army's laser reenactments of historical battles, the FBI's studies of non-firing rates among law-enforcement officers in the 1950s and 1960s, and countless other individual and anecdotal observations all confirm Marshall's conclusion that the vast majority of combatants throughout history, at the moment of truth when they could and should kill the enemy, have found themselves to be unable to kill.

The question is why. Why did these men fail to fire? As I examined this question and studied the process of killing in combat from the standpoints of a historian, a psychologist, and a soldier, I began to realize that there was one major factor that was missing from the common understanding of killing in combat, a factor that answers this question and more. That missing factor is the simple and demonstrable fact that there is within most men an intense resistance to killing their fellow man. A resistance so strong that, in many circumstances, soldiers on the battlefield will die before they can overcome it.

To some, this makes "obvious" sense. "Of course it is hard to kill someone," they would say. "I could never bring myself to do it." But they would be wrong. With the proper conditioning and the proper circumstances, it appears that almost everyone can and will kill. Others might respond, "Any man will kill in combat when he is faced with someone who is trying to kill him." And they would be even more wrong, for in this chapter we shall observe that throughout history the majority of men on the battlefield would *not* attempt to kill the enemy, even to save their own lives or the lives of their friends.

Repression

Part of the reason for our lack of knowledge in this area is that combat is, like sex, laden with a baggage of expectations and myths. In the same way that we did not understand what was occurring in the bedroom, we have not understood what was occurring on the battlefield. Our ignorance of the destructive act matched that of the procreative act. A belief that most soldiers will not kill the enemy in close combat is contrary to what we want to believe about ourselves, and it is contrary to what thousands of years of military history and culture have told us. But are the perceptions handed down to us by our culture and our historians accurate, unbiased, and reliable?

In *A History of Militarism*, Alfred Vagts accuses military history, as an institution, of having played a large part in the process of militarizing minds. Vagts complains that military history is consistently written "with polemic purpose for the justification of individuals or armies and with small regard for socially relevant facts." He states, "A very large part of military history is written, if not for the express purpose of supporting an army's authority, at least with the intention of not hurting it, not revealing its secrets, avoiding the betrayal of weakness, vacillation, or distemper" (cited in Holmes, 1985, p. 6). Vagts paints an image of military and historical institutions that for thousands of years have reinforced and supported each other in a process of mutual glorification and aggrandizement. To a certain extent, this is probably because those who are good at killing in war are quite often those who throughout history have hacked their way to power.[1] The military and the politicians have been the same people for all but the most recent part of human history, and we know that the victor writes the history books.

As a historian, as a soldier, and as a psychologist, I believe that Vagts is quite correct. If for thousands of years the vast majority of soldiers secretly and privately were less than enthusiastic about killing their fellow man on the battlefield, the professional soldiers and their chroniclers would be the last to let us know the inadequacies of their particular charges. The media in our modern information society have done much to perpetuate the myth of easy killing and have thereby become part of society's unspoken conspiracy of deception that glorifies killing and war. There are exceptions—such as Gene Hackman's *Bat 21*, in which an air force pilot has to kill people on the ground, up close and personal for a change and is horrified at what he has done—but for the most part we are given James Bond, Luke Skywalker, Rambo, and Indiana Jones blithely and remorselessly killing men by the hundreds. The point here is that there is as much disinformation and as little insight concerning the nature of killing coming from the media as from any other aspect of our society.

Even after Marshall's World War II revelations, the subject of non-firers is an uncomfortable one for today's military. Writing in *Army* magazine—the U.S. Army's foremost military journal—Colonel Mater states that his experiences as an infantry company commander in World War II strongly supported Marshall's findings and noted several World War I anecdotes that suggest that the problem of non-firers was just as serious in that war.

Mater then bitterly—and appropriately—complains that "Thinking back over my many years of service, I cannot remember a single official lecture or class discussion of how to assure that your men will fire." This included "… such formal schooling as the wartime Infantry Leadership and Battle School I attended in Italy and the Command and General Staff College at Ft. Leavenworth, Kansas, that I attended in 1966. Nor do I remember any articles on the subject in *Army* magazine or other military publications." Colonel Mater concludes, "It is as if there were a conspiracy of silence around this subject: 'We don't know what to do about it—so let's forget it'" (cited in Glenn, 1989, pp. 22–23).[2]

There does indeed seem to be a conspiracy of silence on this subject. In his book *War on the Mind* (1978), Peter Watson observes that Marshall's findings have been largely ignored by academia and the fields of psychology and psychiatry, but they were very much taken to heart by the U.S. Army, and a number of training measures were instituted as a result of Marshall's suggestions. According to studies by Marshall, these changes resulted in a firing rate of 55 percent in Korea and, according to a study by R. W. Glenn, a 90 to 95 percent firing rate was attained in Vietnam. Some modern soldiers use the disparity between the firing rates of World War II and Vietnam to claim that Marshall had to be wrong, for the average military leader has great difficulty in believing that any significant body of his soldiers will not do their job in combat. But these doubters don't give sufficient credit to the revolutionary corrective measures and training methods introduced since World War II.

A kind of madness at work

The training methods that increased the firing rate from 15 percent to 90 percent are referred to as "programming" or "conditioning" by some of the veterans I have interviewed, and they do appear to represent a form of classical and operant conditioning (à la Pavlov's dog and B. F. Skinner's rats). The unpleasantness of this subject, combined with the remarkable success of the army's training programs, and the lack of official recognition, might imply that it is classified. But there is no secret master plan responsible for the lack of attention given to this subject. There is instead, in the words of philosopher-psychologist Peter Marin, "a massive unconscious cover-up" in which society hides from itself the true nature of combat. Even among the psychological and psychiatric literature on war, "[T]here is," writes Marin, "a kind of madness at work." He notes, "Repugnance toward killing and the refusal to kill" are referred to as "acute combat reaction." And psychological trauma resulting from "slaughter and atrocity are called 'stress,' as if the clinicians ... are talking about an executive's overwork." As a psychologist I believe that Marin is quite correct when he observes, "Nowhere in the [psychiatric and psychological] literature is one allowed to glimpse what is actually occurring: the real horror of the war and its effect on those who fought it" (1981, pp. 68–69, 74).

It would be almost impossible to keep something of this nature classified for more than fifty years now, and those in the military who do understand—the Marshalls and the Maters—are crying out their messages, but no one wants to hear their truths. No, it is not a military conspiracy. There is, indeed, a cover-up and a "conspiracy of silence," but it is a cultural conspiracy of forgetfulness, distortion, and lies that has been going on for thousands of years. And just as we have begun to wipe away the cultural conspiracy of guilt and silence concerning sex, we *must* now wipe away this similar conspiracy that obscures the very nature of war.

One of the roots of our misunderstanding of the psychology of the battlefield lies in the misapplication of the fight-or-flight model to the stress of combat. This model holds that in the face of danger a series of physiological and psychological processes prepare and support the endangered creature for either fighting or fleeing. The fight-or-flight dichotomy is the appropriate set of choices for any creature faced with danger *other* than that which comes from its own species. When we examine the responses of creatures confronted with aggression from their own species, the set of options expands to include posturing and submission. This application of animal kingdom intra-species response patterns (that is, fight, flee, posture, and submit) to human warfare is, to the best of my knowledge, entirely new.

The first decision point in intra-species conflict usually involves deciding between fleeing or posturing. A threatened baboon or rooster who elects to stand its ground does not respond to aggression from one of his own kind by leaping instantly to the enemy's throat. Instead, both creatures instinctively go through a series of posturing actions that, while intimidating, *are almost always harmless*. These actions are designed to convince an opponent, through both sight and sound, that the posturer is a dangerous and frightening adversary.

When the posturer has failed to dissuade an intra-species opponent, the options then become fight, flight, or submission. When the fight option is utilized, it is *almost never to the death*. Konrad Lorenz pointed out (1963) that piranhas and rattlesnakes will bite anything and everything, but among themselves piranhas fight with raps of their tails, and rattlesnakes wrestle. Somewhere during the course of such highly constrained and nonlethal fights, one of these intra-species opponents will usually become daunted by the ferocity and prowess of its opponent, and its only options become submission or flight. Submission is a surprisingly common response, usually taking the form of fawning and exposing some vulnerable portion of the anatomy to the victor, in the instinctive knowledge that the opponent will not kill or further harm one of its own kind once it has surrendered. The posturing, mock battle, and submission process is vital to the survival of the species. It prevents needless deaths and ensures that a young male will live through early confrontations when his opponents are bigger and better prepared.

Having been out-postured by his opponent, he can then submit and live to mate, passing on his genes in later years.

As we shall see, modern training or conditioning techniques can partially overcome the inclination to posture. Indeed, the history of warfare can be seen as a history of increasingly more effective mechanisms for enabling and conditioning men to overcome their innate resistance to killing their fellow human beings.

The 2 percent who like it

Swank and Marchand's much-cited World War II study (1946) determined that after sixty days of *continuous* combat, 98 percent of all surviving soldiers will have become psychiatric casualties of one kind or another. Swank and Marchand also found a common trait among the 2 percent who are able to endure sustained combat: a predisposition toward "aggressive psychopathic personalities."

This 2 percent who are predisposed to be "aggressive psychopaths" apparently do not experience the normal resistance to killing and the resultant psychiatric casualties associated with extended periods of combat. But the negative connotations associated with the term "psychopath," or its modern equivalent "sociopath," are inappropriate here, since this behavior is a generally desirable one for soldiers in combat. It would be absolutely incorrect to conclude that 2 percent of all veterans are psychopathic killers. Numerous studies indicate that combat veterans are not more inclined to violence than nonvets. A more accurate conclusion would be that there is 2 percent of the male population that, if pushed or given a legitimate reason, will kill without regret or remorse.

The *Diagnostic and Statistical Manual of Mental Disorders* (DSM) of the American Psychiatric Association (APA) indicates that the incidence of "antisocial personality disorder" (that is, sociopaths) among the general population of American males is approximately 3 percent. These sociopaths are not easily used in armies, since by their very nature they rebel against authority, but over the centuries armies have had considerable success at bending such highly aggressive individuals to their will during wartime. So if two out of three of this 3 percent were able to accept military discipline, a hypothetical 2 percent of soldiers would, by the APA's definition, "have no remorse about the effects of their behavior on others" (DSM-5, 2013, p. 660).[3]

There is strong evidence that there exists a general predisposition for aggression. In all species the best hunter, the best fighter, the most aggressive male, survives to pass his biological predispositions on to his descendants. There are also environmental processes that can fully develop this predisposition toward aggression; when we combine this genetic predisposition with environmental development we get a killer. But there is another factor: the presence of absence of empathy for others. Again, there may be biological and environmental causes for this empathic process, but, whatever its origin, there is undoubtedly a division in humanity between those who can feel and understand the pain and suffering of others, and those who cannot. The presence of aggression, combined with the absence of empathy, results in sociopathy.

Operant conditioning, desensitization, and violent video gaming

In my books *Stop Teaching Our Kids to Kill* (2014, coauthored with Gloria DeGaetano) and *On Combat* (2008) I outline the great body of scholarly research linking media violence with violence in our society. My goal here is to apply the models and methodology of combat killing enabling, as outlined in this chapter, in order to understand the explosion of violent crime in our society. An application of the lessons of combat killing may have much to teach us about the constraint and control of peacetime violence.

One of the most remarkable revelations in Watson's book *War on the Mind* is his report of conditioning techniques used by the U.S. government to train assassins. In 1975 Dr. Narut, a U.S. Navy psychiatrist with the rank of commander, told Watson about techniques he was developing for the U.S. government in which classical conditioning and social learning methodology were being used to permit military assassins to overcome their resistance to killing. The method used, according to Narut, was to expose the subjects to "symbolic modeling" involving "films specially designed to show people being killed or injured in violent ways. By being acclimatized through these films, the men were supposed to eventually become able to dissociate their emotions from such a situation" (Watson, 1978, p. 171). In psychological terms, this step-by-step reduction of a resistance is a form of classical (Pavlovian) conditioning called systematic desensitization.

In Vietnam a systematic process of desensitization, conditioning, and training increased the individual firing rate from a World War II baseline of 15 to 20 percent to an all-time high of up to 95 percent. Today a similar process of systematic desensitization, conditioning, and vicarious learning is unleashing an epidemic, a virus of violence in America. Operant conditioning firing ranges with pop-up targets and immediate feedback, just like those used to train soldiers in modern armies, are found in the interactive video games that our children play today. But whereas the adolescent Vietnam vet had stimulus discriminators built in to ensure that he fired only under authority, the adolescents who play these video games have no such safeguard built into their conditioning.

When I speak of violence enabling I am not talking about video games in which the player defeats creatures by bopping them on the head. Nor am I talking about games where you maneuver swordsmen and archers to defeat monsters. On the borderline in violence enabling are games where you use a joystick to maneuver a gun-sight around the screen to kill gangsters who pop up and fire at you. The kind of games that are very definitely enabling violence are the ones in which you actually hold a weapon in your hands and fire it at human-shaped targets on the screen. There is a direct relationship between realism and degree of violence enabling, and the most realistic of these are games in which great bloody chunks fly off as you fire at the enemy. Another, very different type of game has a western motif, in which you stand before a huge video screen and fire a pistol at actual film footage of "outlaws" as they appear on the screen. This is identical to the shoot-no shoot training program designed by the FBI and used by police agencies around the nation to train and enable police officers in firing their weapons. Through operant conditioning B. F. Skinner held that he could turn *any* child into *anything* he wanted to. In Vietnam the U.S. armed forces demonstrated that Skinner was at least partially correct by successfully using operant conditioning to turn adolescents into the most effective fighting force the world has ever seen. And America seems intent on using Skinner's methodology to turn us into an extraordinarily violent society.

The same tools that more than quadrupled the firing rate in Vietnam are now in widespread use among our civilian population. Military personnel are just beginning to understand and accept what they have been doing to themselves and their men. If we have reservations about the military's use of these mechanisms to ensure the survival and success of our soldiers in combat, then how much more so should we be concerned about the indiscriminate application of the same processes on our nation's children?

The three major psychological processes at work in enabling violence are classical conditioning (à la Pavlov's dog), operant conditioning (à la B. F. Skinner's rats), and the observation and imitation of vicarious role models in social learning. In a kind of reverse *Clockwork Orange* classical conditioning process, adolescents in movie theaters across the nation, and watching television at home, are seeing the detailed, horrible suffering and killing of human beings, and they are learning to associate this killing and suffering with entertainment, pleasure, their favorite soft drink, their favorite candy bar, and the close, intimate contact of their date.

Our society has found a powerful recipe for providing killing empowerment to an entire generation of Americans. Producers, directors, and actors are handsomely rewarded for creating the most violent, gruesome, and horrifying films imaginable, films in which the stabbing, shooting, abuse, and torture of innocent men, women, and children are depicted in intimate detail. Make these films entertaining as well as violent, and then simultaneously provide the (usually) adolescent viewers with candy, soft drinks, group companionship, and the intimate physical contact of a boyfriend or girlfriend. Then understand that these adolescent viewers are learning to associate these rewards with what they are watching. If we had a clear-cut objective of raising a generation of assassins and killers who are unrestrained by either authority or the nature of the victim, it is difficult to imagine how we could do a better job.

We may believe that tabloids and tabloid TV make us exceedingly conscious of the suffering of others as they spread the stories of victims. But the reality is that they are desensitizing us and trivializing these issues as each year they have to find increasingly more bizarre stories to satisfy their increasingly jaded audiences. We are reaching that stage of desensitization at which the infliction of pain and suffering has become a source of entertainment: vicarious pleasure rather than revulsion. We are learning to kill, and we are learning to like it.

Sociopath as role model

And social learning is being used as children learn to observe and imitate a whole new realm of dynamic vicarious role models, such as Jason and Freddy or endless *Friday the 13th* and *Nightmare on Elm Street* sequels, and Hannibal the Cannibal, along with a host of other horrendous sadistic murderers. Even the more classic heroes, such as the archetypal law-abiding police detective, is today portrayed as a murderous, unstable vigilante—a new kind of hero in movies, a hero who operates outside the law. Vengeance is a much older, darker, more atavistic, and more primitive concept than law, and these new anti-heroes are depicted as being motivated and rewarded for their obedience to the gods of vengeance rather than those of law. The fruit of this new cult of vengeance in American society can be seen in Columbine High School, Virginia Tech, and the Oklahoma City bombing. If we look into the mirror provided by the television screen, the reflection we see is one of a nation regressing from a society of law to a society of violence, vigilantes, and vengeance.

And if America has a police force that seems unable to constrain its violence, and a population that (having seen the videotape of Rodney King and the LAPD) has learned to fear its police forces, then the reason can be found in the entertainment industry. Look at the role models, look at the archetypes that police officers have grown up with. Clint Eastwood's Dirty Harry became the archetype for a new generation of police officers who were not constrained by the law, and when Hollywood's new breed of cop was rewarded for placing vengeance above the law, the audience was also vicariously rewarded for this same behavior. Feeding their audience a steady stream of vicarious reinforcement through such vengeful, lawless role models, these movies prepare our society for the acceptance of a truly hideous and sociopathic brand of role model.

Conclusion: the media and the military

Television programmers have always tried to claim the "best of two uncomfortably contradictory worlds," as Michael Medved puts it. It is really not new or profound to point out that television executives have for years claimed that they are not capable of influencing our actions or changing behavior, but for decades America's major corporations have paid them billions of dollars for a paltry few seconds or a minute to do just that. To sponsors, media executives claim that just a few well-placed seconds can control how America will spend its hard-earned money. But to Congress and other watchdog agencies they argue that they are not responsible for causing viewers to change the way they will respond to any emotionally charged, potentially violent circumstance that they may subsequently find themselves in. This in spite of the fact that, as of 1945, there have been more than 200 studies demonstrating the connection between television and violence.[4] The American Psychological Association's commission on violence and youth concluded in 1993 that "There is *absolutely no doubt* that higher levels of viewing violence on television are correlated with increased acceptance of aggressive attitudes and increased aggressive behavior." Violent movies are targeted at the young, both men and women, the same audience the military has determined to be most susceptible for its killing purposes. Violent video games hardwire young people for shooting at humans. The entertainment industry conditions the young in exactly the same way the military does.

Throughout history nations, corporations, and individuals have used noble-sounding concepts such as states' rights, lebensraum, free-market economics, and constitutional rights to mask their actions, but ultimately what they are doing is for their own personal gain and the result—intentional or not—is killing innocent men, women, and children. They participate in a diffusion of responsibility by referring to themselves as "the tobacco industry" or "the entertainment industry," and we permit it, but they are ultimately individuals making individual moral decisions to participate in the destruction of their fellow citizens.

Where did we lose this sense of propriety toward the dignity of death? How did we become so hardened? The answer to that question is that we, as a society, have become systematically desensitized to the pain and suffering of others. The ever-ascending tide of violence in our society must be stopped. Each act of violence breeds ever-greater levels of violence. The study of killing in combat teaches us that soldiers who have had friends or relatives injured or killed in combat are much more likely to kill and commit war crimes. Each individual who is injured or killed by criminal violence becomes a focal point for further violence on the part of their friends and family. Every destructive act gnaws away at the restraint of other men. Each act of violence eats away at the fabric of our society like a cancer, spreading and reproducing itself in ever-expanding cycles of horror and destruction. The genie of violence cannot really ever be stuffed back into the bottle. It can only be cut off here and now, and then the slow process of healing and resensitization can begin.

Notes

1. The great majority of close-combat killing in ancient history was not done by the mobs or serfs and peasants who formed the great mass of combatants. It was the elite, the nobility, who were the real killers in these battles, usually in the pursuit phase after the battle, on horseback or from chariots, and they were enabled by, among other things, social distance. Factors such as cultural distance, moral distance, social distance, and mechanical distance are just as effective as physical distance in permitting the killer to deny that he is killing a human being. Social distance considers the impact of a lifetime of practice in thinking of a particular class as less than human in a socially stratified environment. In nearly all historical battles prior to the age of Napoleon, the serf who looked down his spear or musket at the enemy saw another hapless serf very much like himself, and we can understand that he was not particularly inclined to kill his mirror image.

2. I too have graduated from many a U.S. Army leadership school, including basic training, advanced individual training, the XVIII Airborne Corps NCO Academy, Officer Candidate School, the Infantry Officer Basic Course, Ranger School, the Infantry Officer Advanced Course, the Combined Arms and Services Staff School, the Command and General Staff College at Fort Leavenworth, and the British Army Staff College. Not at any time in any of these schools do I remember this problem being mentioned.

3. Like most personality disorders, this one is a continuum that contains many individuals who, while they would not meet the full diagnostic criteria, are on the borderline of antisocial personality disorder. The DSM tells us that some individuals "who have several features of the disorder [but not enough to be diagnosed with it] achieve political and economic success," and some successful combatants also fit into this category.

4. But the situation is more complex. Correlation does not prove causation. To *prove* that TV causes violence you must conduct a controlled, double-blind experiment in which, if you are successful, you will *cause* people to commit murder. Clearly to perform such an experiment with human beings is unethical and largely impossible. This same situation is the foundation for the tobacco industry's continued argument that no one has ever "proven" that cigarettes "cause" cancer. There comes a point when, in spite of this type of reasoning, we must accept that cigarettes

do cause cancer. Similarly, there comes a point at which we must accept the verdict of 217 correlation studies.

References

American Psychiatric Association (2013). *Diagnostic and Statistical Manual of Mental Disorders: Fifth Edition* (DSM-5). Arlington, VA: American Psychiatric Association.

American Psychological Association (1993). Report of the American Psychological Association Commission on Violence and Youth, Vol. I. http://www.apa.org/pi/prevent-violence/resources/violence-youth.pdf [last accessed 8.8.16].

Ardant du Picq, C. (1946). *Battle Studies*. Harrisburg, PA: Telegraph Press.

Glenn, R. W. (1989). Men and fire in Vietnam. *Army: Journal of the Association of the United States*: 18–27.

Griffith, P. (1989). *Battle Tactics of the Civil War*. New Haven, CT: Yale University Press.

Grossman, D. (1995). *On Killing: The Psychological Cost of Learning to Kill in War and Society*. New York: Back Bay, 2009.

Grossman, D. (2008). *On Combat: The Psychology and Physiology of Deadly Conflict in War and in Peace*. Mascoutah, IL: Warrior Science Publications.

Grossman, D., & DeGaetano, G. (2014). *Stop Teaching Our Kids to Kill: A Call to Action Against TV, Movie, and Video Game Violence*. New York: Harmony.

Holmes, R. (1985). *Acts of War: The Behavior of Men in Battle*. New York: Free Press.

Lorenz, K. (1963). *On Aggression*. New York: Bantam.

Marin, P. (1981). Living in moral pain. *Psychology Today*, 6(11): 68–80.

Marshall, S. L. A. (1978). *Men Against Fire*. Gloucester, MA: Peter Smith.

Swank, R. L., & Marchand, W. E. (1946). Combat neurosis: development of combat exhaustion. *Archives of Neurology and Psychology*, 55: 236–247.

Vagts, A. (1959). *A History of Militarism: Civilian and Military*. New York: Meridian.

Watson, P. (1978). *War on the Mind: The Military Uses and Abuses of Psychology*. New York: Basic Books.

CHAPTER EIGHT

A tangled web: internet pornography, sexual addiction, and the erosion of attachment*

John Beveridge

> *Children today have everything but they are lost, like tiny boats at sea.*
> —Mongolian farmer, BBC World Service, 2014

Introduction

Today and every day, there are apparently sixty-eight million search engine requests for pornography and over four million websites, which are all part of a huge industry whose profits have outstripped those of Hollywood and the music industry. In these troubled times, the three escapist industries that seem to be recession-proof are communications technology, computer games, and pornography. The publishers of porn have never needed sales strategies or planning meetings, and neither do they have to advertise or market pornography; it just sells. There were sexually explicit paintings on the walls of houses of Pompeii because people, mainly men, have always used graphic images of bodies and

---

*This is an edited version of John Beveridge's chapter "A Tangled Web" in *Love in the Age of the Internet: Attachment in the Digital Era*, edited by Linda Cundy (Karnac, 2014).

people having sex as a stimulus to masturbation. The sale of erotic and pornographic images has spread and prospered as delivery systems and technology have become more sophisticated. After the invention of the printing press, followed by photography, film, then video and DVD, there came computers.

Men might not have to address their usage of pornography, or recognise that it is problematic, until they try to stop and find they cannot. Riemersma and Sytsma define sex addiction as "a disorder characterised by compulsive sexual behaviour that results in tolerance, escalation, withdrawal, and a loss of volitional control, despite negative consequences" (2013, p. 308). Addiction to pornography thrives in the consumer's compulsive need for novelty, and, because it is more exciting than satisfying, images quickly become threadbare in their power to arouse and stimulate. In order to constantly increase excitement, the content has to become more extreme.

A pornographic sensibility has permeated films, billboards, fashion, television, magazine adverts, and music videos, affecting how people have sex with themselves, how men and women see each other, and how we relate—and it is affecting young people growing up. Many young people, either with a degree and saddled with debt or without, have been unable to find entry level jobs as a whole generation has been consigned to the scrapheap by a society that does not appear to care. It might not seem to matter if they lose interest in the ordinary pleasures of life; the pursuit of work, study, and the joys of sport might all just seem dull, boring, and unrewarding if they have been prematurely turned on to sex. What effect does the habitual use of pornography have on young people whose characters coalesce and form around the experiences they encounter growing up? And what happens to the appetites of teenagers who can now enjoy unlimited fantasy scenarios that might have made a Roman emperor blush?

Neuroscience

Having worked for years trying to help people to recover from chemical dependence and addiction to sexual behaviours, I would often become frustrated by people who relapsed after having expressed a strong desire to change. Despite my experience and understanding of addiction, I still confused their behaviour with morality and judged them accordingly. My understanding was changed dramatically, and I was able to evoke a more empathic response, when I heard a recorded talk by Dr Kevin McCauley, who defined addiction as

> … a dysregulation of the mid-brain dopamine (pleasure) system, due to unmanaged stress, resulting in symptoms of decreased functioning, which results in loss of control, craving, and persistent drug or behavior use, despite negative consequences. (2004)

I was to learn that people's behaviour is affected by their brain chemistry, which accounts for the disparity between how people intend to act and what they might actually do in a crisis. It is helpful to understand addiction as a disease of the dopamine system, so that we can learn to stop punishing addicts because of their behaviour. Sex addiction, like addiction to gambling, is a process addiction, arising out of self-generated chemicals and hormones that behave like powerful drugs. We produce these drug-like chemicals in response to our environment, and we carry them with us everywhere we go. If a knife-wielding maniac burst into the room, our brains would respond by flooding our bodies with adrenalin to facilitate our flight or fight response. When the danger had passed, we might start to shake, which is our body's way of getting rid of the accumulation of adrenalin. Perhaps we like to think we might behave in a heroic manner, but as the captain of a sinking cruise liner recently found, we do not know how we might act until we are at mortal risk.

We produce a simple organic chemical called dopamine which functions as a neurotransmitter in the brain and rewards us by making us feel good when we engage in activities that help us survive. If we monitor newborn babies, we can see that dopamine is produced when the infant turns his head towards the breast, and the rewards for this first act of searching brings immediate mood alteration in anticipation of food or attention. The repetition of these experiences forms neural pathways, which change the brain, and we call this process learning. When we sit next to someone in a meeting or at the cinema and we notice them casually reach for a phone to check for messages or go online, then their boredom threshold has dropped and they are refreshing their dopamine levels. So, when we go searching online, either for an academic paper or houses for sale in France, it changes the way we feel and, so, too, does looking online for sexual material.

McCauley (2004) describes experiments in which drugs are administered and the subject's brain is then scanned; the mid-brain, or limbic system, is seen to respond dramatically. This part of the brain is linked directly to the basic functions that have maintained our survival as a species: the three "Fs" of "feeding, fighting, and fucking". This has been described as the "mammalian brain", which responds and reacts first to all incoming information from the environment. "Emotions are gener-ated in the limbic system, along with most of the many appetites and urges that direct us to behave in a way that (usually) helps us to sur-vive" (Carter, 2000, p. 42). Our ancestors once had to learn where to get food and sex and, if anyone obstructed their intention, they would fight them because their lives depended upon these things for survival. In addiction, our appetites have this life-or-death quality to them.

When a person watches pornography, he or she builds sexual excite-ment, raising and maintaining tension by producing dopamine, and when orgasm is reached, endorphins are released bringing relaxation and relief, so that a self-contained method of mood alteration has been learnt. In effect, this is an addiction to our body's self-generated opioids. When levels decrease post orgasm, endorphins are replaced by anxiety inducing stress hormones that "activate the urge-making areas of the brain" (Carter, 2000, p. 105), thus perpetuating the addictive cycle. According to Lewis:

> "[W]anting" and "liking" are distinct psychological states under-pinned by distinct neural processes. It's the opioids that cause liking—the sensation of pleasure or wellbeing. And it's the dopamine that produces wanting—the feeling of desire or attraction. (2011, p. 134)

James Olds conducted experiments in the 1950s where rats were trained to press levers to obtain a rewarding hit of drugs. They became habitu-ated to repeating these actions to feel the effects of the drug despite harmful consequences, such as foregoing food or having to run across heated plates to reach the lever. Someone who masturbates habitu-ally might know cognitively that they are not having "real sex", but their bodies are fooled into releasing those same exciting chemicals. There is YouTube footage of a tortoise with a faraway look in its eyes, rhythmically humping a training shoe, oblivious to the fact that it is not another member of its species.

Dopamine raises the pleasure threshold, the "hedonic level" of the brain, which operates like a thermostat, and then the ordinary pleasures in life do not mean as much as they once did.

When people take drugs or get high from sexual excitement, or both together, the mutation from habit to compulsion and addiction requires a helping hand, such as opportunity and availability, and what is better suited than the internet? A patient told me that there is always the feeling that there is something elusive and more stimulating just around the corner. Some men I have worked with have found themselves, when looking at porn, falling into a trance-like state, searching for hours on end and sometimes escalating to extreme, perverse, or illegal genres, amplifying porn's hyper-stimulating effects by forcing the release of a never-ending stream of dopamine spikes.

There is something inherently different about looking at images on the printed page, compared to spending hours looking at seemingly infinite exciting images on an illuminated screen in a state of adrenalised sexual arousal. Describing the plasticity of the brain, Doidge (2007) writes,

> The men at their computers looking at porn … had been seduced into training sessions that meet all the conditions required for plastic change of brain maps. Since neurons that fire together wire together, these men got massive amounts of practice wiring these images into the pleasure centres of the brain, with the rapt attention necessary for plastic change. (p. 108)

Internet porn is free, easy to access, available within seconds, twenty-four hours a day and seven days a week. For the susceptible person, the effect of compulsively using internet pornography has been compared to those that crack cocaine has on the nervous system of cocaine users, causing an acceleration of addiction (Mary Ann Leyden, US Senate testimony, October 18, 2004). Some people have always been prone to addiction, because they have responded to early experiences of stress by becoming able to dissociate, which is a process of unconsciously splitting off parts of the mind. As well as protecting them from pain, this can lead people to defensively detach from the natural need for attachments that organise and stabilise our emotional experience across the human lifespan.

Addiction: craving, self-soothing, splitting, and shame

Our sense of self and our personality, our belief systems and the values that inform our behavioural intentions, are all located in the frontal cortex. This is the most advanced structure in the brain and it is shaped by early experiences with our attachment figures; it embodies the superego and fosters the ability to contain, rather than act on, our primitive impulses. However, when someone feels threatened, or during addictive and drug-like experiences, this part of the brain can go "offline". People with no understanding of the addictive process might say, "Well, we all get stressed but we don't become addicts, they are just weak and have no willpower!" Yet, some people in extremis will take drugs or engage in compulsive behaviours because, when they feel threatened, there are certain genes that affect our impulse to seek novelty and risk. People are then prone to becoming addicted because their habitual physical and emotional reaction to stress has now become craving. According to Carnes, Carnes, and Bailey,

> During a craving, the area of the brain that creates drives is activated, while the areas that restrain these urges are deactivated. The result is a person who can't defend against the craving. It is essentially a high-jacking [sic] of the rational part of the brain. This all happens at a subconscious level. (2011, p. 79)

I have seen addicts face extreme symptoms of distress when they cannot act out with their old, self-soothing behaviour. With the erosion of willpower, their ability to resist diminishes, because craving feels like grief and grief is separation anxiety. Anyone who has experienced bereavement might recognise the spiky, volatile, angry, agitated, and restless longing that platitudes cannot put right. To say to an addicted person "Just say no" is missing the point. McCauley (2004) points out that addicts' survival imperative, operating out of the mid-brain, kicks in, urging, "Get me something NOW to get me through the next ten minutes—We'll worry about all that 'life' stuff, like work, family, and children, tomorrow!" When faced with any threat, addicts will feel at mortal risk because "The pleasure producing cycle is now unconsciously and inextricably linked with the mid-brain, the survival mechanism part of the brain, so that survival has become the drug" (McCauley, 2004).

I have worked with many sex-addicted clients committed to religious beliefs, who see themselves as weak and sinful when they succumb, once again, to acting-out behaviour after making firm pledges to stop. This sense of being split that people have experienced as a result of historical religious attitudes to sexuality reflects the struggle between intentions and actions operating out of different parts of the brain. Ulman and Paul say that the addict, unconsciously:

> … induces a self hypnotic trance (i.e., the hypnoid defense) within him or herself that flips unconscious subjective experience from one characterized by an excruciatingly painful mood of narcissistic mortification (reflective of being out of and having lost control) to one characterized by a mood of narcissistic bliss (indicative of a temporary and fleeting feeling of rapture). (2006, p. 118)

With minds obsessed and preoccupied by continuous fantasies of body parts and part-objects, there is a growing sense of separation, increasing fear, and paranoia, activated by those primitive anxieties that the acting out was supposed to keep at bay. Dissociated from their attachments, values, beliefs, morals, and spirituality, a sense of disintegration is common among sex addicts. Self-punishing thoughts lead to shame, and the need to alleviate that shame creates more cycles of acting out, causing damage in the relational field by eroding people's ability to respect themselves, to love and make love, to be intimate, vulnerable, attached, and to be good partners and parents. The first half of the title of this chapter, "A tangled web", is from an oft-remembered family trope: "O what a tangled web we weave, when first we practise to deceive."

Therapy

Many men in their twenties present for therapy after they have entered a real relationship and, wanting to commit sexually to a partner, they realise that their online behaviour cannot be as easily relinquished as they had hoped. Sometimes, in order to be apprehended, addicts might create a crisis by forgetting to erase their online history, thereby unconsciously setting themselves up for the discovery of shocking or illegal images on computers or mobile phones by partners or employers, so that they have to stop. I worked with a woman who found a prostitute's telephone number on her partner's phone, which he had let her borrow, two weeks before their wedding. This can lead to a recovery that is often described as "spouse led". We need to understand that, despite the revulsion that their behaviour might cause us to feel, addiction to the sex chemicals in the body and the behaviours that stimulate and protect them, are as serious and as difficult to treat as heroin addiction, even among clients who are highly motivated to change. Also, unlike heroin, accessing online pornography is less risky and generally free of charge.

Shaming or punishing people who are addicted has never effected a cure, as the prison population, who are, more often than not, alcoholic or chemically dependent, would testify. I once found myself feeling angry and taking it personally when a man informed me that he had relapsed after I thought the therapy was going well. I heard myself saying, "Well, maybe you are just one of those people who never get recovery." I later felt the need to apologise and tell the client about the angry feelings I had experienced at his lapse, and I pointed out the countertransferential dynamic where, like his father and numerous previous employers in his past, I had been set up to be just another authority figure who had rejected him. That was a turning point in this man's recovery, helping him recognise the unconscious payoff he had in his core belief of feeling himself to be unacceptable. Therapists who have not yet taken the time to become informed about the drivers of sexual compulsivity and its treatment can sometimes be dismissive of sexual addiction; an ex-therapist of one of my present clients told her, "Not to worry, all artistic people have high sex drives," when she was full of shame about her sexual behaviour.

Whenever I work with people who identify as being addicted to sex or pornography, who are seeing themselves through the lens of self-hatred, I explain that their compulsive behaviour is an attempt at self-soothing to help them cope with the stress of their life's struggles. I also add that when they appear to be most out of control in their addictive behaviour, they are, emotionally, at their most defended. They immediately ask, "So what do I do to stop doing this?" This response is understandable among people who have always been able to *do* something, or reach for something that they thought could help, often unaware of what they might be avoiding or defending against. Of course, what they have traditionally done in order to cope eventually becomes the presenting problem, the compulsive behaviour, which can sometimes lead a therapist to collude in a moralistic drama of preoccupation with the addicts' behaviour rather than with their hidden emotions or distress.

When we ask about the sex lives of our clients, we also need to ask if they regularly use pornography, and what effect that use might have had on their desire, their relationships, and their attitudes to sexual partners. Despite our fear of appearing prurient, it might also help to know what sexual fantasies actually arouse them; what many people think about when they are having sex might not be what they are actually doing. Having explored the sexual fantasies of over 19,000 adults, Brett Kahr recapitulated Stoller's theory; if we examine our clients' most secret thoughts and the fantasies they use to trigger orgasm, it will often reveal the story of their lives: "Thus, our sexual fantasies protect us and shield us from something potentially dreadful. Yet in doing so, these fantasies reinforce our wish to masturbate, and hence avoid exploration of what lurks beneath" (2007, p. 291).

Our clients' scenarios of acting out sexually—which they might never have told anyone—can often reveal hidden trauma, which they bring under their omnipotent control at the point of orgasm, turning trauma into triumph. According to Stoller,

> Since his infantile traumatic experiences live forever inside him however, his triumphs last only a short while and must be endlessly repeated. Where a sense of despair and inferiority rides too close to the surface, it must be repeated rapidly and endlessly. (1975, p. 126)

As psychodynamic therapists, it is important to recognise the connections between sexual addiction and fantasy, masturbation, perversion, and dissociation, which many practitioners, including myself, encountering sexually compulsive clients had half intuited, but not thought through in terms of brain chemistry and neuroplasticity.

Mark, a gay patient, found that he had become addicted to watching abusive, heterosexual porn, finding himself most excited by images of men taking aggressive sexual pleasure, without thought or consideration for their female partners. He felt shame that his behaviour went against the conscious, liberal values he held about women, but this guilt only seemed to add to his erotic charge, making this secret material difficult to discuss. "Political correctness", of which the unconscious has no conception, is perhaps the last arena in which we can feel truly sinful. In therapy, we were able to associate his intense arousal to his early memories when, as an infant, he was placed in his parents' bed. He now believed this was to forestall marital rape, which he imagined to have happened on the nights when his father has been out drinking. He had been caught in the intense sexual force field between his father's desire to penetrate and the mother's determination to resist. He became conscious of the angry feelings about the use that had been made of him by his mother, and his own need of the secondary gains that he had enjoyed in his relationship with her, where he felt special and chosen over his father. In time, his enjoyment of seeing the besting of the women in pornography became less intense and no longer necessary.

Treatment

As with any addictive or compulsive behaviour, if we want to support someone who wishes to stop using, we need to ask the question, "What happens when they try to give up their problematic behaviour?" I usually find that when addicted people aim for a period of abstinence from all sexual activity, so that we can begin to understand the emotional needs that might have been sexualised, they very quickly go into a physical withdrawal, just like a drug user. They can sometimes experience intense bodily reactions, such as headaches and flu-like symptoms. Often, they are also exposed to deep and debilitating feelings, indicating the strength of the emotions they might have been trying to evade, perhaps for a lifetime. Even renunciation brings grief, and, since grief is connected to loss, the questions here are, "What has been lost, and when?" As it was for Mark, so it is for others: the sense of bringing unconscious primal scene anxieties under one's own omnipotent control through watching porn is illusory.

When, in therapy, we relinquish the illusions that have given us a sense of power, we are losing something dear to us. The feeling states of bereavement, including denial, bargaining, anger, despair, and depression, which might have been unconsciously entrenched but unexpressed for years, can now be recognised. When "solutions" such as addiction and avoidant or disorganised attachment behaviour no longer keep out awareness of early abandonment, sexual abuse, or emotional neglect, these tragedies might then have to be mourned.

New information gained from neuroscience can help us understand the strength and tenacity of the dependence upon sexual acting out, but it does not give people an excuse or a "green card" to behave as they wish by saying, "I can't help it—it's the dopamine!" For addicted clients, I strongly recommend attendance at, and support from, one of Britain's fastest growing, twelve-step sex addiction recovery groups, Sex and Love Addicts Anonymous (SLAA, www.slaa.uk.org), whose membership, surprisingly, comprises almost equal numbers of women and men. They offer a structured treatment programme which helps addicts learn, with peer support, how to go through difficulties without acting out, and helps them take responsibility in their relationships by making reparation for the pain that their actions, or avoidance of action, has caused. This can be helpful for people coming out of hiding and shame. The mind can be altered for the better with the acquisition of alternative coping mechanisms, so that the building of self-respect can become a new and powerful motivational reward system. They can then move on to find or rebuild healthy relationships, where sexuality is brought into balance and where they can operate as reliable attachment figures to their partners and children.

Once sexual sobriety is established, deeper psychodynamic work can be done in psychotherapy to reveal and release the trauma that has remained locked within sexual fantasies, allowing people to grieve and mourn the losses that addiction has left in its wake. Support from groups involving "mindfulness" practice can break the tyranny of isolation and fantasy. All addictions are really addictions to what the fantasy of acting out always promises, but seldom delivers. "In the midst of such an illusory spell, which cannot be so easily broken, an addict exists as a figment of his or her own imagination" (Ulman & Paul, 2006, p. 315).

Mindfulness practice can help people learn how to observe their own thought processes and to determine whether the thought or the feeling comes first. They can begin, in times of stress, to operate from their observing ego, engaging the frontal cortex. People can practise thinking, "I am not someone who is going to die if I don't do something immediately to take away my pain." They can begin to see that "I am just someone having a feeling or thought that I am going to die if I don't do something immediately!" In treating sexual compulsion, I look for, and expect to find, early experiences of overt or covert sexual or emotional abuse and disorganised or avoidant attachment histories. Because of previous dysfunctional relationships where rage has been eroticised, it can take time to lower the hedonic threshold and live an ordinary life, bringing emotions within the window of tolerance. Developing a non-compulsive sexuality may lack the drama and intensity of hyper-stimulation and continuous over-arousal.

In the past twenty years, there has been a recognition that many recovering chemical addicts, successful in living sober lives, found that their compulsion had moved from alcohol or drugs to other self-defeating behaviours, such as overeating and anorexia, or, very often, sex addiction. There has been a growing awareness of, and more research into, this condition, coming out of the "recovery movement", with certified training for therapists becoming available in the past ten years from organisations such as the International Institute for Trauma and Addiction Professionals (IITAP) in Europe and the USA, and the Association for the Treatment of Sex Addiction and Compulsivity (ATSAC) in the UK.

There is clearly much more work to be done. With many pre-teen children regularly accessing sexual material on the internet, it has been said that there is a tidal wave of addiction heading towards the therapeutic world. Riemersma and Sytsma (2013) make an important distinction between the "classic" addict, most often met in the past in adult males, and what we might be recognising today as a new manifestation that they describe as a "contemporary" form of sex addiction, "rapid in its onset", which is "disrupting normal neurochemical, sexual and social development in youth" (p. 307). They alert us to the delayed therapeutic response of the professional community and the paucity of research in this area, saying that

> ... effectual therapy with this population will likely require child and adolescent developmental expertise due to the increasing numbers of young people who are predicted to be impacted by "contemporary" sexual addiction. Alternatives to adult-oriented talk therapy and 12 step groups for example, will be needed. Informed consent and parental release will be important legal issues in this population. (p. 316)

The vulnerability to predation that the condition of sexual compulsion already creates in teenagers might also make attendance at adult groups or adult treatment centres problematical. We will have to develop new forms of treatment and therapeutic responses to this condition.

Young people and online addictions: cumulative trauma

Young people presenting in therapy for sexual compulsion today might not have suffered early relational trauma or come from sexually abusive homes like the "classic" sex addict; their addiction to pornography may have had an opportunistic element. They seem to have become addicted simply because it was there. The effects of being continuously excited by extreme and shocking material, repeatedly opiated after orgasm, together with the isolation that pornography encourages, may, over time, have become traumatic experiences in themselves to brains that are still developing.

It might also be worth considering that some symptoms, such as attention deficit hyperactivity disorder, depression, obsessive-compulsive and mood disorders, lack of sexual desire, and social anxiety in young people, might be the effects of habitual pornography use. Riemersma and Sytsma write,

> It is suggested that these are typically the result of modern sexual addiction (rather than the driving force as may be the case with the "classic" addict), given that compulsive, virtual sexuality drives impairment in the very human, interpersonal and sexual connections that are protective against mood disorders and addictions. (2013, p. 315)

Then there are the physical effects of online compulsivity and screen addiction: the brains and the minds of children and adolescents are more plastic and, therefore, more vulnerable to being overwhelmed by overstimulation and stress. Laurance (2012) described a study on the brain-altering effects of internet addiction on seventeen game-addicted adolescents in China who had been diagnosed with "internet addiction disorder". Their brains were scanned and compared with those of their peers, and "… the results showed impairments of the white matter fibres in the brain connecting regions involved in emotional processing, attention, decision-making and cognitive control".

Screen compulsivity may also be the result of a particular kind of neglect. Today and every day, we can see evidence everywhere of people around thirty, "digital natives", bringing up children to whom screens are given as toys to keep them quiet. One wonders if parents are fully aware of their children's online behaviour and whether, as attachment figures, they have tried hard enough to protect them from the dangers to be found in cyberspace. It is hard to quantify the effect of care and attention that is missing.

Conclusion

Whenever anyone writes a book about sex addiction, it is usually the first third, the exciting part revealing the shenanigans and the crazy things that addicts do, that is often read avidly. The last third, which talks about healthy sexuality and the building of relationships, the difficult bit, often goes unread. Healthy relationships—with other people and with ourselves—are not marked by intense highs and lows, but by a sustained and sustaining reliable commitment to making them work, which is neither glamorous nor exciting.

Psychoanalysis in Freud's time of infant mortality and short life expectancy, when most people were acquainted with sorrow and grief, was focused on working towards the removal of sexual repression that was being converted into hysteria and other symptoms. Since then, all that freedom of sexual expression does not appear to have made us happier. Today, due to the commodification of everything from sex to debt, and the unwillingness or inability to cope with grief or stress, the diseases of our time that we meet in our psychotherapy rooms and treatment centres seem to be narcissism and addiction. It is not just addicts; we increasingly live in a world that has forgotten how to suffer. As a culture, we do not know how to wait, how to work through pain, and few people seem to understand the concept of loss any more, evidenced by the ubiquity of advertisements for "no win-no fee" injury compensation lawyers. We want compensation, and we want it now! The term "retail therapy" is established in the culture where shopping, buying online, and consuming are regarded as recreational activities, recognised as ways to reduce any unwanted feelings of stress, boredom, or discomfort.

According to James (2012), the portrayal of the male sex addict in the film *Shame* can tell us a lot about the way we are living now:

> [T]he rest of us Westerners consumed as if there is no tomorrow—and now, there is no tomorrow. Name your poison—the one that caught you up in the consumer boom. Gadgets? Heels? Guitars? Cocaine? A huge DVD collection? (p. 34)

Even in the most recent recession, although we had maxed out the credit cards, we were still being encouraged to consume our way out of trouble. Indulgence is condoned and endorsed in a "live now and don't pay later" culture, where we take what we want, without struggle or challenge, "because we're worth it!" This ethos goes right to the top of governments who will financially enslave, exploit, or invade other countries so that they can supply us with what we perceive to be our due.

In just a few years, a virtual, push button, so-called interactive way of communicating has become the norm. It has made enormous inroads into our collective behaviours and it is not going away. Young people can spend the equivalent of a working week in front of screens, affecting how they relate to themselves and others because they are often having contact, but not relationship with real people.

This might all seem rather bleak but there is hope for addicts, both "classic" and "contemporary", who feel trapped in secrecy and shame around their sex addiction. The information available to us from the field of neuroscience shows that brains can be rewired when people learn to care for themselves and others. We are born seeking proximity with other human beings and we need to engage in working through the friction and challenges of building real, productive relationships by learning how to manage and transcend conflict, and this can reinforce our sense of self-worth. In SLAA, they say that "Love is a committed, thoughtful decision, not a feeling by which we are overwhelmed." People can recover from addiction and can practise, over time, how to be present with their own discomfort and the wounded parts of themselves by learning how to wait, how to grieve, and how to mourn. But they need relationship with real others to help them with recovery.

Inviting people to suffer is never going to be an easy sell. Is there an App for that?

References

BBC World Service (2014). *From Our Own Correspondent*. www.bbc.co.uk. Broadcast 7 February.

Carnes, P., Carnes, S., & Bailey, J. (2011). *Facing Addiction: Starting Recovery from Alcohol and Drugs*. Carefree, AZ: Gentle Path Press.

Carter, R. (2000). *Mapping the Mind*. London: Phoenix.

Cundy, L. (Ed.) (2014). *Love in the Age of the Internet: Attachment in the Digital Era*. London: Karnac.

Doidge, N. (2007). *The Brain that Changes Itself: Stories of Personal Triumph from the Frontiers of Brain Science*. London: Penguin.

James, N. (2012). Sex and the City. *Sight and Sound Magazine, 22*(2): 34–38.

Kahr, B. (2007). *Sex and the Psyche: the Truth about Our Most Secret Fantasies*. London: Penguin.

Laurance, J. (2012). Addicted! Scientists show how Internet dependency alters the human brain. *The Independent*, 12 January 2012. www.independent.co.uk/news. Accessed 4 February 2012.

Lewis, M. (2011). *Memoirs of an Addicted Brain: A Neuroscientist Examines His Former Life on Drugs*. New York: Public Affairs.

McCauley, K. T. (2004). *The Disease Model of Addiction: Families, Friends & Employers*. Part I. CD available from: www.instituteforaddiction study. com. Accessed 12 December 2013.

Riemersma, J., & Sytsma, M. (2013). A new generation of sexual addiction. *Sexual Addiction and Compulsivity: The Journal of Treatment and Prevention, 20*(4): 306–322.

Shame (2011). Film4/See-Saw Films, UK.

Stoller, R. J. (1975). *Perversion: The Erotic Form of Hatred*. London: Karnac.

Ulman, R. B., & Paul, H. (2006). *The Self-Psychology of Addiction and Its Treatment: Narcissus in Wonderland*. New York: Routledge.

CHAPTER NINE

The corporation as a pathological institution*

Joel Bakan

Introduction

Over the last 150 years the corporation has risen from relative obscurity to become the world's dominant economic institution. Today, corporations govern our lives. They determine what we eat, what we watch, what we wear, where we work, and what we do. We are inescapably surrounded by their culture, iconography, and ideology. And, like the Church and monarchy in other times, they posture as infallible and omnipotent, glorifying themselves in imposing buildings and elaborate displays. Increasingly, corporations dictate the decisions of their supposed overseers in government and control domains of society once firmly embedded within the public sphere.

The corporation's legally defined mandate is to pursue, relentlessly and without exception, its own self-interest, regardless of the often harmful consequences it might cause to others. As a result, I argue, the

*Reprinted with the permission of Penguin Canada, a division of Random House Canada Limited, and Free Press, a division of Simon & Schuster, Inc., from *The Corporation: The Pathological Pursuit of Profit and Power* by Joel Bakan. Copyright © 2004 by Joel Bakan. All rights reserved.

173

corporation is a pathological institution, a dangerous possessor of the great power it wields over people and societies. That raises a number of questions: How did the corporation become what it is today? What is the nature, and what are the implications, of its pathological character and of its power over society? And what should and can be done to mitigate its potential to cause harm? By revealing the institutional imperatives common to all corporations and their implications for society, I hope to provide a crucial and missing link in people's attempts to understand and do something about some of the most pressing issues of our time.

The corporation's dramatic rise to dominance is one of the remarkable events of modern history, not least because of the institution's inauspicious beginnings.[1] By the early years of the twentieth century, however, large publicly traded corporations had become fixtures on the economic landscape. Over two short decades, beginning in the 1890s, the corporation underwent a revolutionary transformation. It all started when New Jersey and Delaware ("the first state to be known as the home of corporations," according to its current secretary of state for corporations[2]), sought to attract valuable incorporation business to their jurisdictions by jettisoning unpopular restrictions from their corporate laws. Among other things, they:

- Repealed the rules that required businesses to incorporate only for narrowly defined purposes, to exist only for limited durations, and to operate only in particular locations
- Substantially loosened controls on mergers and acquisitions; and
- Abolished the rule that one company could not own stock in another.

Other states, not wanting to lose out in the competition for incorporation business, soon followed with similar revisions to their laws. The changes prompted a flurry of incorporations as businesses sought the new freedoms and powers incorporation would grant them.

Soon, however, with most meaningful constraints on mergers and acquisitions gone, a large number of small and medium-size corporations were quickly absorbed into a small number of very large ones— 1,800 corporations were consolidated into 157 between 1898 and 1904 (Marchand, 1998, p. 7). In less than a decade the U.S. economy had been transformed from one in which individually owned enterprises competed freely among themselves into one dominated by relatively few huge corporations, each owned by many shareholders. The era of corporate capitalism had begun.

The corporation becomes "a person"

By the early twentieth century, corporations were typically combinations of thousands, even hundreds of thousands, of broadly dispersed, anonymous shareholders. Unable to influence managerial decisions as individuals because their power was too diluted, they were also too broadly dispersed to act collectively. Their consequent loss of power in and control of large corporations turned out to be managers' gains. In 1913, a congressional committee set up to investigate the "money trust," led by Congressman Arsène Puijo, reported:

> None of the witnesses called was able to name an instance in the history of the country in which the stockholders had succeeded in overthrowing an existing management in any large corporation, nor does it appear that stockholders have ever even succeeded in so far as to secure the investigation of an existing management of a corporation to ascertain whether it has been well or honestly managed … [I]n all great corporations with numerous and widely scattered stockholders … the management is virtually self-perpetuating and is able through the power of patronage, the indifference of stockholders and other influences to control a majority of stock. (cited in Herman, 1981, p. 7)

Shareholders had, for all practical purposes, disappeared from the corporations they owned. With shareholders, real people, effectively gone from corporations, the law had to find someone else, some other person, to assume the legal rights and duties firms needed to operate in the economy. That "person" turned out to be the corporation itself.

As early as 1793, one corporate scholar outlined the logic of corporate personhood when he defined the corporation as "a collection of many individuals united into one body, under a special denomination, having perpetual succession under an artificial form, and vested, by the policy of law, with the capacity of acting, in several respects, as an individual, particularly of taking and granting property, of contracting obligations, and of suing and being sued, of enjoying privileges and immunities in common" (cited in Ireland, 1996, pp. 45–46). In partnerships, another

scholar noted in 1825, "The law looks to the individuals"; in corporations, on the other hand, "… it sees only the creature of the charter, the
body corporate, and knows not the individuals" (ibid., p. 45).

By the end of the nineteenth century, through a bizarre legal alchemy,
courts had fully transformed the corporation into a "person," with
its own identity, separate from the flesh-and-blood people who were
its owners and managers and empowered, like a real person, to conduct business in its own name, acquire assets, employ workers, pay
taxes, and go to court to assert its rights and defend its actions. The
corporate person had taken the place, at least in law, of the real people
who owned corporations. Now viewed as an entity, "not imaginary
or fictitious, but real, not artificial but natural," as it was described by
one law professor in 1911, the corporation had been reconceived as a
free and independent being (cited in Horwitz, 1987, p. 51). Gone was
the centuries-old "grant theory," which had conceived of corporations
as instruments of government policy and as dependent upon government bodies to create them and enable them to function. Along with
grant theory had also gone all rationales for encumbering corporations
with burdensome restrictions. The logic was that, conceived as natural
entities analogous to human beings, corporations should be created
as free individuals, a logic that informed the initiatives in New Jersey
and Delaware, as well as the Supreme Court's decision in 1886 that,
because they were "persons," corporations should be protected by the
Fourteenth Amendment's right to "due process and law" and "equal
protection of the laws," rights originally entrenched in the Constitution
to protect freed slaves.[3]

As the corporation's size and power grew, so did the need to
assuage people's fears of it. The corporation suffered its first full-blown
legitimacy crisis in the wake of the early twentieth-century merger
movement, when, for the first time, many Americans realized that corporations, now huge behemoths, threatened to overwhelm their social
institutions and governments. Corporations were widely viewed as
soulless leviathans—uncaring, impersonal, and amoral. Suddenly, they
were vulnerable to popular discontent and organized dissent (especially from a growing labor movement), as calls for more government
regulation and even their dismantling were increasingly common.
Business leaders and public relations experts soon realized that the
institution's new powers and privileges demanded new public relations strategies.

In 1908, AT&T, one of America's largest corporations at the time and the parent company of the Bell System, which had a monopoly on telephone services in the United States, launched an advertising campaign, the first of its kind, that aimed to persuade a skeptical public to like and accept the company. In much the same way that law had transformed the corporation into a "person" to compensate for the disappearance of the real people within it, AT&T's campaign imbued the company with human values in an effort to overcome people's suspicion of it as a soulless and inhuman entity. "Bigness," worried one vice president at AT&T, tended to squeeze out of the corporation "the human understanding, the human sympathy, the human contacts, and the natural human relationships." It had convinced "the general public [that] a corporation is a thing." Another AT&T official believed it was necessary "to make the people understand and love the company. Not merely to be consciously dependent upon it—not merely regard it as a necessity— not merely to take it for granted—but to love it—to hold real affection for it." From 1908 into the late 1930s, AT&T trumpeted itself as a "friend and neighbor" and sought to give itself a human face by featuring real people from the company in its advertising campaigns. Employees, particularly telephone operators and linemen, appeared regularly in the company's advertisements, as did shareholders. One magazine advertisement entitled "Our Shareholders" depicts a woman, presumably a widow, examining her AT&T certificates as her two young children look on; another pronounces AT&T "a new democracy of public service ownership" that is "owned directly by the people—controlled not by one, but controlled by all" (Marchand, 1998, pp. 8, 4, 76).

Other major corporations soon followed AT&T's lead. General Motors, for example, ran advertisements that, in the words of the agency responsible for them, aimed "to personalize the institution by calling it a *family*." "The word 'corporation' is cold, impersonal and subject to misunderstanding and distrust," noted Alfred Swayne, the GM executive in charge of institutional advertising at the time, but "'Family' is personal, human, friendly. This is our picture of General Motors—a big congenial household" (ibid., p. 139).

By the end of World War I, some of America's leading corporations, among them General Electric, Eastman Kodak, National Cash Register, Standard Oil, U. S. Rubber, and the Goodyear Tire & Rubber Company, were busily crafting images of themselves as benevolent and socially responsible. "New Capitalism," the term used to describe the trend, softened corporations' images with promises of good corporate citizenship and practices of better wages and working conditions. As citizens demanded that governments rein in corporate power and while labor militancy was rife, with returning World War I veterans, having risked their lives as soldiers, insisting upon better treatment as workers, proponents of the New Capitalism sought to demonstrate that corporations could be good without the coercive push of governments and unions (McQuaid, 1977, p. 323).

A leader of the movement, Paul W. Litchfield, who presided over Goodyear Tire for thirty-two years through the middle part of the twentieth century, believed capitalism would not survive unless equality and cooperation between workers and capitalists replaced division and conflict. Though branded a socialist and a Marxist by some of his business peers at the time, Litchfield forged ahead with programs designed to promote the health, welfare, and education of his workers and their families, and to give his workers a greater voice in company affairs. One of his proudest achievements was a workers' Senate and House of Representatives, modeled on the national one, that had jurisdiction over employment issues, including wages. Litchfield defended his benevolent policies as necessary for Goodyear's success. "Goodyear has all about her the human quality," he said, "and it has been to this human quality fully as much as to her business models, that Goodyear owes her meteoric rise in the ranks of American Industry" (Rodengen, 1997).

Corporate social responsibility blossomed again during the 1930s as corporations suffered from adverse public opinion. Many people believed at the time that corporate greed and mismanagement had caused the Great Depression. They shared Justice Louis Brandeis's view, stated in a 1933 Supreme Court judgment, that corporations were "Frankenstein monsters" capable of doing evil.[4] In response, business leaders embraced corporate social responsibility. It was the best strategy, they believed, to restore people's faith in corporations and reverse their growing fascination with big government. Gerard Swope, then president of General Electric, voiced a popular sentiment among big-business leaders when, in 1934, he said that "Organized industry should take the lead, recognizing its responsibility to its employees, to the public, and to its shareholders *rather than that democratic society should act through its government*" (Swope, 1931, p. 22; italics added).[5]

Adolf Berle and Gardiner Means had endorsed a similar idea two years earlier in their classic work *The Modern Corporation and Private Property*. The corporation, they argued, was "potentially (if not yet actually) the dominant institution of the modern world"; its managers had becomes "princes of industry," their companies akin to feudal fiefdoms. Because they had amassed such power over society, corporations and the men who managed them were now obliged to serve the interests of society as a whole, much as governments were, not just those of their shareholders. "[T]he 'control' of the great corporations should develop into a purely neutral technocracy," they wrote, "balancing a variety of claims by various groups in the community and assigning to each a portion of the income stream on the basis of public policy rather than private cupidity." Corporations would likely have to embrace this new approach, Berle and Means warned, "if the corporate system [was] to survive" (1968, pp. 4, 312–313). Professor Edwin Dodd, another eminent scholar of the corporation at the time, was more skeptical about corporations becoming socially responsible, but he believed they risked losing their legitimacy, and thus their power, if they did not at least appear to do so. "Modern large-scale industry has given to the managers of our principal corporations enormous power," Dodd wrote in 1932 in the *Harvard Law Review*. "Desire to retain their present powers accordingly encourages [them] to adopt and disseminate the view that they are guardians of all the interests which the corporation affects and not merely servants of its absentee owners" (p. 1157).[6]

Despite corporate leaders' claims that they were capable of regulating themselves, in 1934 President Franklin D. Roosevelt created the New Deal, a package of regulatory reforms designed to restore economic health by, among other things, curbing the powers and freedoms of corporations. As the first systematic attempt to regulate corporations and the foundation of the modern regulatory state, the New Deal was reviled by many business leaders at the time and even prompted a small group of them to plot a coup to overthrow Roosevelt's administration. Though the plot failed, it was significant for reflecting the depth of hostility many business leaders felt for Roosevelt. The spirit of the New Deal, along with many of its regulatory regimes, nonetheless prevailed. For fifty years following its creation, through World War II, the postwar era, and the 1960s and 1970s, the growing power of corporations was offset, at least in part, by continued expression of government regulation, trade unions, and social programs. Then, much as steam engines and railways had combined with new laws and ideologies to create the corporate behemoth one hundred years earlier, a new convergence of technology, law, and ideology—economic globalization—reversed the trend toward greater regulatory control of corporations and vaulted the corporation to unprecedented power and influence.

Brand identities: the development of corporate personhood

Corporations now *govern* society, perhaps more than governments themselves do; yet ironically, it is their very power, much of which they have gained through economic globalization, that makes them vulnerable. As is true of any ruling institution, the corporation now attracts mistrust, fear, and demands for accountability from an increasingly anxious public. Today's corporate leaders understand, as did their predecessors, that work is needed to regain and maintain the public's trust. And they, like their predecessors, are seeking to soften the corporation's image by presenting it as human, benevolent, and socially responsible. "It's absolutely fundamental that a corporation today has as much of a human and personal characteristic as anything else," said public relations czar Chris Komisarjevsky, CEO of Burson-Marsteller, in an interview. "The smart corporations understand that people make comparisons in human terms ... because that's the way people think, we think in terms that are often very, very personal ... If you walked down the street with a microphone and a camera and you stopped [people] on the street ... they will describe [corporations] in very human terms."

Today, corporations use "branding" to create unique and attractive personalities for themselves. Branding goes beyond strategies designed merely to associate corporations with actual human beings—such as AT&T's early campaign that featured workers and shareholders or the more recent use of celebrity endorsements (such as Nike's Michael Jordan advertisements), and corporate mascots (such as Ronald McDonald, Tony the Tiger, the Michelin Man, and Mickey Mouse). Corporations' brand identities are "personification[s]" of "who they are and where they've come from," said Clay Timon, chairman of Landor Associates, the world's largest and oldest branding firm, in an interview. "Family magic" for Disney, "invent" for Hewlett-Packard, "sunshine foods" for Dole are a few examples of what Timon calls "brand drivers." "Corporations, as brands ... have ... soul[s]," says Timon, which is what enables them to create "intellectual and emotional bond[s]" with the groups they depend upon, such as consumers, employees, shareholders, and regulators.[7]

Timon points to Landor's brand drivers for British Petroleum— "progressive, performance, green, innovative"—as evidence of how corporate environmental and social responsibilities are emerging today as key branding themes. However, he says, even companies that do not explicitly brand themselves as such must now embrace corporate social responsibility. "Out of necessity," says Timon, "companies, whether they want it or not, have had to take on social responsibility." And that is partly the result of their new status as dominant institutions. They must now show that they deserve to be free of governmental constraints and, indeed, to participate in governing society. "Corporations need to become more trustworthy," says Sam Gibara [former CEO of Goodyear Tire], a successor to social responsibility pioneer P. W. Litchfield. "There has been a transfer of authority from the government ... to the corporation, and the corporation needs to assume that responsibility ... and needs to really behave as a corporate citizen of the world; needs to respect the communities in which it operates, and needs to assume the self-discipline that, in the past, governments required from it."[8]

Beginning in the mid-1990s, mass demonstrations against corporate power and abuse rocked North American and European cities. The protestors, part of a broader "civil society" movement, which also included nongovernmental organizations, community coalitions, and labor unions, targeted corporate harms to workers, consumers, communities, and the environment. Their concerns were different from those of post-Enron workers, for whom shareholders' vulnerability to corrupt managers was paramount. But the two groups had something in common: they both believed the corporation had become a dangerous mix of power and unaccountability. Corporate social responsibility is offered today as an answer to such concerns. Now more than just a marketing strategy, though it is certainly that, it presents corporations as responsible and accountable to society and thus purports to lend legitimacy to their new role as society's rulers.

Corporate psychopaths

Business leaders today say that their companies care about more than profit and loss, that they feel responsible to society as a whole, not just to their shareholders. Corporate social responsibility is their new creed, a self-conscious corrective to earlier greed-inspired visions of the corporation. Despite this shift, the corporation itself has not changed. It remains, as it was at the time of its origins as a modern business institution in the middle of the nineteenth century, a legally designated "person" designed to valorize self-interest and invalidate moral concern. Most people would find its "personality" abhorrent, even psychopathic, in a human being, yet curiously we accept it in society's most powerful institution. The troubles on Wall Street today, beginning with Enron's spectacular crash, can be blamed in part on the corporation's flawed institutional character, but the company was not unique for having that character. Indeed, all publicly traded companies have it, even the most respected and socially responsible among them, such as Pfizer Inc.

Not everyone, however, is convinced of corporate social responsibility's virtue. Milton Friedman, for one, a Nobel laureate and one of the world's most eminent economists, believes the new moralism in business is in fact immoral. When Friedman granted me an interview, his secretary warned that he would get up and walk out of the room if he found my questions dull. So I was apprehensive as I waited for him in the lobby of his building. This must be how Dorothy felt, I thought, just before Toto pulled back the curtain to reveal the real Wizard of Oz. Friedman is an intellectual giant, revered and feared, deified and vilified, larger than life. So I felt some relief when he entered the room smiling, a charming little man who, like the wizard himself, barely broke five feet. Friedman surveyed the lobby, now a chaotic makeshift television studio (the interview was for a government-funded TV documentary). Lights and cameras cluttered the room, tangles of wire covered the floor. Two crew members stood ready, cotton balls in hand, to remove the shine on the great man's nose. Bemused, Friedman curmudgeonized, "ABC came in here the other day with two guys and one camera. Here we see government fat and waste at its worst."

Friedman thinks that corporations are good for society (and that too much government is bad). He recoils, however, at the idea that corporations should try to *do* good for society. "A corporation is the property of its stockholders," he told me. "Its interests are the interests of its stockholders. Now, beyond that should it spend the stockholders' money for purposes which it regards as socially responsible but which it cannot connect to its bottom line? The answer I would say is no." There is but one "social responsibility" for corporate executives,

Friedman believes: they must make as much money as possible for their shareholders. This is a moral imperative. Executives who choose social and environmental goals over profits—who try to act morally—are in fact, immoral.

There is, however, one instance when corporate social responsibility can be tolerated, according to Friedman—when it is insincere. The executive who treats social and environmental values as means to maximize shareholders' wealth—not as ends in themselves—commits no wrong. It's like "putting a good-looking girl in front of an automobile to sell an automobile," he told me. "That's not in order to promote pulchritude. That's in order to sell cars." Good intentions, like good-looking girls, can sell goods. It's true, Friedman acknowledges, that this purely strategic view of social responsibility reduces lofty ideals to "hypocritical window dressing." But hypocrisy is virtuous when it serves the bottom line. Moral virtue is immoral when it does not.

Though Friedman's views are rejected by many sophisticated businesspeople, who think his brand of cynicism is old-fashioned, mean-spirited, and out of touch with reality, his suspicion of corporate social responsibility attracts some weighty support. William Niskanen, a former Ford economist and now chairman of the Cato Institute, said he "would not invest in a firm that pioneered in corporate social responsibility." "I think Ford Motor Company still makes fine cars and trucks," he continued, "but I think the [socially responsible] actions by the new Mr. Ford are likely to undermine the value of the corporation to the owners."[9] Peter Drucker, the guru of all business gurus, who believes that Friedman is "probably our greatest living economist," echoes his view that corporate social responsibility is a dangerous distortion of business principles. "If you find an executive who wants to take on social responsibilities," Drucker said, "fire him. Fast." Harvard Business School professor Debora Spar insisted that corporations "are not institutions that are set up to be moral entities ... They are institutions which have really only one mission, and that is to increase shareholder value." And Noam Chomsky—Friedman's intellectual and ideological nemesis—shares his view that corporations must "be concerned only for their stockholders and ... not the community or the workforce or whatever."[10]

Corporations are created by law and imbued with purpose by law. Law dictates what their directors and managers can do, what they cannot do, and what they must do. And, at least in the United States and other industrialized countries, the corporation, as created by law, most closely resembles Milton Friedman's ideal model of the institution: it compels executives to prioritize the interests of their companies and shareholders above all others and forbids them from being socially responsible—at least genuinely so.

Dissociation, compartmentalization, corporation

The benevolent rhetoric and deeds of socially responsible corporations create attractive corporate images, and likely do some good in the world. They do not, however, change the corporation's fundamental institutional nature: its unblinking commitment to its own self-interest. Anita Roddick, founder and former head of The Body Shop, blames the "religion of maximizing profits" for business's amorality, for forcing otherwise decent people to do indecent things: "Because it has to maximize its profits ... everything is legitimate in the pursuit of that goal, everything ... So using child labor or sweatshop labor or despoiling the environment ... is legitimate in the maximizing of profit. It's legitimate to fire fifteen thousand people to maximize profits, keep the communities in just such pain."

The managers who do these things are not monsters, Roddick says. They may be kind and caring people, loving parents and friends. Yet, as philosopher Alasdair MacIntyre observed, they compartmentalize their lives. They are allowed, often compelled, by the corporation's culture to dissociate themselves from their own values—the corporation, according to Roddick, "stops people from having a sense of empathy with the human condition"; it "separate[s] us from who we are ..." "The language of business is not the language of the soul or the language of humanity," she says. "It's a language of indifference; it's a language of separation, of secrecy, of hierarchy." It "is fashioning a schizophrenia in many of us."[11]

Psychology, as Roddick's last comment suggests, may provide a better account of business executives' dual moral lives than either law or economics. That is why we asked Dr. Robert Hare, a psychologist and internationally renowned expert on psychopathy, for his views on the subject. He told us that many of the attitudes people adopt and the actions they execute when acting as corporate operatives can be characterized as psychopathic. You try "to destroy your competitors, or you want to beat them one way or another," said Hare, echoing Roddick, "and you're not particularly concerned with what happens to the general public as long as they're buying your product." Yet, despite the fact that executives must often manipulate and harm others in pursuit of their corporation's objectives, Hare insists they are not psychopaths. That is because they *can* function normally outside the corporation— "They go home, they have a warm and loving relationship with their families, and they love their children, they love their wife, and in fact their friends are friends rather than things to be used." Businesspeople should therefore take some comfort from their ability to compartmentalize the contradictory moral demands of their corporate and non-corporate lives, for it is precisely this "schizophrenia," as Roddick calls it, that saves them from becoming psychopaths.[12]

The corporation as psychopath

The corporation itself may not so easily escape the psychopath diagnosis, however. Unlike the human beings who inhabit it, the corporation is *singularly* self-interested and unable to feel genuine concern for others in any context. Not surprisingly, then, when we asked Dr. Hare to apply his diagnosis checklist of psychopathic traits (italicized below) to the corporation's institutional character, he found there was a close match. The corporation is *irresponsible*, Dr. Hare said, because "in an attempt to satisfy the corporate goal, everybody else is put at risk." Corporations try to "*manipulate* everything, including public opinion," and they are *grandiose*, always insisting that "we're number one, we're the best." A *lack of empathy* and *asocial tendencies* are also key characteristics of the corporation, says Hare—"Their behavior indicates they don't really concern themselves with their victims"; and corporations often *refuse to accept responsibility for their own actions* and are *unable to feel remorse*: "If [corporations] get caught [breaking the law], they pay big fines and they … continue doing what they did before anyway. And in fact in many cases the fines and the penalties paid by the organization are trivial compared to the profits that they rake in."

Finally, according to Dr. Hare, corporations relate to others *superficially*—"Their whole goal is to present themselves to the public in a way that is appealing to the public [but] in fact may not be representative of what th[e] organization is really like." Human psychopaths are notorious for their ability to use charm as a mask to hide their dangerously self-obsessed personalities. For corporations, social responsibility may play the same role. Through it they can present themselves as compassionate and concerned about others when, in fact, they lack the ability to care about anyone or anything but themselves.

Conclusion

As a psychopathic creature, the corporation can neither recognize nor act upon moral reasons to refrain from harming others. Nothing in its legal makeup limits what it can do to others in pursuit of its selfish ends, and it is compelled to cause harm when the benefits of doing so outweigh the costs. Only pragmatic concern for its own interests and the laws of the land constrain the corporation's predatory instincts, and often that is not enough to stop it from destroying lives, damaging communities, and endangering the planet as a whole. Enron's implosion, and the corporate scandals that followed, were, ironically, violations of corporations' own self-interest, as it was shareholders, the very people— indeed, the only people—corporations are legally obliged to serve, who were chief among its victims. Far less exceptional in the world of the corporation are the routine and regular harms caused to others—workers, consumers, communities, the environment—by corporations' psychopathic tendencies. The corporation, like the psychopathic personality it resembles, is programmed to exploit others for profit.

Notes

1. For a full account of the historical emergence of the corporation see the chapter "The Corporation's Rise to Dominance" in Bakan, 2004, pp. 5–27.
2. Interview with Dr. Harriet Smith Windsor. All interview quotations are from the 2006 documentary film *The Corporation*, directed by Jennifer Abbott and Mark Achbar, and written and co-created by Joel Bakan, and based on his book.
3. *Santa Clara County v. Southern Pacific Railroad*, 118 U.S. 394 (1886). Between 1890 and 1910, business interests invoked the Fourteenth Amendment 288 times before the courts, compared to nineteen times by African Americans, according to Mary Zepernick of the Program on Corporations, Law and Democracy in an interview. And in the name of the Fourteenth Amendment, beginning with its 1905 decision in *Lochner v. New York*, the Supreme Court fashioned a jurisprudence that, over

the next three decades, would bar states from enacting various kinds of regulatory measures, such as maximum-hour and minimum-wage protections for workers. In 1937, President Roosevelt, fearful that the Court might thwart his New Deal with its antiregulatory bias, threatened to pack it with five new judges, all of them New Deal sympathizers, prompting it to adopt a more deferential posture toward government. More recently, however, courts have once again begun to recognize corporations' rights under the Constitution and strike down laws that, in their view, offend them.

4. *Louis K. Liggett Co. et al. v. Lee, Comptroller et al.*, 288 US 517 (1933), p. 548, p. 567.

5. Dodd (1932) also quoted economic historian Charles Beard's wry observation about Swope and his plan: "Mr. Swope spoke as a man of affairs, as president of the General Electric Company. No academic taint condemned his utterance in advance; no suspicion of undue enthusiasm clouded his product. As priest-kings could lay down the law without question in primitive society, so a captain of industry in the United States could propose a new thing without encountering the scoffs of the wise or the jeers of the practical" (ibid., p. 1155).

6. The corporation's prestige was partly restored by the outbreak of World War II. Corporations were widely believed to be key to defeating fascism; they were called "arsenals of democracy" at the time, for having transformed their operations in ways that would meet the needs of a nation at war. The war, however, had also strengthened ties between workers and the institutions they looked to for protection: government and organized labor, which were now more powerful than ever. In response, business began a systematic campaign during the postwar years to become a powerful, well-organized political presence. Corporate lobbying and campaign financing were used to help foster a political climate that viewed corporations as benevolent, responsible, and best left alone by government, and an all-out public relations campaign, led by the National Association of Manufacturers, was launched to help convince Americans that individualism, competition, and free enterprise were synonymous with the American Way. See Fones-Wolf, 1994.

7. For an excellent critical discussion of branding and its implications for society, see Klein, 2000. More generally, the notion that corporations are persons—individuals—has served throughout history to obscure, in both law and public opinion, the fact that corporations exercise the

collective economic power of vast numbers of shareholders and thus are profoundly more powerful than the rest of us.

8. Interviews with Clay Timon and Samir Gibara.
9. Interview with William Niskanen.
10. Interviews with Peter Drucker, Debora Spar, and Noam Chomsky.
11. Interview with Anita Roddick.
12. Interview with Dr. Robert Hare.

References

Bakan, J. (2004). *The Corporation: The Pathological Pursuit of Profit and Power.* London: Constable.

Berle, A. A., & Means, G. C. (1968). *The Modern Corporation and Private Property.* New York: Harcourt, Brace & World.

Dodd, E. M. (1932). For whom are corporate managers trustees? *Harvard Law Review, 45*: 1145–1163.

Fones-Wolf, E. A. (1994). *The Selling of Free Enterprise: The Business Assault on Labor and Liberalism 1945–1960.* Urbana, IL: University of Illinois Press.

Herman, E. (1981). *Corporate Control, Corporate Power.* Cambridge: Cambridge University Press.

Horwitz, M. J. (1987). Santa Clara revisited: The development of corporate theory. In: W. Samuels & A. Miller (Eds.), *Corporations and Society: Power and Responsibility.* New York: Greenwood Press.

Ireland, P. (1996). Capitalism without the capitalist: the joint stock company share and the emergence of the modern doctrine of separate corporate personality. *Journal of Legal History, 17*(1): 41–73.

Klein, N. (2000). *No Logo: Taking Aim at the Brand Bullies.* Toronto: Knopf Canada.

Marchand, R. (1998). *Creating the Corporate Soul: The Rise of Public Relations and Corporate Imagery in American Big Business.* Berkeley, CA: University of California Press.

McQuaid, K. (1977). Young, Swope and General Electric's "New Capitalism": A study in corporate liberalism, 1920–1933. *American Journal of Economics and Sociology, 36*(4): 417–428.

Rodengen, J. L. (1997). *The Legend of Goodyear: The First 100 Years.* Fort Lauderdale, FL: Write Stuff Syndicate.

Swope, G. (1931). *The Swope Plan: Details, Criticisms, Analysis.* New York: Business Bourse.

CHAPTER TEN

We've Had a Hundred Years of Psychotherapy—And the World's Getting Worse*

James Hillman and Michael Ventura

Two men are on an afternoon walk in Santa Monica, on the Pacific Palisades. They began their walk on the Santa Monica Pier, with its rundown carnival air, where the affluent and the homeless pass among each other—and among Latinos from East L.A. and the new Central American ghettos; blacks from South Central; Asians from Chinatown, Koreatown, and the Japanese enclaves; pale whites from Culver City and North Hollywood; tan, svelte whites from West L.A.; old people of all descriptions and accents; and tourists from everywhere. The poor fish for food off the pier, though signs in English and Spanish tell them it's dangerous to eat their catch. The beach is often closed from sewage spills. But the ocean doesn't show its filth, it looks as lovely as always, and it's anywhere from ten to thirty degrees cooler at the Pacific than even just a few miles inland—so everybody comes.

The two men have walked the steady incline up the Palisades, along the cliffs overlooking the Pacific Coast Highway and the sea, and, at the far end of the park, where the cliffs are highest and there aren't so many people, they've sat down on a beach.

---

*This is an edited version of *We've Had a Hundred Years of Psychotherapy—And the World's Getting Worse* by James Hillman and Michael Ventura and is reprinted by permission of HarperCollins Publishers.

The men are James Hillman and Michael Ventura. Hillman is in his mid-sixties, tall and slender. Though born Jewish in Atlantic City he carries himself like an old-timey New Englander, with that Yankee sense of tolerant but no-nonsense authority—softened somewhat by the eagerness of his interest in whatever and, usually, whoever's around him. Ventura is in his mid-forties, shorter, darker, and scruffier than Hillman. He wears the kind of hat men wore in 1940s movies and a good but battered set of cowboy boots, and he gives the impression of trying to balance between these incongruities. Hillman is a psychoanalyst, author, and lecturer; Ventura is a newspaper columnist, novelist, and screenwriter.

Ventura carries a small tape recorder, and when he's with Hillman these days it's almost always on, even when they're walking or driving. Their conversation has a theme: psychotherapy. And it has something like a form: each man is to push the other not to make more sense but to get further out in his thinking. And their conversation has an ambition: that their talks and, later, their letters, will make a book, an informal but (they hope) fierce polemic to give psychotherapy a shake. For they share the conviction that psychotherapy needs desperately to push past the boundaries of its accepted ideas; it needs a new wildness before it's co-opted entirely as just another device for compressing (shrinking) people into a forced, and false, normality.

They sit on the beach, Ventura puts the tape recorder between them, and Hillman takes off on what, these days, is his favorite theme.

JH: We've had a hundred years of analysis, and people are getting more and more sensitive, and the world is getting worse and worse. Maybe it's time to look at that. We still locate the psyche inside the skin. You go *inside* to locate the psyche, you examine *your* feelings and *your* dreams, they belong to you. Or it's interrelations, interpsyche, between your psyche and mine. That's been extended a little bit into family systems and office groups—but the psyche, the soul, is still only *within* and *between* people. We're working on our relationships constantly, and our feelings and reflections, but look what's left out of that.

Hillman makes a wide gesture that includes the oil tanker on the horizon, the gang graffiti on a park sign, and the fat homeless woman with swollen ankles and cracked skin asleep on the grass about fifteen yards away.

JH: What's left out is a deteriorating world.

So why hasn't therapy noticed that? Because psychotherapy is only working on that "inside" soul. By removing the soul from the world and not recognizing that the soul is also *in* the world, psychotherapy can't do its job anymore. The buildings are sick, the institutions are sick, the banking system's sick, the schools, the streets—the sickness is out *there*.

You know, the soul is always being rediscovered through pathology. In the nineteenth century people didn't talk about psyche, until Freud came along and discovered psychopathology. Now we're beginning to say, "The furniture has stuff in it that's poisoning us, the microwave gives off dangerous rays." The world has become toxic.

Both men, watching the sun flash on the sea, seem to be thinking the same thing.

MV: That sea out there is diseased. We can't eat the fish.

JH: The world has become full of symptoms. Isn't that the beginning of recognizing what used to be called animism? The world's alive—my god! It's having effects on us. "I've got to get rid of those fluorocarbon cans." "I've got to get rid of the furniture because underneath it's form-aldehyde." "I've got to watch out for this and that and *that*." So there's pathology in the world, and through that we're beginning to treat the world with more respect.

MV: As though having denied the spirit in things, the spirit—offended— comes back as a threat. Having denied the soul in things, having said to things, with Descartes, "You don't have souls," things have turned around and said, "Just you *watch* what kind of soul I have, muthafucka."

JH: "Just watch what I can do, man! You're gonna have that ugly lamp in your room, that lamp is going to make you suffer every single day you look at it. It's going to produce fluorescent light, and it's going to drive you slowly crazy sitting in your office. And then you're going to see a psychotherapist, and you're going to try and work it out in your relationships, but you don't know I'm really the one that's got you. It's that fluorescent tube over your head all day long, coming right down on your skull like a KGB man putting a light on you, straight down on you—shadowless, ruthless, cruel."

MV: And yet we sense this in all we do and say now, all of us, but we're caught in a double bind: on the one hand this is "progress," a value that's been ingrained in us—and if you think it's not ingrained in you, take a drive down to Mexico and see if even poor Americans would want to live the way most of those people have to live (the life of the American poor seems rich to them, that's why they keep coming); but on the other hand, we know that the things of our lives are increasingly harmful, but we haven't got Idea One about what to do. Our sense of politics has atrophied into the sort of nonsense that goes on in presidential elections.

JH: There is a decline in political sense. No sensitivity to the real issues. Why are the intelligent people—at least among the white middle class—so passive now? Why?

Because the sensitive, intelligent people are in therapy! They've been in therapy in the United States for thirty, forty years, and during that time there's been a tremendous political decline in this country.

MV: How do you think that works?

JH: Every time we try to deal with our outrage over the freeway, our misery over the office and the lighting and the crappy furniture, the crime on the streets, whatever—every time we try to deal with that by going to therapy with our rage and fear, we're depriving the political world of something. And therapy, in its crazy way, by emphasizing the inner soul and ignoring the outer soul, supports the decline of the actual world. Yet therapy goes on blindly believing that it's curing the outer world by making people better. We've had this for years and years and years: "If everybody went into therapy we'd have better buildings, we'd have better people, we'd have more consciousness." It's not the case.

MV: I'm not sure it's causal, but it's definitely a pattern. Our inner knowledge has gotten more subtle while our ability to deal with the world around us has, well, *deteriorated* is almost not a strong enough word. *Disintegrated* is more like it.

JH: The vogue today, in psychotherapy, is the "inner child." That's the therapy thing—you go back to your childhood. But if you're looking backward, you're not looking around. This trip backward constellates what Jung called the "child archetype." Now, the child archetype is by nature apolitical and disempowered—it has no connection with the political world. And so the adult says, "Well, what can I do about the world? This thing's bigger than me." That's the child archetype talking. "All I can do is go into myself, work on my growth, my development, find good parenting, support groups." This is a disaster for our political world, for our democracy. Democracy depends on intensely active citizens, not children.

By emphasizing the child archetype, by making our therapeutic hours rituals of evoking childhood and reconstructing childhood, we're blocking ourselves from political life. Twenty or thirty years of therapy have removed the most sensitive and the most intelligent, and some of the most affluent people in our society into child cult worship. It's going on insidiously, all through therapy, all through the country. So *of course* our politics are in disarray and nobody's voting—we're disempowering ourselves through therapy.

MV: The assumption people are working out of is that inner growth translates into worldly power, and many don't realize that they go to therapy with that assumption.

JH: If personal growth did lead into the world, wouldn't our political situation be different today, considering all the especially intelligent people who have been in therapy? What you learn in therapy is mainly feeling skills, how to really remember, how to let fantasy come, how to find words for invisible things, how to go deep and face things—

MV: Good stuff to know—

JH: Yes, but you don't learn political skills or find out anything about the way the world works. Personal growth doesn't automatically lead to political results. Look at Eastern Europe and the Soviet Union. Psychoanalysis was banned for decades, and look at the political changes that have come up and startled everybody. Not the result of therapy, their revolutions.

MV: So you're making a kind of opposition between power, political power or political intelligence, and therapeutic intelligence. Many who are therapeutically sensitive are also dumb and fucked up politically; and if you look at the people who wield the most power in almost any sphere of life, they are often people whose inner growth has been severely stunted.

JH: You think people undertake therapy to grow?

MV: Isn't growth a huge part of the project of therapy? Everybody uses the word, therapists and clients alike.

JH: But the very word *grow* is a word appropriate to children. After a certain age you do not grow. You don't grow teeth, you don't grow muscles. If you start growing after that age, it's cancer.

MV: Aw, Jim, can't I grow *inside* all my life?

JH: Grow what? Corn? Tomatoes? New archetypes? What am I growing, what do you grow? The standard therapeutic answer is: you're growing yourself.

MV: But the philosopher Kierkegaard would come back and say, "The deeper natures don't change, they become more and more themselves."

JH: Jung says individuation is becoming more and more oneself.

MV: And becoming more and more oneself involves a lot of unpleasantness. As Jung also says, the most terrifying thing is to know yourself.

JH: And becoming more and more oneself—the actual experience of it is a shrinking, in that very often it's a dehydration, a loss of inflation, a loss of illusions.

MV: That doesn't sound like a good time. Why would anyone want to do it?

JH: Because shedding is a beautiful thing. It's of course not what consumerism tells you, but shedding feels good. It's a lightening up.

MV: Shedding what?

JH: Shedding pseudo skins, crusted stuff that you're accumulated. Shedding dead wood. That's one of the big sheddings. Things that don't work anymore, things that don't keep you—keep you alive.

Sets of ideas that you've had too long. People that you don't really like to be with, habits of thought, habits of sexuality. That's a very big one, 'cause if you keep on making love at forty the way you did at eighteen you're missing something, and if you make love at sixty the way you did at fifty you're missing something. All that changes. The imagination changes.

Or put it another way: *Growth is always loss*. Anytime you're gonna grow, you're gonna lose something. You're losing what you're hanging onto to keep safe. You're losing habits that you're comfortable with, you're losing familiarity. That's a big one, when you begin to move into the unfamiliar. You know, in the organic world when anything begins to grow it's moving constantly into unfamiliar movements and unfamiliar things. Watch birds grow—they fall down, they can't quite do it. Their growing is all awkwardness. Watch a fourteen-year-old kid tripping over his feet.

Symptoms as signs

JH: Let's keep working away at why the world is getting worse—getting worse not only in the usual sense, about Amazon forests and dead dolphins. That is the easy part to see, if not easy to correct. Our job is to show how *psychology* contributes to making the world worse.

Suppose we entertain the idea that psychology makes people mediocre; and suppose we entertain the idea that the world is *in extremis*, suffering an acute, perhaps fatal, disorder at the edge of extinction. Then I would claim that what the world needs most is radical and original extremes of feeling and thinking in order for its crisis to be met with equal intensity. The supportive and tolerant understanding of psychotherapy is hardly up to this task. Instead it produces counterphobic attitudes to chaos, marginality, extremes. Therapy as sedation: benumbing, an-aesthesia so that we calm down, relieve stress, relax, find acceptance, balance, support, empathy. The middle way. Mediocrity.

I can think of a middle ground, but not the one therapy tries to work, because that middle ground, I believe, is mediocrity, compromising symptom and system in such a way that in the end the symptom disappears and the "successful" case reenters society. The middle ground I would propose is the arts, in which the symptom becomes the marginal informing spirit or hounding dog that never lets go, driving the psyche to the edge.

I've been straining for decades to push psychology over into art, to recognize psychology as an art form rather than a science or a medicine or an education, because the soul is inherently imaginative. The primary function of the human being is to imagine, not to stand up straight, not to make tools and fire, not to build communities or hunt and till and tame, but to *imagine* these other possibilities. And we go on imagining and imagining, irrepressibly. The repressed returns as symptoms, so our symptoms are actually the irrepressible imagination breaking through our adapted mediocrity. Hence, the pronouncement: "In your pathology is your salvation"—not salvation as adaptation, but salvation from adaptation. All our pathologies are imaginings, and so therapy's job is primarily to deal with the symptoms, just as Freud tried at the beginning, but now because the symptoms are the imaginings of the psyche seeking a better form.

Let us go the other way with therapy, toward art. Then we may consider some of the pathology we have mentioned as political protests, as refusals to comply, and the consulting room as a safe house for revolutionaries. The symptom becomes a demonstration of a life force within the Winstons of our society (Orwell's hero in *1984*) that will not bend to big brother. Even when we try, even when we want to, the symptoms insist on depressing me so I can't get to work, sexualizing me so I harass and buy porn, enraging me so I shout in public, putting my money on horses instead of what the ads tell me to buy. I haven't kept faith with the economy (as they say a consumer must). I haven't served Jesus by Christmas shopping. I have stopped consuming, stopped watching TV, stopped voting. My symptoms want something else, something more. In my symptoms is the soul's deepest desire.

I have suggested an artistic paradigm for therapy, though I don't mean literal artists and art. For the arts and artists can be just as blithely self-centered and apolitical as the Berlin Philharmonic playing for a *Wehrmacht* audience. I have suggested the artistic paradigm because it satisfies the three requirements discussed in this letter. First, art *forms* madness rather than represses it. Second, the arts often act as the sensitive antennae of social justice and moral outrage, keeping the soul awake to hypocrisy, cant, suppression, and jingoism. And third, the fundamental enemy of all art is mediocrity.

You see, Michael, for me the job of psychotherapy is to open up and deal with—no, not deal with, *encourage*, maybe even inflame—the rich and crazy mind, that wonderful aviary (the image is from Plato) of wild flying thoughts, the sex-charged fantasies, the incredible longings, bloody wounds, and the museums of archaic shards that constitute the psyche.

The city as psyche

JH: It took the last several decades for therapy to learn that body is psyche, that what the body does, how it moves, what it senses is psyche. More recently, therapy is learning that the psyche exists wholly in relational systems. It's not a free radical, a monad, self-determined. The next step is to realize that the city, where the body lives and moves, and where the relational network is woven, is also psyche. City strongly affects psyche. Better said: city *is* psyche.

The Greeks knew this. The *polis* was the other half of *mythos*. *Mythos* was lived in *polis*. The Gods take part in and are felt in civic life. We sense this often in nature; why are we so numb to recognize soul in the city? Blacks and Latinos do. What goes on in the city is not merely politics or economics or architecture. It's not even "environment"; it's psychology. Everything "out there" is you.

The collective unconscious, as Jung said, is the world, and—also as he said—the psyche is not in you, you are in the psyche. The collective unconscious extends beyond the great symbols of your dreams, beyond the repercussions of ancestral history. It includes the ground swells that ebb and flow through the city, the fashions, language, biases, choreographies that rule your waking soul as much as the images ruling your soul. It's more than ozone levels and days of sunshine; a city is a soul. You, Michael, *are* Los Angeles. You may be Brooklyn and Austin too, but as long as you pull yourself out of the night world each morning in L.A. you are L.A.

What does this mean? It means each city ought to have its own school of therapy, like the Vienna school, the Zurich school, the schools of Nancy and of Paris. It also means you can't honestly do therapy apart from the city in which it takes place. It means therapy has reached its city limits.

This issue goes to the roots of *the political role of therapy*. If I am right that a major task of therapy is to work with the pathological ferment in the body politic, then compliance with normalization subverts its political task. If therapy imagines its task to be that of helping people cope (and not protest), to adapt (and not rebel), to normalize their oddity, and to accept themselves "and work within your situation; make it work for you" (rather than refuse the unacceptable), then therapy is collaborating with what the state wants: docile plebs.

Outrage

JH: There's another thing therapy does that I think is vicious. It internalizes emotions.

Hillman looks down at the Pacific Coast Highway packed with cars going as fast as they can bumper to bumper.

JH: I'm outraged after having driven to my analyst on the freeway. The fucking trucks almost ran me off the road. I'm terrified. I'm in my little car, and I get to my therapist's and I'm shaking. My therapist says, "We've gotta talk about this." So we begin to talk about it. And we discover that my father was a son-of-a-bitch brute and this whole truck thing reminds me of him. Or we discover that I've always felt frail and vulnerable, there've always been bigger guys with bigger dicks, so this car that I'm in is a typical example of my thin skin and my frailty and vulnerability. Or we talk about my power drive, that I really wish to be a truck driver. We convert my fear into anxiety—an inner state. We convert the present into the past, into a discussion of my father and my childhood. And we convert my outrage—into rage and hostility. Again, an internal condition, whereas it starts in *out*rage, an emotion. Emotions are mainly social. The word comes from the Latin *ex movere*, to move out. Emotions connect to the world. Therapy introverts the emotions, calls fear "anxiety." You take it back, and you work on it inside yourself. You don't work psychologically on what that outrage is telling you about potholes, about trucks, about Florida strawberries in Vermont in March, about burning up oil, about energy policies, nuclear waste, that homeless woman over there with the sores on her feet—the whole thing.

MV: You're not saying that we don't need introspection, an introspective guy like you?

JH: Put this in italics so that nobody can just pass over it: *This is not to deny that you do need to go inside*—but we have to see what we're doing when we do that. By going inside we're maintaining the Cartesian view that the world out there is a dead matter and the world inside is living.

MV: A therapist told me that my grief at seeing a homeless man my age was really a feeling of sorrow for myself.

JH: And dealing with it means going home and working on it in reflection. That's what dealing with it has come to mean. And by that time you've walked past the homeless man in the street.

MV: It's also, in part, a way to cut off what you would call Eros, the part of my heart that seeks to touch others. Theoretically this is something therapy tries to liberate but here's a person on the street that I'm feeling for and I'm supposed to deal with that feeling as though it has nothing to do with another person.

JH: Could the thing that we all believe in most—that psychology is the one good thing left in a hypocritical world—be not true? Psychology, working with yourself, could that be part of the disease, not part of the cure? I think therapy has made a philosophical mistake, which is that cognition precedes conation—that knowing precedes doing or action. I don't think that's the case. I think reflection has always been after the event.

They reflect on that a bit.

JH: The thing that therapy pushes is relationship, yet work may matter just as much as relationship. You think you're going to die if you're not in a good relationship. You feel that not being in a significant, long-lasting, deep relationship is going to cripple you or that you're crazy or neurotic or something. You feel intense bouts of longing and loneliness. But those feelings are not only due to poor relationships; they come also because you're not in any kind of political community that makes sense, that matters. Therapy pushes the relationship issues, but what intensifies those issues is that we don't have (a) satisfactory work or (b), even more important perhaps, we don't have a satisfactory political community.

You just can't make up for the loss of passions and purpose in your daily work by intensifying your personal relationships. I think we talk so much about inner growth and development because we are so boxed in to petty, private concerns on our jobs.

MV: In a world where most people do work that is not only unsatisfying but also, with its pressures, deeply unsettling; and in a world where there's nothing more rare than a place that feels like a community, we load all our needs onto a relationship or expect them to be met by our family. And then we wonder why our relationships and family crack under the load.

JH: It's extraordinary to see psychotherapy, that came out of those nuts from Vienna and Zurich, and out of the insane asylums of Europe, talking the same language today as the Republican right wing about the virtues of family. The government and therapy are in symbiotic, happy agreement on the propaganda that we had from Ronald Reagan for so many years about family. Yet family, we know sociologically, doesn't exist anymore. The statistics are astounding. And the actual patterns of family life, how people feel and act in the families that still exist, have changed radically. People don't live in families in the same way; people won't live in families. There are broken families, half-families, multiple families, all kinds of crazy families. The idea of family only exists in the bourgeois patient population that serves psychotherapy. In fact, the family is largely today a white therapist's family.

Why do we need this Norman Rockwell family, this make-believe ideal, that's so rampant now in politics and in therapy? I don't know what it's doing for the body politic, but I know what it's doing for therapy. For therapy, it's keeping an ideal in place so that we can show how dysfunctional we all are. It keeps the trade going.

MV: But even the Norman Rockwell ideal of the happy, self-sufficient family is a distortion of what families were for thousands, probably tens of thousands of years. During that time, no family was self-sufficient. Each family was a working unit that was part of the larger working unit which was the community—the tribe or the village. Tribes and villages were self-sufficient, not families. It's not only that everyone worked together, everyone also played and prayed together, so that the burden of relationship, and of meaning, wasn't confined to the family, much less to a romantic relationship, but was spread out into the community. Until the Industrial Revolution, family always existed in that context.

JH: And family always existed in the context of one's ancestors. Our bones are not in this ground. Now our families don't carry the ancestors with them. First of all, we Americans left our homelands in order to come here, and we let go of the ancestors. Second, we're all now first name people. I was just at a psychotherapists' conference with seven thousand people, and everybody had on their name tags. Everybody's first name was in large caps and the last name was in small letters below it.

MV: And in the last name are the ancestors, the country, the residue of the past.

JH: It's all in the last name. The first name is fashion, social drift. One generation you have a lot of Tracys and Kimberlys, Maxes and Sams, another generation you have Ediths and Doras, Michaels and Davids. You've got your ancestors with you in your psyche when you use your last name. You've got your brothers and sisters with you, they have the same name. When I'm called Jim, I'm just plain Jim, it has no characteristics.

To have only a first name is a sign of being a peasant, a slave, an oppressed person. Throughout history slaves had only first names. Now our entire nation has only first names. At this conference, the only people who had last names were the faculty—the twenty-five people that these other seven thousand had paid to see and hear. We had our last names in big letters and our first names in small letters. I asked about this and was told, "We don't want you people called James or Jim or Bob or Bill, we want you addressed as Mr. Hillman."

Therapy's no different here; it complies with the convention, too. The early cases of analysis, Freud's, Jung's, had only first names—Anna, Babette. It's supposed to show intimacy and equality—

MV: —and anonymity—

JH: What it actually does is strip down your dignity, the roots of your individuality, because it covers over the ancestors, who are in the consulting room too. Worse, this way of talking concentrates all attention on me, Jim, my little apple, ignoring the whole complexity of my social bag, my racial roots. We ought to have three or four last names, all hyphenated, like in Switzerland or Spain, with my mother's family name in there too, and my wife's and my ex-wife's and so on and so on. No one is just plain Jim.

MV: I'm too American for that, I *like* being able to leave some of that behind. Still, we should carry both our parents' names, at least—but not hyphenated. You know, speaking of slaves: bosses and owners are almost always called Mister, but they have the freedom to address their employees by their first names. And among workers of equal or supposedly equal status, it's not unusual for a man to be called by his last name while women are almost always called by their first names unless they're really heavy-duty. So we're also dealing with power when we use names. We're reinforcing certain kinds of authority and inequality.

But I want to go back to something: that to tout the ideal family is a way of *making* ourselves dysfunctional, because that ideal makes anything outside it, by definition, not ideal, i.e., dysfunctional. Without that ideal, we're just who we are.

JH: The ideal of growth makes us feel stunted; the ideal family makes us feel crazy.

MV: We have these idealizations that make us feel crazy, even though we don't see any of these ideals in life. I feel crazy that I can't be in one relationship all my life, even though I look around and where do I see anybody in one relationship all their lives?

JH: I know people who've been married fifty years and more.

MV: So do I, and one partner's an alcoholic, or one's played around a lot or been away a lot, they haven't made love in decades (literally), or one is a closet gay. These aren't abstract examples, these are people I know. Most fifty-year wedding anniversaries would look very different if you knew what everybody's covering up. Yet we keep measuring ourselves against these ideals.

JH: And psychology idealizes family in another, perhaps even more destructive, way: psychology assumes that your personality and behavior are determined by your family relationships during childhood.

MV: Well, people grow up somehow, some way, and how they grow up determines their life, doesn't it?

There's an uncomfortably long silence between them. The oil tanker has gone over the horizon, but traffic is still backed up on the Pacific Coast Highway. A single-engine plane flying low over the Santa Monica Pier pulls a yellow banner wishing somebody named Eliza a happy birthday. Farther down the coast, 747s take off from LAX one after another and do a slow banking turn far out at sea. The homeless woman has woken up (her eyes are open), but she hasn't moved.

Hillman clears his throat.

The consulting room: a cell of revolution

JH: Look. Our assumption, our fantasy, in psychoanalysis has been that we're going to process, we're going to grow; and we're going to level things out so that we don't have these very strong, disturbing emotions and events.

MV: Which is probably not a human possibility.

JH: But could analysis have new fantasies of itself, so that the consulting room is a cell in which revolution is prepared?

MV: What?

JH: Could—

MV: —could the consulting room be a cell in which *revolution* is prepared? Jesus. Could it?

JH: By *revolution* I mean turning over. Not development or unfolding, but turning over the system that has made you go to analysis to begin with—the system being government by minority and conspiracy, official secrets, national security, corporate power, *et cetera*. Therapy might imagine itself investigating the immediate social causes, even while keeping its vocabulary of abuse and victimization—that we are abused and victimized less by our personal lives of the past than by a present system.

It's like, you want your father to love you. The desire to be loved by your father is enormously important. But you can't get that love fulfilled by your father. You don't want to get rid of the desire to be loved, but you want to stop asking your father; he's the wrong object. So we don't want to get rid of the feeling of being abused—maybe that's very important, the feeling of being abused, the feeling of being without power. But maybe we shouldn't imagine that we are abused by the past as much as we are by the actual situation of "my job," "my finances," "my government"—all the things that we live with.

Then the consulting room becomes a cell of revolution, because we would be talking also about, "What is actually abusing me right now?" That would be a great venture, for therapy to talk that way.

MV: Let's double back a second. You said, "Could analysis have new fantasies about itself?" What do you mean by *fantasy*? For most people that word's associated with "unreal."

JH: Oh, no, no. Fantasy is the natural activity of the mind. Jung says, "The primary activity of psychic life is the creation of fantasy." Fantasy is how you perceive something, how you think about it, react to it.

MV: So *any* perception, in that sense, is fantasy.

JH: Is there a reality that is not framed or formed? No. Reality is always coming through a pair of glasses, a point of view, a language—a fantasy.

MV: But if therapy is to take this new direction, have this new perception or fantasy about itself, it seems we need some basic redefinition of some basic concepts.

> Hillman smiles, looks out into the distance. The light has changed, the sun will be down soon, and the breeze off the sea is suddenly cool. The homeless woman is wrapping herself in plastic garbage bags, muttering something. The highway traffic below is moving smoothly again. The oil tanker's lights are on, and in a few moments it will be out of sight. And the lights of the Santa Monica Pier have come on, too, as sad as forced cheer.

Redefining the self

JH: Maybe the idea of self has to be redefined.

MV: That would be revolutionary. That would eventually change the entire culture, if it caught on.

JH: The idea of self has to be redefined. Therapy's definition comes from the Protestant and Oriental tradition: self is the interiorization of the invisible God beyond. The inner divine. Even if this inner divine is disguised as a self-steering, autonomous, homeostatic, balancing mechanism; or even if the divine is disguised as the integrating deeper intention of the whole personality, it's still a transcendent notion, with theological implications if not roots. I would rather define self as *the interiorization of community*. And if you make that little move, then you're going to feel very different about things. If the self were defined as the interiorization of community, then the boundaries between me and another would be much less secure. I would be with myself when I'm with others. I would not be with myself when I'm walking alone or meditating or in my room imagining or working on my dreams. In fact, I would be estranged from myself.

And "others" would not include just other people, because community, as I see it, is something more ecological, or at least animistic. A psychic field. And if I'm not in a psychic field with others—with people, buildings, animals, trees—I *am* not. So it wouldn't be, "I am because I think." (*Cogito ergo sum*, as Descartes said.) It would be, as somebody said to me the other night, "I am because I party." *Convivo ergo sum.*

MV: That's a redefinition of self, all right.

JH: Look, a great deal of our life is manic. I can watch thirty-four channels of TV, I can communicate with people anywhere, I can be everywhere at once, I can fly across the country, I've got call waiting, so I can take two calls at once. I live everywhere and nowhere. But I don't know who lives next door to me. Who's in the next flat? Who's in 14-B?

I don't know who they are, but, boy, I'm on the phone, car phone, toilet phone, plane phone, my mistress is in Chicago, the other woman I'm with is in D.C., my ex-wife is in Phoenix, my mother in Hawaii, and I have four children living all over the country. I have messages coming in day and night, I can plug into all the world's stock prices, commodity exchanges, I am everywhere, man—but I don't know who's in 14-B.

You see, this hyper communication and information is part of what's keeping the soul at bay.

MV: Oh yeah. Very much so. But—maybe it's because I'm a writer, maybe it's the way I've trained myself—but I feel most myself when I'm alone.

JH: It's not because you're a writer or because you've trained yourself. That training began two thousand years ago.

MV: How?

JH: That training is the emphasis upon withdrawal, innerness—in Augustine's sense of confessions, in Jerome's sense of hiding out in the desert. This is the result of a long discipline to sever a person from the natural world of community. It's a monkish notion. A saintly notion.

And there's a second reason you are convinced that you're more yourself when you're alone: because it's more familiar. You are in a habitual, repetitious rut: "This is me, because I'm in the same pattern"; it's recognizable. When you're with another person you're out of yourself because the other person is flowing into you and you are flowing into them, there are surprises, you're a little out of control, and then you think you're not your real true self. The out of control—that's the community acting through you. It's the locus that you're in, acting through you.

The Jungians would say that a life having more integrity with itself is what they mean by individuating. I don't think so. The concept of individuating is based on a larger ideology that assumes original *wholeness*—an *a priori*, if you like, wholeness that we begin with, then it gets shattered, then we spend our lives reconstituting it. *Individuating*—the very word—locates that entire wholeness in the individual, apart from the world. But what if that's not so? What if, as you and I have been saying, we're not born whole, and what if the quality of wholeness is not located in the individual but in a community that includes the environment? How does all that, the-individual-as-part-of-community-as-part-of-environment, "individuate"? If, instead, we conceive of therapy as an attempt to invent and speak a language appropriate to a particular life, the world must be part of it because any life is a life *in the world*.

Additional resources

The following is a selection of organisations and websites for anyone wanting to explore further the themes of this book. As many of its contributors note, one of the most effective ways of integrating the outer and inner is through practical involvement and engagement, rather than sitting in a bedroom or indeed a consulting room: through transforming the world we transform ourselves.

Insight/resources

*Social Power and Psychological Distress: A Social
Materialist Approach to Clinical Psychology
(David Smail's website)*

"Hardly any of the 'symptoms' of psychological distress may correctly
be seen as medical matters. The so-called psychiatric 'disorders' are
nothing to do with faulty biology, nor indeed are they the outcome
of individual moral weakness or other personal failing. They are the
creation of the social world in which we live, and that world is structured by *power*.

"Social power may be defined as the means of obtaining security or
advantage, and it will be exercised within any given society in a variety
of forms: coercive (force), economic (money power) and ideological (the
control of meaning). Power is the dynamic which keeps the social world
in motion. It may be used for good or for ill.

"One cannot hope to understand the phenomena of psychological
distress, nor begin to think what can be done about them, without an
analysis of how power is distributed and exercised within society. Such
an understanding is the focus of this website."
www.davidsmail.info

Midlands Psychology Group: For a Social Materialist Psychology

"We are a group of clinical, counselling and academic psychologists who believe that psychology—particularly but not only clinical psychology—has served ideologically to detach people from the world we live in, to make us individually responsible for our own misery and to discourage us from trying to change the world rather than just 'understanding' our selves. What are too often seen as private predicaments are in fact best understood as arising out of the public structures of society."
www.midpsy.org

Psychotherapists and Counsellors for Social Responsibility (PCSR)

PCSR was set up in the UK in 1995 as "a forum for psychotherapists, counsellors and members of other professions who wish to influence and broaden the political process". Among its founders was the Jungian analyst Andrew Samuels, who has long argued for the importance of psycho-politics. One of the main ways in which PCSR seeks to fulfil its aims is through "incorporating emotional and psychological perspectives into current debates on social, cultural, environmental and political issues". It also seeks to campaign and lobby around specific issues on which it feels that psychotherapists and counsellors should have a voice.
www.pcsr-uk.ning.com

Psychotherapy and Counselling Union

"All counsellors, psychotherapists, psychologists etc are warmly invited to become members of the Psychotherapy and Counselling Union. This is a single organisation working to bring together counsellors, psychotherapists, and other practitioners from every corner of the field, including trainees on an equal basis. It campaigns for true diversity and equal opportunities in the therapy world, and supports individuals in disciplinary and complaints procedures or who are harassed or discriminated against.

"It also campaigns against the use of therapy to get people off benefits and/or back to work; supports and defends therapy against attacks from government and media and against creeping medicalisation;

defends and extends the provision of open-ended therapy which is free at the point of contact; supports and defends practitioners in disciplinary hearings, and against bullying and harassment; and campaigns to reform IAPT and to change the system whereby starting practitioners have to work unpaid, often with very complex issues and without adequate support. For more information please visit the website."
www.pandcunion.ning.com

Social brain—RSA: Providing Insights into Human Nature in Context, to Help People Live a Larger Life

"The notion of a profit-maximising individual who makes decisions consciously, consistently and independently is, at best, a very partial account of who we are. Science is now telling us what most of us intuitively sense: humans are a fundamentally social species. We are embedded in complex social networks. We are largely habitual creatures and highly sensitive to social and cultural norms. We are better at rationalising than being rational.

"However, recent social, political and environmental challenges fail to grasp that social context is not an afterthought, a variable to be controlled, but the defining feature of how we think, learn and behave. We need to make these theories of human nature more accurate through research, more explicit through public dissemination and more empowering through practical engagement.

"The Social Brain Centre focuses on three principal aspects of human nature—Habits, Attention and Decisions—and applies these behavioural insights to our most pressing social, political and environmental challenges. The Centre was launched formally in November 2012, and was marked by a workshop exploring the practical relevance of Iain McGilchrist's ideas on the relationship between brain hemispheres and cultural evolution."
www.thersa.org/action-and-research/rsa-projects/social-brain-centre/social-brain

Perspectiva: Systems, Souls and Society

"Perspectiva examines complex problems in the external world from the perspectives of our inner worlds; integrating systems, souls and society for the common good. Our research platform exists to inform and

inspire, generating networks and practices to deepen human engagement with the major challenges of our time."
www.systems-souls-society.com

Mental Fight Club (MFC) and the Dragon Café

"**Mental Fight Club** was founded by Sarah Wheeler in Southwark in 2003 as a creative force for change led by service users. The group has been running pop-up creative events since 2003 to explore issues around mental illness, recovery and wellbeing. These varied events play to packed audiences, using creativity to break down the barriers between the ill and the well, the supporters and the supported. In this way the group hopes to 'open everyone's mind to the wisdom and riches that can be gained in the journey through mental illness into recovery'.

"In 2012 Maudsley Charity began funding the Dragon Café project: MFC's most innovative endeavour to date. Fuelled by a regular volunteer workforce, two-thirds of whom have themselves experienced mental health problems, the Dragon Café is open every Monday in the Crypt of St George the Martyr Church, London, and offers a support structure to the work of MFC, creating a hub which draws together people from a diverse range of backgrounds and mental health experiences.

"A programme of creative or wellbeing-related events is delivered every Monday, with different themes each month; from poetry to painting, Tai Chi to boxing, there is a new experience to suit every palate. The café is free and open to all, people can come and go for creative activities with payment only required for the delicious and healthy vegetarian menu. The Dragon Café prides itself on being a 'free, open, creative, welcoming and high quality community space where all can feel at home'."
www.dragoncafe.co.uk
www.mentalfightclub.com

Shaping Our Lives: A National Network of Service Users and Disabled People

"Shaping Our Lives is a national organisation and network of user-led groups, service users and disabled people. We are a non-profit company, chaired by Peter Beresford, Professor of Social Policy at Brunel University and Director of the Citizen Participation Centre. We are a user-led organisation committed to inclusive involvement and specialise in the research and practice of involving diverse communities in policy, planning and delivery of services.

"Our vision is of a society where all people have the same rights, responsibilities, choices and opportunities; a society where people have choice and control over the services they use and how they live their lives.

"Shaping Our Lives has 12 years' experience of undertaking research with and consulting with service users and representing their views. Our inclusive approach enables people from all communities to have an equal say, including people with physical, sensory and cognitive impairments, older people, people in care, homeless people, mental health service users, people with alcohol or drug use issues, people from black and minority ethnic communities and lesbian, gay, bi-sexual and transgender people and their carers. We understand that people have complex identities and recognise that people often face multiple disadvantages and that there is inter-connection between economic, social, cultural and environmental influences."

www.shapingourlives.org.uk

Social Perspectives Network: For Modern Mental Health

"The Social Perspectives Network is a unique coalition of service users/ survivors, carers, policy makers, academics, students and practitioners interested in how social factors both contribute to people becoming distressed, and play a crucial part in promoting people's recovery.

"We aim to share work and information looking at mental health from a social perspective, to support people to put social perspectives into practice, and influence the development of mental health policy from a social perspective.

"SPN's work takes the form of study days, published papers, media campaigning and information provision through our website. Through links with other organizations and individuals, SPN also seeks to promote the importance of social care and social work."

www.spn.org.uk

National Survivor User Network (NSUN)

"NSUN is an independent mental health service user/survivor led organisation that connects people with experience of mental health issues to give us a stronger voice in shaping policy and services.

"The network was set up by service users to build a more united and confident mental health service user movement. It recognises the isolation and discrimination experienced by mental health service users and their needs beyond clinical treatment.

"In 2003 service user-led research, coordinated by Jan Wallcraft for the User Survey Steering Group and funded by the Sainsbury Centre for Mental Health, resulted in the report 'On Our Own Terms'. It urged the formation of a national network to bring individual mental health service users and groups together to encourage good practice and build the capacity of the sector. Inspired by this report, the Sainsbury Centre funded a number of meetings and a conference in London in 2005 to agree on some practical actions based on the recommendations.

"A Steering Group organised a conference focused on how to set up a national service user/survivor network. Nearly 200 service users and survivors attended the 'Our Future' conference in Birmingham in March 2006. The National Planning Group that grew out of the conference included representatives from a whole range of service user and survivor led groups."

www.nsun.org.uk

The Free Psychotherapy Network

"We are a group of psychotherapists offering free and low-fee psychotherapy to people on low incomes. We are currently developing our own ways of doing no-fee work and we are supporting each other in the experience. We would like other qualified psychotherapists and counsellors to join us in building a network.

"We envisage a loose, mutually supportive, network of practitioners offering their time, experience and energy to their local communities in whatever settings work for them. This might be through individual or group sessions, through facilitating peer-support groups or by working with existing community groups. We see ourselves as contributing to a broad movement of activism, pressing for social justice and community values in response to the social injustice and cynical market values that seem to have a tightening grip on our society.

"We want to work with local communities by supporting people who would benefit from the experience of practitioners, who cannot get the kind of support they need from their GPs or from voluntary services, and who do not have the money to pay for psychotherapy.

We want to work, as far as possible, from local bases in communities we are connected to. We want to encourage people to collaborate, support each other and share experience and understanding of psychological difficulties. We will work with people as psychotherapists, but also as equals in the common experience of wanting to understand ourselves and others better, and to live our lives with more freedom, more creativity and more responsibility toward the common good."
www.freepsychotherapynetwork.com

Mental Health Resistance Network

"The Mental Health Resistance Network was set up by people who live with mental distress in order to defend ourselves from the assault on us by a cruel government whose only constituents are the super rich and who value everyone else according to how much they serve the interests of this selfish minority."
www.mentalhealthresistance.org

Psychologists Against Austerity: Mobilising Psychology for Social Change

"This group was formed in 2014 after discussions within various UK Community Psychology forums, which are still ongoing on this interactive community website.

"We are a mixed group of different applied psychologists, including Clinical and Counselling Psychologists, Academic and Research Psychologists, Educational Psychologists and Forensic Psychologists, as well as trainees, other health care professionals and community members. We speak as a collective of individuals and not on behalf of our workplaces or institutions.

"We are non party political but believe psychologists must use their power, tools and resources to be actively involved in political and societal issues. We believe that as applied psychologists in the UK it is our *public and professional duty* to be speaking out against the further implementation of austerity policies. From professional experience and our knowledge of empirical psychological evidence, we know that cuts have been toxic for people's wellbeing and mental health.

"Recent (Dec 2015) scientific evidence continues to demonstrate links between austerity policies and the nation's worsening mental health

and increasing mental health inequalities. Responding to this, this campaign aims to mobilise psychologists and psychological knowledge to make a case against further austerity policies."
www.psychagainstausterity.wordpress.com
www.communitypsychologyuk.ning.com

Psychoanalysis and Politics: Conference Series

"PSYCHOANALYSIS AND POLITICS is a conference series that aims to address how crucial contemporary political issues may be fruitfully explored through psychoanalytic theory, and vice versa: how political issues may reflect back on psychoanalytic thinking. The series is interdisciplinary; we invite theoretical contributions and historical, literary or clinical case studies from philosophers, sociologists, psychoanalysts, psychotherapists, group analysts, literary theorists, historians and others. Perspectives from different psychoanalytic schools are most welcome.

"We emphasise room for discussion among the presenters and participants, thus the symposium series creates a space where representatives of different perspectives come together and engage with one another's contributions, participating in a community of thought."
www.psa-pol.org

Outsight/resources

EDUCATION AND CHILDHOOD

Boarding School Survivors: Therapeutic Help
for Those Affected by Boarding

"'Boarding School Survivors' was founded in 1990 and has three principal activities: to offer therapeutic help for ex-boarders; raise public awareness about boarding; and provide specialist training for therapists. In order to raise public consciousness, we research, lecture, write, and broadcast about the psychological effects of sending children away to school—such as the 2014 'Ban Boarding for Under 16s' debate, which was overwhelmingly carried at Edinburgh University—and the social system which has encouraged this habit.

"We also run a programme of therapeutic workshops for adults who have recognised that they may have paid a price for their education and are looking for ways to understand and heal their wounds. To find out more about the work of Boarding School Survivors please explore this website. We offer a range of resources, information for boarding school survivors, and events, as well as information for therapists and links to other support services."

www.boardingschoolsurvivors.co.uk

Oxford Parent Infant Project (OXPIP)

"OXPIP is one of the pioneers of parent–infant psychotherapy. Founded in 1998 we have been working in Oxfordshire for fifteen years supporting parents who struggle with the demands of a new baby. We work with babies up to the age of two and their parents, normally the mother, but we have worked with many fathers as well.

"We are part of a growing national movement of people and organisations who are bringing greater focus to the importance of early intervention. We work with professionals and policy makers to raise awareness about the importance of parent–baby attachment and infant mental health. This work continues to inform mainstream national policy."

www.oxpip.org.uk

VIOLENCE AND MEDIA

Veterans for Peace UK

"Veterans for Peace UK is an organisation of voluntary ex-services men and women who have experienced first-hand the reality of contemporary military conflict and who now work to educate young people on the true nature of military service and war. They believe that violence and warfare are not the solutions to the problems of the twenty-first century.

"Each year on Remembrance Sunday, members of Veterans for Peace UK walk to the Cenotaph under the banner 'Never Again'. Unlike other organisations laying wreaths that day, they remember soldiers from all countries, as well as everyone killed in war, including civilians and enemy soldiers. In tribute to Harry Patch, the last surviving British soldier of the 1914–1918 war, they wear a quotation from him on their backs: it simply says 'War is Organised Murder'.

"We are an organisation of former servicemen and women who have come to the realisation that war is irrational and immoral and want to campaign against it. We have members from all three services with experiences ranging from D-Day to Afghanistan. We work to educate the general population on the true nature of warfare and to resist war and militarism through nonviolent action."

www.vfpuk.org

The Center for the Study and Prevention of Violence (CSPV)

"The Center for the Study and Prevention of Violence works from a multidisciplinary platform on violence to bridge gaps between the research community, practitioners and policy makers. It collects research literature on the causes and prevention of violence, particularly youth violence.

"At CSPV we build bridges between the research community, practitioners and policy makers who share the goal of preventing violence and antisocial behavior and promoting positive youth development by putting the best that we know from research into practice.

"We engage in high quality multidisciplinary research and provide a wide range of supports to those who are implementing evidence-based programs, practices and policies to promote positive youth development and reduce problem behaviors (e.g., violence, delinquency, and substance abuse). This includes a focus on enhancing nurturing environments, emotional well-being, positive relationships, and academic performance and reducing the risk factors for violence, delinquency, substance abuse, and other problem behaviors. CSPV produces numerous publications, most of which are available to download free of charge."
www.colorado.edu/cspv

Media Education Foundation (MEF)

"Media Education Foundation produces and distributes documentary films and other educational resources to inspire critical thinking about the social, political, and cultural impact of American mass media.

"Directed by well-known media scholar and author Sut Jhally, this foundation produces and distributes award-winning resources for students of media literacy, educators, parents, and community leaders. *The Killing Screens: Media and the Culture of Violence* and *Media Violence and the Cultivation of Fear* are exemplary educational DVDs available based on the groundbreaking work of Dr. George Gerber."
www.mediaed.org

Killology Research Group

"*Killology* is the study of the psychological and physiological effects of killing and combat on the human psyche, and the factors that enable and restrain killing in these situations. It is therefore the scholarly study of the destructive act, just as sexology is the scholarly study of the pro-creative act.

"In particular, killology focuses on the reactions of healthy people in killing circumstances (such as police and military in combat) and the factors that enable and restrain killing in these situations. This field of study was pioneered by Lt. Col. Dave Grossman, in his Pulitzer-nominated book, *On Killing: The Psychological Cost of Learning to Kill in War and Society.*

"The research group's consulting practice and speakers bureau is dedicated to protecting our families and our children and to the strong defense of our country. Warrior Science Group consultants are human behavior studies specialists with credentials in psychology, educational psychology, training, military history, and modern warfare. Each project is unique, and each project is customized to meet the needs of the client. Col. David Grossman, Director, personally contributes to and supervises all projects."

www.killology.com

ADDICTION AND PORNOGRAPHY

Sex and Love Addicts Anonymous (SLAA)

"Sex and Love Addicts Anonymous, or SLAA, is a Twelve Step, Twelve Tradition oriented Fellowship based on the model pioneered by Alcoholics Anonymous. SLAA is open to anyone who knows or thinks they have a problem with sex addiction, love addiction, romantic obsession, co-dependent relationships, fantasy addiction and/or sexual, social and emotional anorexia. You are welcome here.

"If you have a desire to be free from Sex and Love addiction you may find it helpful to attend one of the meetings listed on the meeting list convenient for you. All meetings welcome newcomers—you can just show up."

www.slaauk.org

International Institute for Trauma and Addiction Professionals (IITAP)

"The International Institute for Trauma and Addiction Professionals is one of several organizations that set standards for the professional treatment of sexual addiction and multiple addictions. IITAP certifies qualifying healthcare professionals who complete a rigorous training, clinical supervision process, and additional criteria to become Certified Sex Addiction Therapists (CSAT) or Certified Multiple Addiction Therapists (CMAT). IITAP is a certified educational resource for the American Psychological Association (APA), the National Board for Certified Counselors (NBCC), the National Association of Social Workers (NASW), the Association for Addiction Professionals (NAADAC) and the California Board of Behavioral Sciences (CaBBS)."

www.iitap.com

Association for the Treatment of Sexual Addiction and Compulsivity (ATSAC)

"The Association for the Treatment of Sexual Addiction and Compulsivity is a not-for-profit organisation that provides information and support on sex addiction and compulsivity. Sex addiction is a growing problem that can devastate lives. ATSAC is committed to providing hope, information, and treatment options to sex addicts and those who love them. We also provide professional standards and training to the growing number of therapists choosing to specialise in this field."

www.atsac.co.uk

CORPORATIONS

The Corporation.com: A Film by Mark Achbar, Jennifer Abbott, and Joel Bakan

"Joel Bakan's book *The Corporation: The Pathological Pursuit of Profit and Power*, not only inspired a feature documentary film, *The Corporation*, written by Bakan and co-created with Mark Achbar (which won numerous awards including best foreign documentary at the Sundance Film festival), but also a whole movement aimed at challenging corporate power, and moving from being a consumerist to activist. To find out more about this exciting democratic project, and its crowdfunding campaign to create new educational materials and community screening resources, please visit their website."

www.thecorporation.com

Joel Bakan's website

Author Joel Bakan's website is also an invaluable resource for further information about the project, as well as providing helpful links to groups, interviews, activities and reviews.

"Dear reader, herein you will find a sampling of my scribblings and obsessions. What value they have derives from immersion in the great crisis of our time: the struggle between global capital, on the one side, and humanity and nature, on the other. I began my activism and writing in the sixties, opposing racism and the US wars in Indochina, and continue today, as the struggle is increasingly waged in terms of capital's assault on ecologies. Looking back, I see a string of defeats; yet I would not have us despair, for though the road is long and hard, the journey is worth taking. I hope that you will find the contents of this website helpful as you travel on."
www.joelbakan.com

Corporate Watch

Corporate Watch is an independent research group who investigate the social and environmental impacts of corporations and corporate power. Founded in 1996, its unique approach (encapsulated by its motto "information for action") has had a significant influence on grassroots campaigns and social movements in the UK and beyond.

Its research is also a vital resource for campaigns looking to target particular companies and provides a reliable source of original and cutting-edge knowledge about the latest forms and manifestations of corporate power. It is a small workers' co-operative and not-for-profit company that strives for a society that is truly democratic, equitable, non-exploitative and ecologically sustainable. As its website states, "progress towards such a society may be achieved, in part, through dismantling the vast economic and political power that corporations have come to exert, as well as developing alternatives to the present socio-economic system."
www.corporatewatch.org

Campaign for a Commercial-Free Childhood (CCFC): Reclaiming Childhood from Corporate Marketers

"CCFC's mission is to support parents' efforts to raise healthy families by limiting commercial access to children and ending the exploitative practice of child-targeted marketing. In working for the rights of children to grow up—and the freedom for parents to raise them—without being undermined by corporate interests, CCFC promotes a more democratic and sustainable world.

"The rise of ubiquitous, sophisticated, and portable screen technologies allows marketers unprecedented direct access to children. At the same time, key policies and agencies created to protect kids from harmful marketing have been weakened. The result is a commercialized culture causing harm to children. Childhood obesity, eating disorders, youth violence, sexualization, family stress, underage alcohol and tobacco use, rampant materialism, and the erosion of creative play are all exacerbated by advertising and marketing. And when children adopt the values that dominate commercial culture—materialism, self-indulgence, conformity, impulse buying, and unthinking brand loyalty—the health of democracy and sustainability of our planet are threatened."

www.commercialfreechildhood.org

The New Economics Foundation (NEF)

"NEF is the UK's leading think tank promoting social, economic and environmental justice. Our aim is to transform the economy so that it works for people and the planet.

"The UK and most of the world's economies are increasingly unsustainable, unfair and unstable. It is not even making us any happier—many of the richest countries in the world do not have the highest wellbeing.

"From climate change to the financial crisis it is clear the current economic system is not fit for purpose. We need a great transition to a new economics that can deliver for people and the planet.

"The New Economics Foundation has been arguing for some time for a shorter working week, even as little as 21 hours per person. The claim is that this will be good for wellbeing, balance out employment opportunities, and rapidly reduce carbon emissions, without diminishing living standards."

www.neweconomics.org
www.neweconomics.org/publications/21-hours

INDEX

223